CU00646004

Fishing Communities
of Angus and the Mearns

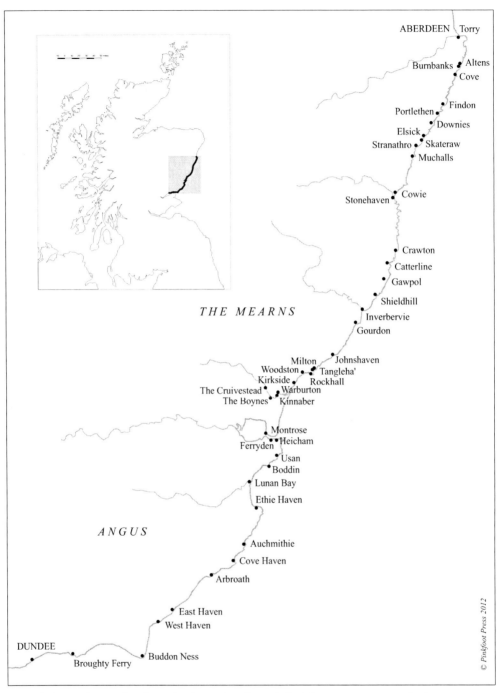

ABERDEEN Torry

Burnbanks Altens
Cove

Portlethen Findon
Downies
Elsick
Stranathro Skateraw
Muchalls

Cowie
Stonehaven

Crawton
Catterline
Gawpol
Shieldhill
Inverbervie
Gourdon

THE MEARNS

Milton Johnshaven
Woodston Tangleha'
Kirkside Rockhall
The Cruivestead Warburton
The Boynes Kinnaber

Montrose
Heicham
Ferryden
Usan
Boddin
Lunan Bay
Ethie Haven

ANGUS

Auchmithie
Cove Haven
Arbroath

East Haven
West Haven

DUNDEE
Buddon Ness
Broughty Ferry

© *Pinkfoot Press 2012*

Frontispiece: *The coastline from Aberdeen to Dundee with the fishing communities and salmon stations listed in the Gazetteer*

Fishing Communities
of Angus and the Mearns
with notes on salmon stations

DAVID G ADAMS

Edited by
GILLIAN ZEALAND

With a foreword by
NORMAN ATKINSON

The Pinkfoot Press
Brechin, 2013

Published in Scotland 2013 by

The Pinkfoot Press, 1 Pearse Street, Brechin, Angus DD9 6JR

ISBN 9781874012597

Copyright

Text

© Angus Council Cultural Services and Gillian Zealand 2013

Illustrations

© Angus Council Cultural Services, The Estate of Colin Gibson and other contributors 2013

Front Cover Illustrations

Catterline – drawing by David Lund, © The Estate of David Lund 2013

Fisher folk of Forfarshire – wood-engravings by Withy, after drawings by Patrick Allan,
in Scott's *The Antiquary* (illustrated edition, Edinburgh: Adam & Charles Black, 1878)

Back Cover Photograph

Mending herring nets at Johnshaven, c.1910

THE
STRATHMARTINE
TRUST

This volume is published with the help of financial support from The Strathmartine Trust

Typeset and designed at The Pinkfoot Press
Printed by ScandinavianBook, Copenhagen

Contents

List of Illustrations

Note on the illustrations: Every effort has been made to trace individual copyright holders. While this has not always been possible, we believe that the author had permission to publish from those who contributed illustrative material for his research.

List of Maps

Foreword

This book has been some time in the making. Its author, David Gordon Adams, died in 2002, leaving his unpublished papers to Angus Council's Cultural Services. These are now safely deposited in Angus Archives at the Hunter Library at Restenneth. Part of this collection comprises the research material for *Fishing Communities of Angus and the Mearns*.

As Davy, for that was how all referred to him, described this project as his *'magnum opus'*, it made me determined to somehow find a way of having the work completed and published. Before ending that tale, it is worthwhile to go back a wee bit, and put the story into context.

Davy was born in Brechin in 1940, and school friends failed to recognise the talent which was to flourish in later life. He initially studied at Duncan of Jordanstone College of Art in Dundee, and later worked as a draughtsman with Ferranti in Edinburgh and London.

The pull of history was too strong, however, and he became a student once more at the new University of Stirling where he gained a Master of Arts degree in Scottish History. This was followed by a postgraduate year at Robert Gordon's in Aberdeen studying librarianship and becoming an Associate of the Libraries Association. This prepared him well for a career ahead with Angus District Council's Libraries and Museums Department.

I first met Davy when he joined us in 1978, which was the beginning of a long friendship which blossomed as a result of a mutually deep passion for the heritage of our native county.

While involved in several local history projects at work, Davy began to write and publish many articles and papers mainly on Scottish and local history. When ill health forced his premature retiral, undaunted, he founded his own publishing business in Brechin. Under the imprint of Chanonry Press (in his own words, 'the press, *c'est moi*'), he went on to produce no fewer than twenty-three books and booklets, mainly on Angus topics.

There is not space to list them here, but one stands out as a precursor to this work, being his *Auchmithie: Home of the Smokie* published in 1995. We spent many hours discussing this topic, since my mother was a Cargill whose family came from Auchmithie to the fit o' the toon in Arbroath in 1882.

It soon became apparent that Davy's plan was to survey all the fishing villages of the two counties, and to this end he spent a great deal of time in his camper-van exploring the coast, gathering stories and photographs and talking to locals, many of whom still had a family background involving fishing.

Davy added to this by painstakingly researching every village, attempting to trace its origins and its traditional families and customs. Sadly, his ambitious project, so near to completion, was brought to an end by his untimely death.

However, to return to where I left off, I realised that it was extremely important to have this work published since it was of immense value in documenting these rapidly vanishing communities.

Margaret King, another colleague, with a deep interest in Arbroath fisher folk and her background as our Museum Curator at Signal Tower, seemed an ideal choice as editor. Margaret readily agreed, but long before she could make significant progress she left Angus for pastures new!

Fortunately, Gillian Zealand, another previous Curator at Signal Tower, came to the rescue and took over the task of making sense of Davy's disparate material – including field-notes, handwritten and electronic files, lists, fragmentary annotated typescripts, references, sketches and photographs – all contained in two large cardboard boxes. Gillian had worked with Davy and understood his methods and thinking and she has assembled the material along the lines that he had intended and, by following in his footsteps to explore the fishertouns, has managed to sympathetically fill the gaps. Gillian has also contributed many beautiful illustrations by her late father, Colin Gibson, which significantly enhance the appearance of the book.

It is also fortunate that David Henry of Pinkfoot Press, who knew Davy from his time as an art student in the early 1960s, took an early and keen interest in the project and was committed to publish the book. It is hoped that the resulting volume is worthy of Davy's work and would have met with his approval.

Norman Atkinson
Angus Council Cultural Services
April 2013

Preface

Throughout the 1980s and 90s the historian David (Davy) G Adams amassed a wealth of information about the early fishing communities between the Tay and the Dee. The idea for the present book took shape as he came to focus on three main areas of study: fishing technology, fisher life and the history of the individual settlements up to around 1900. Though he recognised the scale of this project (he called it his *magnum opus*), it was a subject he had worked on fairly constantly and some of his research had already been published. Just *how* much he had accomplished, however, and the sheer quantity of material he had accumulated, was only revealed to me on examining the contents of two large cardboard boxes which were bequeathed to Angus Council Cultural Services after his death in 2002. Sifting through the files of computer print-outs, hand-written drafts, notes compiled in libraries and archive centres and rough jottings scribbled down on field trips has been a journey of discovery in itself and a source of ever-increasing admiration at the scholarship, dedication and sheer hard graft that had gone into compiling *Fishing Communities of Angus and the Mearns*.

© John Cruse

1 *Davy (l) leading a field trip of the Aberdeen Branch of the Society of Antiquaries of Scotland to some of the old north-east fishertouns*

Davy, though, had a number of attributes which fitted him well to the task. The first was his enquiring mind, coupled with his historical training and a natural interest in the subject. The second was his tenacity: an essential requirement when trawling through volumes of census returns, burgh archives or old parish records. The third was his heritage, though Davy would have scoffed at such a high-falutin' term. He was a Brechiner, and proud of it, who tempered his broad Scots for nobody. But he could converse with anyone – from professors to ploughmen – about anything – from Dark Age monasteries to playing the melodeon, and when it came to fieldwork he brought people out. His book about bothy life[1] arose out of conversations with retired ploughmen and is even written largely in the Angus dialect, as if an old farmhand was reminiscing. It's also, however, a carefully structured piece of research and so can be taken either as an ethnological document or a grand trip down memory lane, depending on your viewpoint. A good deal of information in the present book, particularly the descriptions of long-lining and spratting, also came from what Davy would have called *word o'mou'*. (This is also reflected in the author's 'voice', which strays at times into vernacular territory. I have made no attempt to anglicise this as I feel it adds character and immediacy to the writing.)

In the main, however, the present book deals with a subject which had its heyday in the 19th century and its origins in the middle ages, so the bulk of the author's material has come from books and archives. Since he was not spared to write (as he intended) a general historical résumé, it may be appropriate here to include a brief summary of his researches and how he interpreted his raw material. A list of his sources and references is given in Appendix III.

Just establishing the number and whereabouts of all these disparate communities must have been a task in itself. Early maps, the Statistical Accounts, parish registers, census records, the Fishery Board for Scotland's 'creek returns', a list of Mearns fishertouns in 1642 from *MacFarlane's Geographical Collections*, burgh archives, medieval cartularies and oral tradition all helped to add details and the author had also thoroughly familiarised himself with the ground. Many settlements were always tiny and some had completely vanished. A good example of this is the village of Gawpol, last mentioned in the Statistical Account of 1792. From early maps, land grants and place-name evidence, Davy traced the site of this 'lost' village to the south side of Braidon Bay, near Catterline, and identified it as the *Fischertoun of Kinneff* recorded in 1400. But the history of even neighbouring communities could be surprisingly varied, and nearby Shieldhill had a quite different story. Shieldhill was a planned settlement, first mentioned (as Newhaven of Kinneff) on a land-lease of 1678 and surviving until 1926. From a mere three households in 1841, a redevelopment by Lord Arbuthnott led to its subsequent revival and the 1855 creek return shows over 30 people employed in fishing and in ancillary industries such as packing cod for the London market. The mid-19th century, which also marked the start of the herring boom in Angus and the Mearns, saw the expansion of many settlements like Shieldhill, until the increasing size of boats and the consequent need for better harbour facilities brought about migration to larger centres such as Torry, Stonehaven and Arbroath and the small villages mostly declined. This

---

1 *Bothy Nichts and Days: farm bothy life in Angus and the Mearns.* Edinburgh: John Donald, 1991.

pattern is reflected both in the Fishery Board's returns and in the census records, which at ten-year intervals from 1841 chart not only changing population figures but also the appearance of new surnames: clear evidence of communities on the move.

Around half of the fishing communities were found to be of medieval origin. One valuable source of information was the register of Arbroath Abbey. The abbey owned Auchmithie (which was given to it on its foundation in 1178), as well as lands at Torry, Cove, Catterline, Ferryden and Broughty Ferry and a salmon fishing on the North Esk. Thus the monks were assured of a plentiful supply of fish, and once their needs had been met the fishers of Auchmithie and Broughty Ferry were allowed to sell their surplus, the latter presumably finding a ready market in the growing burgh of Dundee.

Burgh archives were also revealing. In the middle ages the authorities of Dundee and Montrose each considered it the prime duty of their fishers to provide a cheap, regular and plentiful supply of white fish to the inhabitants and took steps to prevent the buying of fish for resale. A list of Dundee harbour dues of 1447 includes 'greite bates' and 'small bates', showing even at this early date the distinction between great line boats used for distant summer fishing and small boats for working closer to home.

The mussel beds of Montrose Basin – a primary source of bait – were long recognised as a valuable asset and feature in the burgh minutes from an early period. In the 15th and 16th centuries Montrose and Dundee were major exporters of salmon (much of it going to the Mediterranean). Montrose was also exporting dried cod from at least 1420, the year that Customs records begin. The amounts involved are staggering – up to 10,000 fish exported annually in the late 15th century – but Montrose's trading precinct extended from Monifieth to the Findon burn and probably included a dozen fishertouns, all contributing to this total. Dundee in 1560 was second only to the Forth and Clyde ports as an exporter of cured herring.

The origins of some communities were found in records of sales and leases. Some could be dated exactly: Shieldhill, as mentioned above, was first leased in 1678, Ethie Haven in 1701, when two men called Torn (probably brothers) were granted house sites by the Earl of Northesk. The fishings of Portlethen were first mentioned in a deed of sale in 1557, those of Muchalls in 1606. The latter, however, may have been much older: a 17th-century reference linked Muchalls to two other fishertouns, Cowie and Elsick, and Davy concluded that this association might well have originated in the 14th century, when all of this part of Fetteresso parish fell within a single barony. The most venerable of all, however, was East Haven, which was mentioned (under the alternative and less than flattering name of *Stinkendehavene*) in a charter of 1214. Davy thought this must be one of the very earliest references to a fishing community anywhere in Scotland.

Land leases also helped to link these early fishertouns to their farming background. At Auchmithie the land, or *ville*, was leased in quarters; each tenant of a quarter had to provide a fully equipped fishing boat and crew while the abbey itself provided a fifth.

Although fishing was a priority, the fishers probably cultivated some land and helped with seasonal tasks such as haymaking. There are many such references to *fischerlands*.

While working through these varied records and archives Davy painstakingly noted every occurrence of the name of each settlement in its original spelling. Apart from their value to place-name scholars, these early forms give an interesting glimpse into a world before Ordnance Survey maps and standardised spellings. Usan, for all its brevity, seems to have presented a particularly taxing problem! Examples are included in the Gazetteer.

From the 1790s onward more detailed information was available, particularly from the Statistical Accounts. At this time fishing was beginning to pick up again after a slump. The causes of this had been three-fold: a dearth of haddock around 1783–93; the increasing vigilance of Customs officers and consequent drop in smuggling activity (always a lucrative sideline on this secluded coast); but, most vitally, the predations of the press gangs, the agents who recruited men for the Navy, often by brutal and illegal means. Some communities had been completely devastated by the press gangs, either through actually losing their young men to the Navy or through abandonment as families moved away to avoid them. The Johnshaven minister, in the Statistical Account of 1793, gives a most vivid and damning account of this iniquitous system. As the threat receded and fish stocks recovered, improving lairds began to look at fishing as a potential investment. A number of villages were rebuilt or even established from scratch at this time. From mid-19th century the burgeoning herring fishery encouraged further expansion, though even before this crews from local villages had travelled to Buchan for the six week summer season, landing at Peterhead. The introduction of bag- and stake-nets had already given a boost to the coastal salmon fishery, and the development of the commercial ice-house (of which a number survive along the Angus and Mearns coast) meant that fresh salmon could now be supplied to the insatiable London market, packed in ice and delivered by fast sailing smacks or steamships. Live lobsters were also transported south. The railway, when it came, was a boon for getting fish (and fishwives) to market, though it also caused a certain inconvenience by literally slicing through some of the fishing communities and in some cases cutting them off from their shore: at East Haven, for instance, part of the village was left looking straight onto the railway embankment, the only access to the beach being through a tunnel.

From the mid-19th century a new source of information was available in the form of the Fishery Board's statistical tables. These list precise numbers of fishermen as well as the number and size of craft at every port. By this time three categories of boat were recognised: yauls[1] (also called 3rd class) were under 18 feet and were used close inshore by old men and boys; medium (2nd class), with crews of five or six, corresponded to

---

1 The author's spelling, which I have used throughout; 'yawl' is more usual. Other idiosyncrasies include 'sheil' (shell, i.e. mussels), usually 'shiel', 'dan' (usually 'dahn'), the anchored pole which marked the start of a 'shot' line, and 'bye-names' (usually, though not always, 'by-') (ed.).

the standard, all-purpose boats of the previous century, while large or 1st class boats might have crews of up to nine for great line fishing and were also used for herring. And at this point I should mention what I have come to call the 'Davy Adams formula'. Knowing the boat types and sizes used in the 19th century and at earlier times allowed the author to estimate the population of fishertouns when his data was incomplete. Medieval Auchmithie, for example, was known to have had five boats (one from each 'quarter', a fifth from the abbey). These would be the standard boats of the day with crews of five or six, giving, by a simple calculation, a total of 25 to 30 fishermen and perhaps 25 households. It was a bit rough and ready and the fact had to be taken into account – in the later period at least – that the same men might crew more than one type of boat, but none the less it was a good guideline. Thus by a combination of published data and the application of simple maths it was possible to gauge the numbers of fishermen and boats, and hence the rough size of a settlement, throughout much of its history. These figures are listed at the end of each section of the gazetteer.

A patient trawl through the census returns and old parish records (the latter going back in some cases to the 17th century) produced a lengthy catalogue of fisher surnames. This formed the basis of the invaluable index (Appendix II) at the end of this book. As well as the provenance and dates it also gives the origin of each name, which in almost every case could be traced to the local, land-based community. This fact ties in nicely, of course, with the evidence from land-leases already mentioned, but it also gives the lie to the persistent myth that fishers were of some strange, exotic origin. Moreover, by identifying the predominant groups of names in these close-knit communities, Davy was able to trace the movements of populations. He could show, for instance, that the residents of Shieldhill, on its foundation in the 1670s, came from Gawpol and Catterline; and that around 1800 the new settlements of Downies, Burnbanks and Stranathro were colonised from Portlethen. In the 18th century an attempt was made at Arbroath (which was strangely short of fishers for a coastal burgh) to bring two fisher families from 'Hacterland, near Bervie'. This place was unknown, but the distinctive names of the fishers – Alexander and Bridgefoord – showed beyond doubt that what was meant was Catterline. Incidentally they never arrived, and Arbroath had to wait for an influx of fishers from Auchmithie before its fishing industry took off.

Finally, a word about *my* role.

Shortly before he died, Davy reckoned, with satisfaction, that the book was three-quarters complete. Looked at another way, however, this left 25 percent still to do, and consequently, as editor, I have had to do a fair amount of checking, cross-referencing and reconstruction. Where serious gaps occurred I have also had decisions to make.

The plan, as indicated above, was for a three-part study, covering fisher life, fishing technology and the history of the individual communities, the last in the form of a gazetteer. Fisher life was the least visited part of Davy's researches. There was very little written up in any finished form and it was a fairly easy decision not to include this as a self-contained section. Having said that, there are enough references scattered throughout the rest of the text (see Auchmithie and Usan, for instance) to give a good impression of what life was like in the fishertouns of Angus and the Mearns. Some of Davy's previous publications also explore this subject in more detail (see Appendix III: Sources and references, for these).

Fishing technology presented more of a dilemma. While some subjects, such as line fishing and boat development, were thoroughly dealt with, other major areas (such as herring fishing) were frustratingly absent. This problem was resolved in two ways: firstly by extracting and judiciously editing (with due acknowledgement) relevant passages from the author's previous publications; and secondly by appropriating information from elsewhere in the current text and setting this out, using the author's own words as far as possible, in the way I hope he would have done himself. These reconstructed sections are clearly identified.

The individual histories were the most worked-on part of the project. Most entries were either on disc, typed up, or at least existed in hand-written drafts. A few, however, had not yet reached this stage of development. In such cases I have tried to present what material exists, with the minimum of interference but in what I hope is a readable form. Again these sections are clearly indicated in the text and I would ask the reader's forbearance that they may not be as complete or as polished as the author would have liked. It should also be borne in mind that when the author mentions 'recent' or 'current' developments he is referring to the 1980s and early 90s, when most of this research was carried out, and that major changes in the fishing industry have occurred since then. Line-fishing, for example, has died out at Gourdon. No white-fish are currently landed at Arbroath; there is still some fishing for shell-fish but these days the harbour is largely full of yachts. Perhaps the most striking change has been in coastal salmon netting, which has seen a buy-out by conservation bodies and river management boards in an attempt to redress the down-turn in fish stocks. Commercial netting of salmon is now (2010) limited to the section of coast between Scurdie Ness and Auchmithie (fished by Usan Salmon Fishing Co.) and to a net and coble fishing in the lower reaches of the North Esk at Kinnaber; coastal fishings at Gourdon and Johnshaven are still in private ownership but have not been fished for a number of years.

Apart from the above-mentioned modifications nothing new has been added to the text – with two small exceptions. On the grounds that one cannot have a gazetteer with gaps, I have felt justified in adding short entries (they would otherwise be completely missing) on the important salmon fishing stations at Buddon Ness and Lunan Bay, and I am very grateful to Colin R McLeod, Dr Marshall Halliday, Willie Shearer and the Usan salmon fishers for providing information on these. I have also taken the liberty of 'slimming down' a few of the entries, without, I hope, diminishing the value of their contents. This applies particularly to the section on Dundee, which had originally been conceived as a separate book, and to the chapters on Auchmithie, Johnshaven, and the North Esk salmon fishings, which are based on work already published. The reader is referred to these (see Appendix III: Sources and references) for the full accounts.

Finally I would like to acknowledge Norman Atkinson, Angus Council, Cultural Services, who instigated the whole project and wrote the Foreword; Margaret King, formerly of Signal Tower Museum, Arbroath, who worked on the draft before me, and the staff of Aberdeen, Arbroath, Dundee, Forfar, Montrose and Stonehaven Libraries, Arbroath and Montrose Museums and Angus Archives. J R Coull read part of the text and made many helpful comments. Bob Falconer kindly gave permission to reproduce his drawings from *The Ha'ens o' Panbride* and Angus Council, Cultural Services (holders of the David G Adams archive) kindly allowed me to quote from several of the author's published books and typescripts to which they hold copyright. The black and white illustrations are by Colin Gibson and were first published in the artist's weekly 'Nature Diary' in *The Courier*; they are reproduced courtesy of the estate of Colin Gibson. Photographs of Johnshaven were supplied by Tom Valentine and the late Cecil McBay. Other illustrations (except where indicated) are from the David G Adams archive and include maps drawn by Davy himself. Barbara Crawford has been an enthusiastic supporter from the start. David Henry has ably steered the book through production and publication. I hope Davy would have been pleased with the results, and I would like to dedicate *Fishing Communities of Angus and the Mearns* to his memory.

Gillian Zealand
2010

Fishing Communities of Angus and the Mearns

Dedicated to
the memory of its author

DAVID G. ADAMS

(1940–2002)

2 Davy holding forth to 'Aberdeen Antiquaries' at Portlethen

Introduction

Origins of communities

On 40 miles of Mearns coast from the North Esk to the Dee at Torry lie 21 white-fisher communities, with a further ten[1] on the 35 miles of Angus coast from Dundee to Montrose. At least 14 are of medieval origin; three were abandoned in the 18th century; four were founded around 1800 and 25 were in existence around 1850. Before 1850 many were very small, having only one or two boats and crews and consisting of only five to ten families.

Even the smallest of these settlements had several basic requirements. There were no white-fishing communities, for instance, on stretches of open sandy bays such as St Cyrus, where only flat-bottomed salmon cobles could be launched. Since white-fishing boats went some miles out to sea a fairly deep keel was needed and consequently an inlet or lagoon of sheltered water, preferably a shingle beach, was necessary to launch and land the boats. An area behind to pull the boats clear of the water was also a requirement, as was access to and from the shore to the place of habitation. Some fisher houses were only a few feet above sea level, others perched high above with only steep paths where everything had to be carried up and down.

Many fishing communities, such as Crawton and Catterline, show close physical and organisational proximity to a farm and probably emerged from semi-agricultural part-time or seasonal fishing in the early middle ages. Some places had arable land, usually called Fischerschead/Fisherlands. The early fishers would probably have been similar in status to agricultural sub-tenants and cottars and dependent like them on the husbandman. Like the other sub-tenants they probably cultivated some land and could keep a cow on the common grazing. They may have had seasonal duties: Cowie fishers in the 17th century had to cart peats and assist at the harvest. Often sub-tenants and other dependents in fermtouns would move if the husbandman ended his lease, but the specialised skills of the fishers could not be done without or learned overnight by landsmen, so although tied into the agricultural settlement they were probably the most stable element. As fishing grew in importance so land-based activities gradually decreased. By the 19th century most were entirely employed at fishing, the lands were let or incorporated into local farms.

North folk and south folk

There was a linguistic and cultural divide between the fisherfolk of the district. To the south of Dunnottar parish folk speak the southern Mearns dialect, which is close to the Angus dialect, while to the north folk speak the north-east Scots dialect. The most

---

1 Eleven if one counts Cove Haven, which has left the merest trace (ed.).

obvious shibboleth is that *lassie* is used to the south but *quine* to the north. Inland, 'quines' begin at Fordoun village, and north of the Bervie Water many farm workers, brought up in, or with antecedents from, Aberdeenshire, tend to speak north-east Scots. From Stonehaven to Buchan the fishers refer to Fifers as Dykers (from Cellardyke) but this is not found to the south; Gourdon fishers refer to 'KY' men, from the Kirkcaldy registration of East Fife boats, while the Forth is the Sooth Firth.

Catterline seems to be on both the cultural and linguistic boundary. There the northern method of small line fishing was used but the dialect of some of the older fishers is nearer to that of Gourdon than Stonehaven although others tend towards the north-east dialect and the use of both *lassie* and *quine* can be found. The northern method of working small lines in Catterline may only date from the late-18th century, when the older surnames disappear and an influx of fishers from farther north occurred. A characteristic of the coastal settlements from Catterline to Ferryden and Usan is the vowel sound 'oe' for 'oo', e.g. *toe, doe, yoesed* and *boets* for English too, do, used and boots, whereas inland and farther south this becomes *tae, dae, yaised* and *buits*, and from Stonehaven north *tee, dee, eesed* and *beets*. To the south, English roof, moon, spoon, snood become *ruif, muin, spuin, snuid* but in the north *reef, meen, speen, sneed.* Although the dialect of the southern Mearns is similar to that of Angus the fisherfolk have some distinctive words of their own, such as *pleeng(ie)*, a seagull and *pallach(ie)*, a young partan (edible crab).

© Bob Falconer

3 *Edible crab*

Minor variations in pronunciation and technology also existed and each community once had its own instantly recognisable micro-dialect, now much eroded. The linguistic divide between north and south coincided with a technical divide, mainly in the way the small lines, or sma' lines, were used. From Catterline northwards each fisherman had three sets of sma' lines and these were redd, or sorted out, on a spiletree (wooden rack); white horse hair was preferred for the tippings and fewer snoods were used per line. In the

4 *Reddin' lines at Catterline*

south a set of two lines was used and they were redd over the fisherman's knees, while black horsehair was used for the tippings. Another difference was that the wicker sculls used to hold the baited lines were much deeper and more rounded in the north than those used in the south, which are flat, with sides tapering from a few inches deep at one end to nothing. (For an explanation of these technical terms see 'Fishing methods' below.)

White-fishers and salmon fishers

Salmon fishers were originally a different breed from white-fishers, really landsmen rather than seafarers, although some now go inshore creel fishing. Most of the salmon fishers were only employed during the season: Candlemas (2 February) to Michaelmas (29 September). In early times they had crofts and kept a cow for subsistence and worked on the land or were weavers in winter. In more recent times some worked on the roads and in quarries, or at tattie-dressing, in the off-season. In some areas they may have taken up white-fishing in the winter but usually the local fishers are described as white- *or* salmon fishers, although at some places the two occupations do not seem to have been mutually exclusive. Salmon fishers seem to have been paid partly in meal and partly in cash, known as 'hemp money' and 'spring fees', with a sixth part of the proceeds of the fishing.

To white-fishers the word 'salmon' and anything to do with them was originally taboo and they were referred to as 'red fish' if necessary. Only by around 1900, with the end of herring and great line fishing in the smaller fishertouns, did some young white-fishers begin to go salmon fishing in summer, returning to small line fishing in winter.

3

The division of labour [1]

The laborious processes involved in small line fishing, which concerned the community for most of the year, conditioned their whole life, everyone from children to the aged helped in some way; mere toddlers helped to gather limpets and sheil (shell) bait. The men's daily and seasonal round of work is described under 'Fishing methods' but all commentators noted how little the men did when ashore, forgetting they may have been to sea for ten to 16 hours. Boys might go to sea regularly from the age of 14 with their fathers or uncles. Old men in their 80s, if fit enough to walk, could still fish in the bay in fine weather with young lads while the fitter men were away at the gretlins (great lines) or the herring fishing in the summer. If landbound, they spun tippings for the lines. Barring accidents at sea, which happened with greater frequency in the days of sail, an active outdoor life and a healthy diet based on oatmeal, tatties and fish saw many living beyond the biblical three score years and ten; but if a whole boat's crew went down this was a great blow as most of the crew would belong to one or two families: brothers, sons, fathers and cousins.

Since their menfolk had to face the hardships and danger of going to sea the women accepted as normal everything else which fell to them. At Auchmithie the part the women played in launching and landing the boats is recorded by several commentators. In rough weather they carried their husbands on their shoulders through the surf, often waist-deep in the water in order that the menfolk might remain dry for their day's work.

After the boat's return and the share-out of fish, the men's only task was to redd (clean) the lines and replace lost hooks but the women's work then began. The fish were loaded into rips (baskets) held by a rope across the chest and carried up to the houses, then a second journey was made to collect the line in its scull. The whole afternoon each village would be a busy scene as haddock was gutted for curing or for drying on pebbles by the beach. The sale and distribution of fish also fell to the women who, even in the days of railways, would walk to Dundee and back, a 40-mile round trip, laden with rips full of smoked and fresh fish. Of course they also had to bring up children, wash clothes and cook for their families. It should not be thought, however, that women were in any way subservient: in the house their word might be law, and since the cure and sale of fish was in their hands so were the proceeds. When a son got married he might have no savings of his own unless he had been to the herring fishing and his mother would furnish his home for him.

---

1 Adapted by editor from author's *Auchmithie: home of the smokie* (1995).

The fishing year and seasonal employment

Most of the white-fishers' year was originally taken up with small line fishing, mainly for haddock. Inshore fishing for small codlings occupied late winter and early spring when the haddock were in roe. This was followed by great line fishing from April to early July and then by a return to small line fishing. When creel fishing was introduced in the mid-18th century it interfered with the summer great line fishing as returns were initially so good but later the fittest men tended to go to the great lines while the older men and boys practised creel fishing, depending on the returns. Fishers have always been quick to respond to changes in the market although sometimes cautious in adopting new technology when tried and tested methods were at hand. When herring fishing began in the 1830s the majority only followed a six-week season from mid-July onwards, immediately after the great line season and using the same larger boats. If the herring fishing proved unpromising the great lines were resumed until early September. Small line fishing then resumed over winter. At some of the burghs and bigger communities in the late-18th century the crews of small coasting barks, otherwise unemployed in winter, took up small line fishing. In the 18th century many fishermen were also pilots.

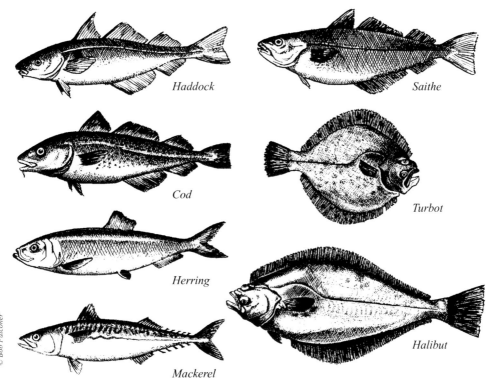

5 *Types of fish caught: from a drawing by Bob Falconer (reproduced from Adams, D G and Falconer, Bob* The Ha'ens o' Panbride and roond aboot: a history of East Haven, West Haven & district *Brechin: Chanonry Press 1990)*

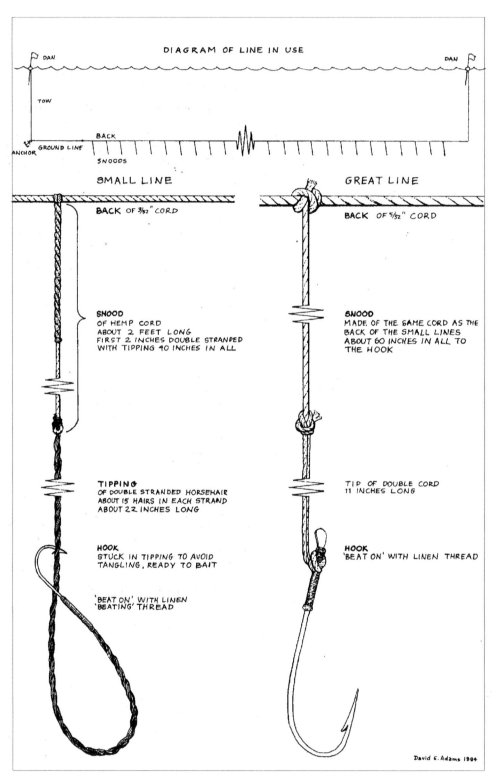

DIAGRAM OF LINE IN USE

DAN

DAN

TOW

BACK

ANCHOR GROUND LINE

SNOODS

SMALL LINE

GREAT LINE

BACK OF ³⁄₃₂" CORD

BACK OF ⁵⁄₃₂" CORD

SNOOD
OF HEMP CORD
ABOUT 2 FEET LONG
FIRST 2 INCHES DOUBLE STRANDED
WITH TIPPING 40 INCHES IN ALL

SNOOD
MADE OF THE SAME CORD AS THE
BACK OF THE SMALL LINES
ABOUT 60 INCHES IN ALL TO
THE HOOK

TIPPING
OF DOUBLE STRANDED HORSEHAIR
ABOUT 15 HAIRS IN EACH STRAND
ABOUT 22 INCHES LONG

TIP OF DOUBLE CORD
11 INCHES LONG

HOOK
STUCK IN TIPPING TO AVOID
TANGLING, READY TO BAIT

HOOK
'BEAT ON' WITH LINEN THREAD

'BEAT ON' WITH LINEN
'BEATING' THREAD

David G. Adams 1984

6 *Davy's own diagram of sma' and great lines*

6

Fishing methods

Small lines

Sma' lines, as pronounced locally, was the form of fishing traditionally practised throughout the greater part of the year mainly to catch haddock, also small codling, whiting and small flat fish. The lines were originally of hemp and the main part was called the back. It was made of lengths of hemp cord spliced together by the fishermen and called *hanks* (Mearns) or *strings* (Angus). The number of hanks or strings and the number of hooks attached to each (and so the total number of hooks) varied from place to place. At Ferryden and Gourdon 1200 hooks were usual in recent times, on a line made up of 12 strings or hanks, each with 100 hooks. Earlier 70 to 80 hooks were attached to each of 14 strings or hanks, giving a total of 980 to 1120 hooks per line. In the northern Mearns line fishing died out some time ago but it appears that fewer hooks were used, under 1000 and as few as 600 perhaps, as in Buchan. At Catterline 60 to 70 hooks to 14 to 15 hanks were used so around 1050 hooks or less. For the sake of comparison at Eyemouth in Berwickshire ten strings of 100 hooks each made up a total of 1000 hooks to a line. The hooks were attached to the back by hemp snoods (Mearns: *snuids*; Ferryden: *snods*; Arbroath: *sneds*), attached to the back by a clove hitch, with about two inches plaited at the top, the other end having a small loop. To the loop was tied a horsehair tipping (Mearns: *tippen*; Ferryden: *tuppin*; Arbroath: *tuppet*), to which the hooks were tied. The combined length of the snood and tipping was about 36 to 40 inches, the tipping being about 22 inches. The tippings consisted of two strands of horsehair each made of about 15 to 18 hairs. Black or dark brown horsehair was preferred in Angus and the southern Mearns but in the northern Mearns white horsehair was preferred. The reason for using horsehair at all is not clear, it was believed that the horsehair floated slightly as it lay along the seabed and attracted the fish, but at the depth and time of day the lines were used it is unlikely that the fish could see the bait at all; they probably located it by olfactory means. When synthetic orange 'corlene' began to be used for the whole line, snood and tipping it was at first tarred black until it was realised that the bright orange made no difference to the fish. This negates also the fishers' belief that black was preferred where 'hard boddam' or rock prevailed while white was preferred on sandy or 'saft boddam'. It seems that the preference for different colours of horsehair is another cultural distinction between north folk and south folk. Curiously at Isle of Whithorn on the Solway a preference for fawn horsehair was expressed.

Each of the 1000 to 1200 hooks had to be baited, usually with two mussels as those from Montrose Basin (the usual source) are small. Sometimes three or even four were needed. Mussels were also brought from the Tay or Eden. In the 1950s the Gourdon Fishermen's Association collected large mussels from the Ythan at Newburgh; only one was needed per hook. *Sheilin* (shelling) the hundreds of mussels or limpets required was the job of women, children and old folk. Baiting the line was always women's work, taking about three or four hours. As it was baited the line was coiled in a special flat oval basket called a *scull*, with the baited hooks arranged on a bed of grass to prevent snagging. Each member of a boat's crew took a scull with a baited line aboard. Since each line was latterly a mile long, a crew of six had as many miles of line.

The boats went to sea very early in the morning in order to get to the fishing ground by first light when fish begin to feed. An anchored pole or *dan* was put overboard and the first line attached. As they were shot the lines were tied end to end. The last line was tied to another dan and the boat was sailed or rowed back to the first one and the line hauled in. It could take up to six or seven hours to haul in the line and detach the fish, each man taking it in turn to pull in 500 hooks. The boat would return home about midday and the catch was shared out. The man's only job on shore was to *redd* (clean) the line of old bait and the starfish, clams etc. which attached to it, and to *beat on wants* (replace any lost hooks). Each man owned two lines, one being baited while the other was in use. They had to be boiled with bark every few weeks to remove the build-up of slime.

In the early part of the year when haddock are in roe a variety of bait on larger hooks was used close inshore. This must be the 'near great fishing' described at Johnshaven in the 1790s. In recent times it was called the 'sma' gretlins' in Angus and the 'sma' gritelins' or 'pawpie lines' in the Mearns. It was believed that the fish went off mussels at that time of year so they were supplemented by a variety of other bait according to what was locally available. 'Loag' (lugworm, *Arenicola marina*) and 'rampers' (ragworm, *Neries* sp.) were dug from tidal sands for bait while women and children collected limpets (*Patella vulgata*) from rock pools along with red beadlet anemones (*Actima equina*), called 'pappies' or 'clipes' at Arbroath, 'clipes' at Ferryden and 'pawpies' in the Mearns. At Gourdon 'slavery buckies' (dogwhelk, *Nucella lapillus*) were smashed with a hammer and cut in half for use as bait. The live lugworms and ragworms squirmed about on the baited lines so the women baiters did not have to be the least squeamish.

Great lines

Heavier calibre great lines, called *gretlins* in Angus and *gritelins* in the Mearns were used to catch the great fish at distant banks: large mature cod (once called keiling) and ling, also halibut, turbot and skate. Fishing with great lines was referred to at Johnshaven in the 18th century as the 'distant great fishing'. The boats went out in midsummer 30 to 50 miles, staying out two or three nights in fine weather. The 'back' of the gretlins was made of heavier hemp cord than that of the sma' lines, $^5/_{32}$ of an inch, as compared with $^3/_{32}$. It was the calibre of the lines which gave them their distinguishing name, not the length, since the great lines were shorter. The snoods were made of hemp cord of the same calibre as the back of the sma' lines. They were fixed to the back in a different way, the line being pierced and the snood pulled through and tied round it. The tippings were of two strands of lighter calibre hemp cord, and the hooks, which were three or four inches long or larger, were likewise beat on with linen thread. The whole snood and tipping was about 60 inches long.

At Ferryden, 'twenty-five score' (500) hooks were apparently used, but at Gourdon, where this mode of fishing continued much later, 1000 hooks were usual. The snoods were spaced several feet apart and this could be varied according to the species sought. The lines were not baited ashore in a scull but were coiled in a quarter cran basket which had cork around half of the rim, into which the hooks were stuck. The hooks were baited as the lines were shot, usually with pieces of herring or other fish, and it must have needed a deft hand to avoid nasty accidents while baiting, such as hooking a finger. 'Inkies' (cuttlefish) were excellent bait for cod when available; these would sometimes be found in lobster creels. The lines were preferably shot the night before or very early in the morning before sunrise. In 1477 an agreement drawn up between Alexander Luvel of Ballumbie and Arbroath Abbey concerning Broughty Ferry (q.v.) allowed the fishers there to take bait from Monifieth Sands for their *linea gracili* (fine or small lines). This must imply the existence of great lines too in the 15th century and they may well have been used long before that. Certainly the large species caught in recent centuries with the great lines were also caught and consumed regularly in the middle ages. From Dundee there is a reference to 'gret line' boats in 1523, which shows beyond any doubt that this method was in use in medieval times.

Great line fishing seems to have ceased at most of the smaller havens when herring fishing ceased around 1900–14 and the large boats used for both were given up. At Arbroath and Gourdon in the inter-war period motor vessels fished locally offshore and then went to fish in the Firth of Clyde out of Campbeltown. After the Second World War the Montrose Bank, about 28 miles out, was successfully fished by boats from Arbroath and Gourdon for a couple of seasons and was then abandoned for good. Large Aberdeen boats used to use great lines off Rockall until the mid-1970s and one Anstruther boat practised this fishing until July 1984. Unlike the Scots the Norwegians have long used a fully mechanised baiting system and so continue to fish for cod etc. by long lines.

Handlines

This may have been the oldest method of catching fish. It was barely a commercial method once more productive catching methods such as long lining had evolved, but could provide extra income, or a bare living, from close offshore in tiny yauls. Clusters of unbaited hooks called 'rippers' can be used fairly close inshore to catch cod. Handlines with dyed or coloured feathers could be used to catch mackerel, shoals of which once drove onshore. Before creels were introduced in the 18th century, lines with a single hook were used to yank lobsters and partans from rock pools, a method never totally abandoned for casual fishing.

Trawling [1]

Trawl nets were bag-shaped and were towed over the sea-bed, originally held open by a beam and heavy ground-line. It was very unusual for Scots to use trawl nets before the advent of steam trawlers at Aberdeen in 1882 as they needed a powerful steam or motor boat to draw them along the bottom. Nowadays the net is held open by large metal 'doors' called otter boards.

Seine netting [2]

Various places, including Gourdon, are credited with having the first seine-net in Scotland, but the Fishery Board's records show that they were adopted at all places with large enough boats by 1921. They were developed in Denmark originally. Seine-nets consist of two wings of net and a 'cod end'. The net is gradually drawn in around a school of fish, rather than being drawn along the bottom like a trawl, and consequently does not need such a powerful boat. In winter they were used to catch valuable flat-fish on sand or 'saft boddam'.

Cod netting [3]

Nothing seems to be recorded about the origins of cod nets. They were introduced in the late-19th century and were widely adopted with the advent of motors on boats. They can be used in winter from small boats, with a crew of three or less, otherwise used for creels in summer. Today single fishermen even operate cod nets. Cod nets consist of a wall of net, originally made of hemp and held up by cork floats, later made of cotton and held up by glass floats. Modern ones are of nylon with plastic floats. Originally seven fleet, later four to six, were used, anchored across the tide on sand or 'saft boddom' and left overnight, now usually four fleet and anchored *with* the tide on rocky or 'hard boddom'.

Herring fishing [4]

Although there seem to have been regular shoals in the Tay in the middle ages (in 1560 Dundee was second only to the Forth and Clyde as an exporter of herring), herring fishing was virtually unknown off the Angus and Mearns coast until the 19th century. The salmon fishers of Bervie had occasionally caught a shoal coming inshore in their salmon nets,

---

1,2,3 Adapted from author's *Johnshaven and Milton, a social and economic history* (1991).

4 Modified from a hand-written rough (originally relating to East Haven), with reference also to the author's *Johnshaven and Milton, a social and economic history* (1991).

and herring were discovered again in the Tay when salmon stake nets were erected in the estuary shortly after 1800. Headrick in 1813 said that

> herring fishing has been tried in the open sea, off the Hayne [East Haven] in the parish of Panbride, and considerable quantities taken in the months of June, July and August, those earliest taken were plump and fat, and in no way inferior to the best loch Fyne herring.

Herring migrate in shoals near the surface and change migration routes unaccountably; unlike bottom feeding fish, which give a reliable daily catch, they could arrive in vast shoals which could not be sold as they glutted the market. Being an oily fish they could not be kept long or dried but had to be salt-pickled in barrels; this required a good deal of capital, so the industry was controlled by the curers, who had the resources to assemble barrels and salt and to engage coopers, fishing crews and their boats and the lassies who carried out the gutting and packing at the herring ports. A system of barrel bounties from 1785, and the establishment in 1809 of the Fishery Board for Scotland with its district offices and quality inspectors saw the development of a huge seasonal fishing off the Caithness and Sutherland coast, landing at Wick where there were large-scale curing facilities. Cholera decimated the northern communities around 1830 and the focus of herring fishing moved to Buchan. In 1832 Montrose-based curers engaged boats and men from the Angus and Mearns coast to work out of Peterhead in late summer. There was no mention of herring fishing the following year, either locally or off Buchan, but by the 1840s curers were engaging local boats to catch 200 crans each at a price ranging from nine shillings to 13 shillings per cran ($37\frac{1}{2}$ gallons, or about 1000 fish), each crew member also being awarded two bottles of whisky. This could mean £20 to each man at the end of a six-week season once the quota was caught, equal to about half a year's wages of a skilled artisan at the time. Stonehaven, Gourdon and Johnshaven became herring ports by the 1850s, Arbroath from 1858 and Montrose by the early 1860s.

The herring season usually lasted about six weeks from mid-July, following on the great line fishing, to early September, when sma' line fishing was resumed. By the 1880s the boats usually started at Fraserburgh and worked down the coast to Arbroath. The Ferryden fishers were the first to follow the Fifers to Eyemouth, Scarborough and Yarmouth, from 1882. Some boats went to Shetland and the west coast from the local herring ports but most Angus and Mearns fishermen only seem to have worked between Buchan and Arbroath for the usual six-week season. A winter fishing was sometimes carried out if shoals appeared off the local coast but most of that catch would be landed locally and sold fresh. The bulk of the summer herring was salt-pickled and exported to the Baltic coast of Germany, Poland and Russia, only a third went to the home market, fresh or kippered. In the 1860s, when nets were made of hemp cord, a boat might carry 24 nets totalling 3000 square yards but by the 1880s factory-made cotton nets, much lighter and with a finer mesh, would be carried by larger boats; 50 of these gave an area of 33,000 square yards. By these means a single boat might catch £100 worth of herring in a night though in poor seasons there might be little or no return. The increase in catching power ultimately resulted in a lower price per cran. By the 1890s auctions replaced fixed contracts and only the largest and best-equipped boats could compete. The smaller fishertouns dropped out by around 1900, and even Arbroath had a recession by 1908 when steam drifters (first introduced in 1897) began to replace sailing boats.

Herring nets, or drift nets, hung vertically just below the surface of the sea, suspended like a curtain with floats and weights. They were customarily shot at sunset, perhaps 30 to 40 miles out from the port of landing. The mainmast was struck and with two men at the oars the boat was rowed across the tide, a laborious process. After a time the men rowing would be relieved by another two – a crew of five was usual[1] – and would have some supper and a few hours rest or sleep. The skipper took the helm and seldom slept. Psalms might be sung during this night fishing. If there was no catch the nets would be hauled in and the boat rowed to another spot and the process resumed. By the 1880s as much as two miles of herring-laden net had to be hauled aboard and the fish shaken or picked out. The boat then set sail for the herring port. The fish would be unloaded in cran baskets and delivered to the curer's yard while the nets were taken ashore to dry. Like the lines, they were barked with cutch from time to time. At the end of the season the nets would be dried on the local fields as farmers usually welcomed the dried fish refuse as good fertiliser.

Creel fishing

Creels similar to those used today were first introduced by English companies from the mid-18th century, at Ethie Haven from 1755 but at Torry only slightly before 1790. The buyers originally offered three pence for each lobster too large to pass through a wooden ring of a certain diameter. Early catches were phenomenal but soon declined to a lower level, presumably due to over-fishing. The lobsters were kept in chests in the sea with their claws tied until dispatched. A system of fast smacks, which could reach Billingsgate in about four days, collected the lobsters (and from the 1790s also iced salmon and turbot). The smacks were designed with wells allowing sea-water to pass over the lobsters on their way to Billingsgate, so keeping them alive and fresh. Paddle steamers replaced sailing smacks from 1837 and later rail and then road transport was used. Before the railways partans (edible crabs), caught in the same creels, were mostly sold locally, later dispatched to English cities. A Johnshaven firm stores lobsters in tanks of sea-water before transporting them to Europe live by road, also in sea-water. The creels then, as now, consisted of a wooden board weighted with a stone or lump of cement with three wooden (or plastic) hoops holding up two netted chambers which have net funnels. The prey enters the chamber, which is baited with pieces of fish, and cannot escape.

---

1 In the early period. Later the large boats might have crews of eight or nine (ed.).

The fishermen of the district still mostly make their own creels, now from a mixture of natural and synthetic materials including synthetic netting, replacing the original hemp. Mass-produced wire creels, as used in the Minch, are no use in the more exposed conditions of the east coast. Cornish-style 'inkwell' wicker pots for some reason do not attract the local crustaceans, and the traditional design still used varies little from that introduced from eastern England in the 18th century. At Gourdon however, creels with a distinctive style of covering of wooden slats are used, somewhat similar to those used in Iceland and maritime Canada. At Auchmithie and Arbroath, for some reason, such creels are uniquely known as 'sunks'.

Salmon fishing [1]

A wide variety of methods was used to catch salmon, all carefully circumscribed by legislation in the old Scottish Parliament and the British Parliament in order to prevent over-exploitation and spoliation of neighbouring fishings.

Net and coble (sweep nets)

This was the most commonly used method to catch salmon, employed in rivers, tidal estuaries and off the coast. The net is held on the bank or shore while the coble makes a sweep holding the other end. A net and coble fishing still (2010) takes place at the mouth of the North Esk.

Yairs

These were enclosures of wattle or stone, built in tidal or estuary waters to trap salmon. This is probably a very ancient way of fishing; similar methods are used by Canadian Inuit and Native Americans to trap Arctic char. The dam built between his properties on the north and south banks of the North Esk, between Warburton and Kinnaber, by William, Earl of Montrose from 1504 may have been a yair. The fact that it was built would suggest that a historical right to such a 'fixed engine' existed. Its destruction by 1507 by order of the burgh authorities probably arose from its misuse or construction the whole way across the river.

Stells

Stell nets could be placed across a river, while a stell was a place over which nets could be drawn, more rarely an enclosure of nets in a river, according to dictionary definitions. East of Rossie Island, at the mouth of the South Esk, was a fishing called the Stell, the site now occupied by the wharf of the oil base. Presumably this particular form of fishing was practised here.

---

1 Drawn largely from the author's *Report on the History of Salmon Fishing in the Montrose Area from c.1360 to 1835*, 1985 (typescript).

Cruives

Rights to cruives were mentioned in Montrose's charter of 1359. Whole series of cruives were built on some rivers, such as the Ness near Inverness; some exist on Irish rivers but this system seems to have been abandoned or outlawed by about 1800 in Scotland. The method may be quite ancient and the name seems to imply a wicker construction but by the later middle ages cruives were elaborate traps in stone dykes, made of slats of wood. It was a system constantly open to misuse. Prior to 1762 the structure at Stone of Morphie, on the North Esk, had seven cruives and the dyke was about 15 feet broad and two feet or more above the water, making it impossible for the salmon to pass. A detailed account and diagram of its replacement survives from 1768. Each sluice or opening was allowed to be one ell (37 inches) wide set in the bottom of the river channel, the dyke to be one foot six inches above the water surface as it was between 1 April and 1 May when there was no spate, and to slope from the top until two feet below the water. Into the sluices were set the cruives, or traps, made of wooden slats called hecks which by law had to be three inches apart. The teeth or rungs of these had to be entirely removed at 'forbidden' times, that was for the whole of the close season (October to January) and, during the fishing season, for the 'Setterday slap', which was from 6pm on Saturday night to sunrise on Monday morning. Misuse of the cruive dyke by Scott of Brotherton resulted in its disuse or entire removal sometime before 1793.

7 *Driving a stake into the sand*   8 *A single row of stakes*

Stake-nets [1]

Stake-nets (also known as fly-nets) were introduced into the Tay by Maule of Panmure just after 1800 and into the Montrose area in 1807. This method is suitable for fishing from sandy beaches. The nets are attached to stakes driven into the sand to form an 'arrow-head' trap. The fish are guided into the trap by the 'leader', a net stretching out from the shore, and removed using a long-handled net. Until recently this method was still practised on the Angus and Mearns coast and the stakes were a familiar feature of sandy beaches such as Lunan Bay. Nowadays (2010) the Usan salmon fishers mostly use jumper nets, which require fewer anchorage points and are more easily removed; the leader floats free, suspended from a line of cork floats. A single fly-net is still used at Boddin, where, uniquely, the stakes are inserted into holes bored in the rock.

Bag-nets [2]

The first effective deep-water floating net was designed by John Hector of Aberdeenshire, who in 1828 set up 12 single-sided nets in the Bay of Nigg. A double-sided three-chambered net was introduced at Cove in 1841 and this arrangement is still in use today. Bag-nets are suitable for fishing off rocky parts of the coast, being anchored a short distance out to sea. The salmon enter as the tide retreats and are caught in the trap at the sea-end. Large sea-going cobles are required to empty the nets, which is done by pulling them into the boat and releasing the fish through a 'trapdoor'.

1, 2 Contributed by editor.

9 *Stake nets at Lunan Bay*

15

Boats and coasting vessels

Sailing boats

Early medieval north European ships and boats traditionally had a single mast and square sail and were clinker built of overlapping strakes. From the mid-15th century Mediterranean influences led to large trading vessels being carvel-built, the strakes set edge-to-edge and caulked with hemp rope and tar. Additional masts and sails were added to ships and so three- and four-masted ships developed, with triangular lateen sails rigged to the mizzen mast while the main and foremast remained square rigged. A great variety of smaller trading vessels with two masts and square or fore-and-aft sails also emerged, but where and when the lugsail, later typical of Scottish fishing boats, was developed seems unknown. Records from the 15th century show that the largest Scottish fishing boats were totally distinct from the smallest cargo boats both in rig and in the facts that the masts could be lowered and the boats could be rowed as well as sailed. In England two-masted fishing luggers were in use by the 17th century, and presumably were also in Scotland, but most useful or reliable depictions of Scottish boats (from gravestones, maps, engravings and paintings) only date from the late-17th century, including Slezer's views of Scottish burghs drawn around 1678. There are stray records indicating that quite large fishing boats, along with much smaller ones, were in use locally in medieval and early modern times. In 1447 the burgh of Dundee was granted the right by the Crown to collect dues for the upkeep of the harbour and specified three types of trading vessel which were to be charged ten shillings, five shillings or one shilling according to size while 'greite bates' were to be charged sixpence and 'small bates' twopence. This would appear to indicate a significant difference in size and capacity. At Milton of Mathers in 1553 there was a single boat and seven fisher households, so a minimum crew of seven. In 1635 Montrose Town Council forbade the building and use of 'great boats', perhaps fearing that the fishers could land their fish at other ports or sell it to ships far out to sea (the main function of the local fishers, as they saw it, being to supply fish to the burgh). In 1686 an Auchmithie fisherman paid the Earl of Northesk for the privilege of using both great and small boats. An arcanely worded letter from the Earl of Cromartie to Northesk in 1713 suggests the use of boats as large as 20 or 30 tons burden along with smaller 'yoles', but it is doubtful if such large boats were used on the Angus and Mearns coast at that time. Slezer's view of Dundee from the east, drawn around 1678, shows two small yauls, each with a single central mast and lugsail. Adair's map of the local coast of 1703 shows four small yauls with crews of three or four; a single mast is lowered onto a mutch in the bows as they apparently fish by line. Another boat has a lowered mainmast and a small standing mast and rectangular sail in the bows. This one has a balustrade at the stern and is fishing with a net, so must be intended to depict a herring buss; there is no evidence for locally-based herring fishing at that time although the Dutch were fishing in Scottish waters. In 1731 the largest boat's crew was expected to be six men and a boy but it is likely that the boats were about the same size as those later in the century.

In the later-18th century most of the boats in the district were all-purpose vessels of just under 25 feet overall. According to Knox, writing in 1786, they used both oars and sails and were wedge-shaped, with sharp bows (hence the name 'pinks') but broader aft. They had a deep, sharp keel and were reckoned to be more seaworthy than any boats of their size.

These boats had a crew of six, usually including a boy (a few only five) and were used in all types of fishing, both inshore and the more distant water great-lining. This practice, typical of the period 1770s to 1830, contrasts with earlier times, when some communities used more than one size of boat, and later, when all communities had three sizes of boat. Johnshaven appears to have been unusual in the mid-18th century, certainly in the Dee to Tay area, in having large ten-man boats of 8 to 10 tons burden for distant water great line fishing in midsummer, while even their haddock boats had crews of eight and were of 5 or 6 tons burden. A few other fishertouns may also have had such boats but evidence is lacking. When Montrose Town Council, for the purposes of selling mussels to outsiders, fixed the following rates in 1766 and 1777, 'large boats' presumably meant the Johnshaven boats, 'middling', or 'pinks' the standard haddock boats of up to 25 feet and 'yauls' small boats (up to 18 feet) which were used by old men and boys:

1766

Large boats	£6–7 Scots (10s to 11s 8d Stg.)
Middling boats	£4 Scots (6s 8d Stg.)
Smallest boats	£2 Scots (3s 4d Stg.)

1777

Big boats	20s Stg.
Pinks	10s Stg.
Yauls	5s Stg.

By the 1790s most fishertouns in the district had the standard boats of up to 25 feet. Some also had yauls, and a few places, such as Ferryden, Montrose and some of the smaller fishertouns, only had yauls. This was due to the fittest fishermen having been seized by the press gangs, leaving only older men and boys to carry out inshore small line, handline and creel fishing.

19th-century developments

When local involvement in herring fishing began off Buchan from 1832, at first the stoutest available haddock boats were used but soon the advantages of larger boats became apparent. In 1834 the Montrose Customs collector, whose district was from the Tay to Todhead, reported that large boats of 18 to 24 tons burden were being used for herring fishing and great line cod fishing from May to early September; they were beached for the winter when small line fishing was resumed. They cost £60 to £80, usually shared between four to six persons. The smaller boats were said to be below 15 tons burden. Under the stimulus of the herring fishing, boats continued to get larger. By 1848 boats of around 35 to 40 feet overall were in use, still mostly with a crew of five for herring fishing but with up to nine at the great line fishing. The Fishery Board began to class boats over 30 feet as 1st class, those of 18 to 30 feet as 2nd class and those under 18 feet as 3rd class.[1] There was considerable variation from place to place but in 1855 around half of the boats were 2nd class standard haddock boats and one third 1st class, so only around a sixth were yauls. Due to the use of seasonal boats the ratio of boats to fishers in the second half of the century was around 1:2 rather than 1:6 as earlier since most fishermen had shares in two sizes of boats.

Herring boats continued to grow in size, often over 40 feet and partially decked by the 1850s, later fully decked and carvel- as opposed to clinker-built. By 1900 they were up to 60 or 70 feet long. The largest had steam donkey engines to raise the heavy yard-arm and sails and to winch in the large fleets of nets. Their great weight meant that they had to be beached with the aid of teams of horses, steam winches or traction engines. Regional types developed. In the Forth a type of half-decked boat of intermediate size, used from the 1860s, was known as the 'baldi', a name apparently inspired by the contemporary hero Garibaldi. There is a reference to these from Stonehaven so it seems that they were used in the district in question. Along the Moray Firth boats of this size were called 'skiffs', a term whose exact meaning varied from place to place but which usually referred to light clinker-built vessels. The terms used from the Dee to the Tay are unrecorded, except that at Ferryden the term 'skift' was applied to the standard clinker-built small line or haddock boats. The large herring/great line boats may simply have been referred to as big boats. The smallest boats were consistently called 'yauls', 'yoles' or 'yolies'.

Hull design

The earliest measured drawings of Scottish east coast boats are from a report to the House of Commons made in 1848 by a Captain Washington after hundreds of herring boats were lost off the east coast in a great storm. Boats from Wick, Buckie, Fraserburgh, Peterhead, Aberdeen and Newhaven were examined. Washington condemned them all, although they had probably been developed from earlier boats which had evolved to suit local conditions. The Buckie or Moray Firth boat was the most distinctive. It had a 30 - foot keel but was 42 feet overall and very lightly built. The stem was sharply curved while the stern was straight but with a rake of 45 degrees. This was the type later recorded as the 'scaithe', 'scaff' or more familiarly in the diminutive form 'scaffie', a word

---

1 These are what the author, in his lists of fishermen and boats (see Gazetteer), describes as 'large', 'standard' and 'yauls' (ed.).

ultimately cognate with skiff and Gaelic *sgoth*, a type of boat used in the Minch. Scaffies were used in the comparatively sheltered waters of the Moray Firth. Their design and light build made them very manoeuvrable. The Buchan boats were more heavily built with only a slight curve to stem and stern, more suited to open sea and having a better grip in the water. The Aberdeen boat, however, had a pronounced curve to the stem, slightly less to the stern, and most of the earlier 19th-century depictions of boats from the Dee to the Tay also show a slight raking curve to the stem and stern, some more pronounced than others. An 1840 depiction of Ferryden boats shows a fairly pronounced curve to the stem, similar to the Aberdeen boat. Photographs from around the turn of the 20th century show that while the large herring drifters used in the district typically were of the 'fifie' type (see below) and had straight, near-vertical stems and sternposts, the smaller boats still had a noticeable curve to the stem, and this is particularly evident on small yauls new-built in Montrose for ageing Usan fishermen around 1910. There were many boatyards in the district, not only in the burghs and larger villages but at some small fishertouns and elsewhere on the coast. There must always have been slight variations between boats made by different builders, but it seems that, except for the large carvel-built drifters, the boats built and used in Angus and the Mearns tended to resemble the Aberdeen boat of 1848.

The origin of the term 'fifie', denoting large boats having straight vertical stems and straight sternposts barely off the vertical, is unknown. No one has documented the earliest usage of the term though many commentators have applied it loosely and anachronistically. It was only certainly in use by the late-19th century, in reference to the large carvel-built drifters of this design regularly used on the east coast. These had probably evolved from earlier East Fife boats and the term may have been coined to distinguish them from the Moray Firth boats when large fleets of Scottish drifters first began to follow the herring shoals from Shetland to East Anglia, the Moray Firth men and the Fifers having been pioneers in this. As drifters grew larger a hybrid design, dubbed 'zulu' from the contemporary war in the news, was adopted in the Moray Firth. Zulus were also carvel-built and had the near-vertical stem of the fifie, to give better grip in the more exposed waters off the east coast, but the 45 degrees sternpost of the scaffie; they were as long over-all as fifies of similar capacity and had similar sail rig. They were built and used as far east as Fraserburgh; few, if any, would have been used by fishermen in the Dee to Tay district, although they would have been seen landing at the local herring ports in season.

Mast and sail arrangement

Several engravings of Dundee waterfront show fishing luggers as well as trading vessels. One dated 1790 shows a boat with the mainmast and sail well forward and a smaller mizzen hard to the stern, while another of 1793 shows a similar arrangement. A lost

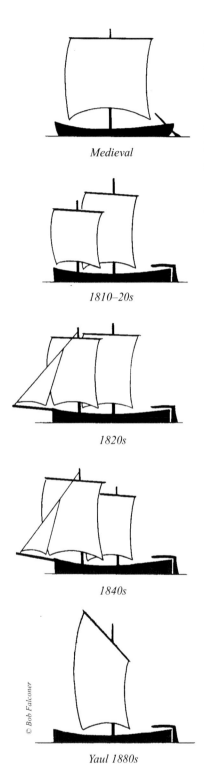

Medieval

1810–20s

1820s

1840s

© Bob Falconer

Yaul 1880s

10 *Diagram of fishing boat sail plans*

gravestone once in Bervie kirkyard however, commemorating a Gourdon skipper who died in 1811, depicted a boat with the mainmast amidships, with a large dipping lugsail held up by a halyard, and a much smaller mast and lugsail forward: the reverse, therefore, of that found on the earlier Dundee boats. A view of Dundee of 1824 includes a boat with a similar arrangement to that at Bervie: mainmast and sail in the centre and slightly smaller lugsail forward. A monument in Portlethen kirkyard, erected by a Burnbanks fisher in 1821, shows a boat with a crew of six, also having the larger sail aft though here there is only a fraction of difference in size between the two sails; there is another very similar and contemporary monument to a Torry fisher in St Fittick's kirkyard at Nigg Bay. The gravestone of a Ferryden fisher in Inchbraoch cemetery, dated 1822, also shows two sails of almost identical size but in addition has a triangular foresail held out on a bowsprit. The use of bowsprit and foresail is evident in a view of Dundee from the Tay of 1836, which shows a fishing boat being rowed with long sweeps; the sail plan, however, has been reversed again, with the large mainmast and sail placed well forward and a (tiny) mizzen mast well aft. This is also demonstrated in an 1840 engraving of Montrose harbour from Ferryden which shows boats being worked with only the mainsail, their mainmasts placed well forward and the smaller mizzens amidships. An engraving of Arbroath harbour of 1843, however, shows a boat still retaining the older arrangement of two lugsails of roughly the same size.

It seems therefore that before 1800 there was a considerable difference in size between the two sails, with the mainsail forward. Thereafter there was a gradual tendency for the sails to become similar in size, which is apparent by the 1820s. By this time bowsprits and foresails were also being used, in Angus if not in the northern Mearns. The change back to placing the large mainsail forward again had taken place, in Angus at least, by the 1840s. Other districts were later in adopting

11 *The Leiper monument in Portlethen kirkyard erected by a Burnbanks fisher in 1821 shows a six-man crew*

12 *A contemporary monument to a Torry fisher in St Fittick's kirkyard at Nigg Bay shows a similar boat but crewed by a helmsman and six rowers. The aft sail appears to be larger than the foresail*

this sail plan: Aberdeen and Peterhead boats in 1848 still had a small mast well forward and their main mast amidships, like the Gourdon boat of 1811. The development of fully decked herring boats, however, meant that masts had to be well fore and aft to accommodate the fish hold between, and the general adoption of the forward mainsail seems to date from sometime in the 1870s. It was certainly in widespread use by the 1880s on large herring boats, as is evident from the many contemporary photographs. There are far fewer photographs of smaller boats in full sail; they are mostly seen in harbour with both masts down, while bowsprits could be taken inboard. It is not clear when similar features were adopted for small boats in other parts of the east coast.

Lugsails

Lugsails seem to have offered some of the benefits of both square-rig and fore-and-aft or gaff-rig. It was basically a very simple rig, a single halyard acted as a mast stay and also served to raise the sail. Lugsails were originally only slightly trapezoidal and only towards the end of the 19th century did they acquire the characteristic high-pointed peak seen in so many photographs of large drifters from the 1880s. Lugsails could be set square

© Bob Falconer

13 *An early-19th-century fishing lugger under sail*

to the mast to run before the wind or at a sharp angle to tack into the wind with most of the sail set to one side of the mast. Unlike a gaff-sail, which could simply be swung the other way, the mast had to be lowered and the yard and sail passed around the mast before being set to tack on the opposite course. Despite the fact that this tricky manoeuvre needed great skill and experience, and could lead to men being swept overboard, the Scots fishers preferred lug-rig to all others, maintaining that they could sail closer to the wind with it. Experiments were made with gaff-rig in the 1870s off Buchan and in the 1880s some of the larger boats at Gourdon seem to have had gaff-sails. But nearly all persisted with lugsails until the final demise of sail, only in Shetland was there a general adoption of gaff-rig. What appear to be gaff-sails are shown on a monument to Auchmithie fishers in St Vigeans kirkyard datable to around 1800–10, but this was probably a mistake by the sculptor, more familiar with sloops and schooners. In fact there are only five depictions of fishing vessels known from monuments in the district, one now lost and only known from a drawing. Skippers of trading vessels could far more often afford elaborately carved gravestones depicting their vessels.

Steam trawlers and drifters

The steam trawler originated in eastern England. In 1877 paddle-tugs laid off during a trade depression, and at a time when coal was cheap, began to try trawling with success. Up until then large two-masted schooner-rigged sailing smacks had been used with trawl nets to catch white fish on the Dogger Bank off the east coast of England from the Thames to the Humber. They were crewed by indentured orphan boys, not by born and bred fishermen as with the smaller line-fishing boats used from Whitby northwards into Scotland. Soon purpose-built paddle-trawlers were built and from around 1880 some English trawlers began to land at Aberdeen. They were soon copied there and from 1882 Aberdeen began to develop its own large fleet of trawlers. Screw steamers, also pioneered in England, began to be built at Aberdeen from the 1890s and were steel-hulled, unlike early drifters. Soon Leith and purpose-built Granton in the Forth also became important trawling ports. Dundee and Montrose were very minor in comparison and their trawlers often worked out of Aberdeen.

The first purpose-built steam drifter was built at Lowestoft in 1897. Some were used in Scotland from around 1900 and a great many were built between 1905 and 1920, mainly copying English lines. They were mostly wooden-hulled and 75 to 90 feet overall. They had steam capstans for net hauling but less powerful engines than trawlers as they were not required to drag a heavy trawl net along the bottom but drifted with the tide when fishing. The superstructure which housed the wheelhouse, galley, engine room and a tall funnel was aft of centre. They had a small mizzen gaff-sail which kept the boats into the wind when fishing. A short foremast was used as a derrick for unloading herring in quarter-cran baskets. They could also be used for great-lining but were not economical for seining. Purpose-built steam great-liners were used out of Aberdeen, the last until the 1960s. In the Moray Firth, Buchan and East Fife, where herring fishing was all-important, steam drifters rapidly replaced sailing drifters; though they cost £3,000 new, as compared to £450 for a sailing drifter, they could catch three times as much as sailing boats. In the district between the Dee and the Tay herring fishing meant only a six-week summer season for the majority of fishers and there was no switch to steam. Only three steam drifters were used in the district, working out of Montrose from 1907 into the 1920s. There is no record of purpose-built steam liners in the district.

Motor boats

Auxiliary paraffin motors began to be used from shortly after 1900 and soon more powerful diesel engines were introduced. At first smaller fifies were converted but after 1918 diesel-powered motor boats of around 45 to 50 feet, based on fifie lines, began to be built. From the later 1920s the cruiser or canoe stern was copied from English boats. This left the stern clear for seine nets as the rudder was beneath the water line. They had a small wheelhouse aft of the fish hold. This type of wooden-hulled multi-purpose boat, used for herring, seine-net and great line fishing, was the predominant style of Scottish boat up to the 1960s. Most in the district were little more than 50 feet as seiner/drifters of over 60 feet were not used. Lighter trawling gear and more powerful diesel engines led to small inshore trawlers of this type being built but seine-netting was the commonest method of white-fishing from the 1920s to the 1960s; only a few were used for great-lining. Motor yauls of the same type, under 40 feet long, the smallest clinker-built, were used for working sma' lines, creels and cod nets. Miscellaneous types of boats, including ships' lifeboats, were also used for the same fishings. From the 1970s metal wheelhouses, painted to simulate wood, and superstructures, usually painted white, have been characteristic of medium sized white-fishing boats. The graceful canoe stern was abandoned for the slab-ended or transom stern and boats became much broader of beam, more suited to the gear in use but certainly less graceful in appearance.

Commercial coasting vessels

At many of the small havens and on shingle beaches small vessels could land and be launched at high tide and did not need harbours. Such vessels, in some cases from the 17th century and certainly by the mid-18th, carried out grain to the Forth or Tyne and brought in coal, and from the 1770s lime for the fields. When bringing in coal they often sat for a week until the cargo was sold to local farmers who brought their carts down to the beach and loaded and paid for it directly. In the later middle ages the smallest class of trading vessel was the crear. They were specifically mentioned at Dundee in 1447 and were to pay one shilling harbour dues, twice as much as the largest fishing boats. They were presumably single-masted and clinker-built but their use overlapped from the 17th century with barks, so there must have been some difference in rig or hull-shape.

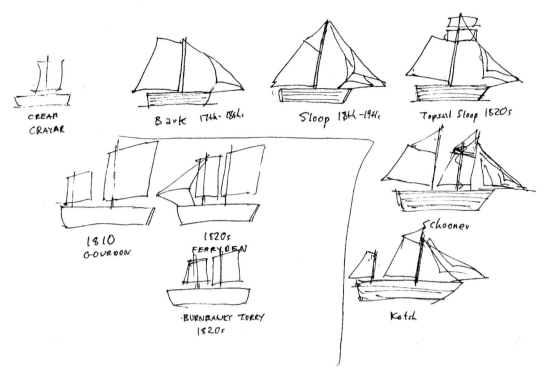

CREAN CRAYAR

Bark 17th-18th

Sloop 18th-19thc

Topsail Sloop 1820s

1810 GOURDON

1820s FERRYDEN

·BURNBANKS TORRY 1820s

Schooner

Ketch

14 *Davy's own sketch of sailing boat types including commercial coasting vessels. The three to the left and below the line represent types of early 19th-century fishing boats from Gourdon, Ferryden and Burnbanks/Torry*

Barks were the small single-masted vessels used in the 17th and early-18th century. They were of 10 to 20 tons burden, were clinker-built like boats and in fact were frequently built by boatbuilders. They had a single gaff-sail on a centrally located mast, with a bowsprit supporting a single triangular foresail. By the early-18th century sloops were replacing barks as the smallest class of coasting vessel. There may have been some difference in the design of their hulls, since the rig was similar, except that early sloops had triangular topsails in addition. Initially they were only of about 20 tons burden and clinker-built but by the 1790s were usually nearer to 40 tons burden and carvel-built. They could be crewed by a skipper, two men and a boy and were quite capable of making voyages to Italy or Norway, although mainly used in coasting. By about 1835 sloops were usually nearer 50 tons burden and later could sometimes be much larger. After 1800 they often had a square-rigged topsail or two and a couple of triangular foresails. Small schooners, an American design, were first introduced to the east of Scotland in the 1790s and were also used in coasting. They were two-masted and gaff-rigged, the slightly taller mainmast and main gaff-sail being aft. They had several triangular foresails and originally had triangular topsails, but after 1800 the foremast sometimes had square-rigged topsails. Such small coasting schooners were seldom much larger than sloops, unlike large ocean-going schooners, which had three or more masts and sails. Towards 1900 smaller ketches began to replace small schooners in coasting trade. They were also two-masted and gaff-rigged but had the mainmast forwards and a much smaller mizzen mast and sail aft and were operated by a smaller crew than schooners. By around 1900 places with small harbours such as Johnshaven, or even a pier like Catterline, had coal delivered by small wooden-hulled steamers. From before 1900 into the 1920s Clyde puffers, specially designed to use the Forth-Clyde and Crinan canals and land where there were no harbours, carried coal from the Forth up the east coast at least as far north as Stonehaven and took away barley to distilleries on Islay on return journeys. Presumably all such vessels were cleaned with sea-water and allowed to dry out to enable sacks of grain to be shipped in them after a bulk cargo of coal or lime. Even if the latter were barrelled, which seems unlikely, the holds must have required scrupulous cleaning.

15 *Sloop on a gravestone in Montrose, 1837*

Markets and cures [1]

In the middle ages the authorities in Dundee and Montrose always considered the supply of fish to the inhabitants as the local fishers' primary function, and took pains to prevent 'forestalling', or buying for re-sale. In 1522–23 it was ordained in Dundee that no-one was to buy more fish than for their own sustenance, and 'hucksters' were only allowed to buy fish 24 hours after the boats had landed. The fishers of Montrose were regularly reminded that they were not allowed to sell fish from their boats but had to expose them for sale at the market cross; in 1751 two hours was the period laid down before any fish could be sold to cadgers. A similar restriction was placed on Arbroath fishers, who in 1574 had to expose their fish at the market on pain of a fine of eight shillings. At Auchmithie, which had been granted to Arbroath Abbey on its foundation in 1178, the fishers' main function was to supply fresh fish to the abbey, though any surplus could be sold once this requirement had been met. After the Reformation part of the abbey (possibly the vaulted undercroft of the Abbot's House) became known as the fish-hall and may have been used as the burgh fish market. Montrose's fish market was set up near the market cross in 1660, about the same time as specialist meat and meal markets. A new market with stone tables and running water was created off John Street in 1802. Dundee's 'fish and flesh stocks' were leased annually by public roup. Originally the fish market was near the market cross, later in the 'highway to the shore', known as Fish Street by the 17th century and on the site of Whitehall Crescent. The growing burgh of Dundee, unsurprisingly, could not depend solely on its own fishing community for supplies, and fish of various kinds was brought in from the smaller fishertouns by cadger. Broughty Ferry and West and East Haven are the most likely outside sources of fresh fish, while dried and pickled fish may have come from much further afield.

By the 18th century the expanding local burghs and the surrounding countryside provided the main market for white fish and partans. In 1722 the fishertouns in Fetteresso parish were said to supply fish 20 to 30 miles up country south and westwards. Angus fishers had a ready market in the burghs of Angus and Perthshire, particularly when these expanded due to the linen trade of the late-18th century. Fish had long been the cheapest source of animal protein available to the rural and urban poor and nearly every home had a triangular wooden fish hake on the wall to hang fish on. Cadgers distributed fish to the inland burghs, mostly in the adjoining parishes but in 1835 it was reported that cadgers from Forfar, Coupar Angus, Perth and Dundee came at all times of year to Ferryden for fresh fish. The fish was also carried to market, or sold directly, by the fishwives, whose stamina for journeys on foot carrying heavy creels of fish was

---

1 Compiled by editor from author's notes and previous publications.

legendary. Before the coming of the Dundee-Arbroath railway in 1838 the fishwives of East and West Haven would regularly walk to Dundee. The opening of the railway to Aberdeen likewise made distribution easier from the more distant Mearns fishertouns; from its opening to passengers in 1850, women from Skateraw and Downies went by train to sell at stances at the Green in Aberdeen. A special fish train ran from Portlethen and a local farmer was paid one shilling to take creels from Downies to the station. Even after the coming of the railway, however, it was said that the women of Auchmithie used to walk to Dundee and back to save the rail fare, a round trip of 40 miles!

Drying

Any surplus fish which could not be sold fresh had to be preserved. In the 18th century and earlier, white fish, including large cod and ling caught at the summer great lines, were traditionally air-dried. The fish were first soaked in strong brine and then laid out on grass or pebbles by the shore and turned frequently. They were gathered into heaps at night and put under a weighted board. The process took about a fortnight. Although the area has a cool climate, often with overcast skies, the actual rainfall is low, under 30 inches (75cm) annually on the coast. If it did rain the fish had to be gathered up in baskets by the women and children and laid out again when it faired. In the late-15th century the Abbey of Arbroath, apart from a daily supply of fresh fish from Auchmithie, bought in dried haddock and speldings. Speldings were haddock or whitings, dried and pressed. At Downies they were laid out on a gaw, a drying frame of criss-cross slats supported on posts; when dried, they were arranged on a chair, tails to middle, in layers separated by paper and weighted with a stone on top. In the 18th century at Johnshaven dried white-fish were taken at the end of the summer great line fishing to ports in the Firth of Forth where they could be sold and a cargo of coal brought home for the winter. In 1747 six Johnshaven boats took 5000 codlings each to Alloa and Bo'ness. Open boats from other fishertouns, including Ferryden, are recorded as bringing coal into the district and so were probably likewise returning from selling fish in the Forth or on Tyneside. After the coming of the railway very little fish may have been dried as the bulk could be sold fresh the same day it was caught. At places not connected to the railway, such as Auchmithie and some small havens on the Mearns coast, a higher proportion of the catch was dried or smoked.

Smoking

In 1642 the comment 'Findon, *vide*[1] Findon haddocks' showed that the dry cure was already famous. The Statistical Account of 1791 mentions that Findon gave its name to peat-dried smoked haddock which were already known and esteemed in most parts of Scotland. Finnans were traditionally smoked for six to eight hours over fires of soft grey

---

1 ?recte *unde*, whence.

peats in domestic 'hinging lums' (large open fireplaces with laths alongside from which the fish were hung above the peat), until late 19th-century food acts banished curing from living quarters and into smoke houses. Well-prepared finnans had a glossy surface like varnish and a flavour quite different from wood-smoked fish. Finnans were also made at neighbouring villages such as Cove and Burnbanks. At the latter, most of the haddock landed was made into finnans and the houses were said to have had Findon-type fireplaces. In the 1840s large quanities of finnans were sent from Cowie by cadger to Angus and Perthshire, by coach and sea to Edinburgh and Glasgow and by steam vessel from Aberdeen to London. Bervies (probably from Gourdon) were also popular in the 18th century. These were similar but used very recent peat of partly decayed sphagnum, and at the end of the cure this was fanned into flames to cook the fish. A company founded in Gourdon in 1836 engaged fishermen to supply haddock daily and established a successful trade in dressing, smoking and barrelling haddocks for distant markets such as Glasgow and London.

Although the Findon and Bervie peat-smoked cures were already well-known in Angus in the early-18th century, and some individuals smoked haddock and codling for their own use, there was no commercial curing in the county. When, in 1849, James Thomson noted that Montrose was famous for pickled cod, smoked haddocks and cured herrings, the smoking of fish was recent, since there had been no commercial smoking in Angus in 1813 according to Headrick's *View of the Agriculture of Angus or Forfarshire*, published that year. In fact Headrick suggested that this method of curing should be *introduced* to Angus, noting that finnans, sent by mail coach from Aberdeen to Edinburgh and London, were sold at high prices. It is possible that the practice of smoking haddocks was already carried on at Auchmithie (home of the smokie), but on such a small scale that it passed unnoticed by Headrick. It is hardly surprising that no mention of smoking haddocks was made by the author of the Statistical Account in 1793 since there was a severe dearth of haddock at that period. The sending of Auchmithie smoked haddocks to Dundee is mentioned in 1842, the earliest actual record that smoked haddock were prepared there. The Finnan haddie was mentioned in 1642, while Bervies were consumed by Forfar Town Council at its meetings in the mid-18th century. It would be nice to assume the smokie cure was as old, but unfortunately there is simply no evidence. The method of making smokies is described under Auchmithie.

Commercial curing and pickling of cod

Thousands of dried cod were exported annually from Montrose from the early-15th century, and possibly earlier, to England, the Netherlands and France. Much of this may have come from the outlying fishertouns within its trading precinct, which extended from the Dighty Water to the Findon Burn. Dundee exported only insignificant amounts of dried cod in the 15th and 16th centuries. By 1560 the salt pickling of fish was certainly being practised as it was ordained that the barrels used for wet-pickling both herring and keiling (large cod) were to contain nine gallons minimum; but as Dundee was then known as an exporter of herring and there may have been regular herring shoals in the Tay at the time it is likely that the curing industry was mainly exploiting these. Herring was also brought in and re-exported.

In 1782 the Customs collector for Montrose district stated that fish, mainly cod, ling and haddock, were exported coastwise from the district, cured with 42 pounds of salt per 100 fish. In 1793, when the tax was repealed on coal carried north of the Red Head, two salt pans were almost immediately built at Usan by David Scott of Dunninald. By evaporating sea water it was hoped to make 9000 bushels of salt annually (1 bushel = 8 gallons), supplying a third of local consumption. But even after a third pan was built only 3700 bushels was produced. Seventy percent of this was sold locally at Montrose and Ferryden for fish curing. It took up to six tons of coal to produce one ton of salt. The duties on salt entering Scotland were repealed in 1823 and cheap rock salt from Cheshire flooded in; all the Scottish saltworks soon closed down. Throughout the 18th century there were six or seven fish curers in Montrose who bought in fish and dealt in salt. Although they must have been employed largely in pickling salmon they also wet-pickled large quantities of cod and ling for export, bought by contract from such places as Johnshaven. The barrelled cod was sent to London but the ultimate destination was the Mediterranean. The trade in dried cod traditionally sent to London gradually fell off. In some areas the introduction of creel fishing for lobsters from 1755 led to the abandonment of the summer cod fishing if the returns were good; at Ethie Haven, however, in 1790 dried cod were still fetching five shillings per 100.

In the 19th century the best of the winter cod of a minimum size were sold by contract to curers. The greater proportion of cod and ling from Ferryden and Usan was sold to fish curers in Montrose and not less than 46,000 might be supplied in one year. By mid-century a number of villages, including Crawton, Shieldhill, Gourdon, Johnshaven, Usan, Ferryden and East and West Haven, had a resident cooper, curing and packing the best of the winter cod for the fish merchants. In 1843 George Shand, a Montrose curer, had 61 barrels containing 1153 fish packed at West Haven. In Gourdon in the 1830s and 40s a curer engaged the fishermen and employed a gutter to dress and salt cod for the London market, almost 100 three-hundredweight barrels being sent annually via Montrose. The same person dried cod in summer for home consumption.

Salmon [1]

In the 14th century salmon seems to have been kippered. From the 15th century to about 1800 the main method of packing salmon for export was to parboil and salt-pickle it. The main destinations were England, the Low Countries and France.

---

1 Much of this section comes from the author's *Report on the History of Salmon Fishing in the Montrose Area from c.1360 to 1835*, 1985 (typescript).

All burghs had a monopoly within their precincts of curing, packing and exporting salmon (among other things), and in 1505 the Crown, which stood to lose from the Great Customs otherwise, specially forbade the packing and export of salmon from Gourdon, 'Stanehiffe' and other places along the coast within Montrose's precinct. Dundee had its own burgh fishings while salmon from downstream stations and on the Fife bank of the Tay may have contributed to its export totals.

The final packing of the salt-pickled, par-boiled fish seems to have been undertaken by coopers hired by the owners or tacksmen of the fishings. In 15th- and 16th-century Montrose these were sometimes merchant burgesses, later mainly the local landowners, but the actual export was in the hands of merchants. Obviously the reputation of a burgh's *bind* or cure was crucial in marketing its product. In 1510 a rental agreement in the Arbroath Abbey register for nets in the Dee at Torry included 16 barrels of sweet red salmon of the common measure of Aberdeen. A lease of the St Thomas net on the North Esk in 1532 stipulated a rent of three barrels of salmon 'full reid and sweit and of the rycht bind of Montrose'. Between 1559 and 1562 the Head Court of Dundee noted that by Act of Parliament salmon barrels were to be standardised, that coopers were to brand them with their own irons so that any fish improperly packed could be traced and that masters of the coopers' craft were to make salmon barrels to contain $11\frac{1}{2}$ gallons. In 1668 James Mill, a Montrose cooper persistently accused of 'insufficient packing' in spite of having been fined, imprisoned and forced to give up his marking iron, was declared by the Council to be altogether incapable of packing salmon in time coming; his marking irons were ordered to be publicly broken at the market cross and he was to sign a bond never again to pack salmon in or about Montrose on pain of banishment. (Immediately before the opening of the new season Mill petitioned the Council that, since salmon packing was his greatest means of livelihood, he had resolved to pack 'faithfully' in future. The Council very forgivingly agreed to restore him to his 'office'.)

Until merchant fish curers began to take over control of the curing, at least some of the stages of the curing and packing of the salmon took place in fish-houses or 'boil-houses' at the proprietors' fishings. The salmon were cured in large tubs as they were caught and remained there until the end of the season when they were packed in barrels for export. It took approximately two bushels of salt per 42 gallon barrel to cure the salmon, which seems a prodigious amount but no doubt much was lost in the process. Salt was bonded and its use rigorously recorded. The salt all came from Portugal by the 18th century, previously it came from La Rochelle and French Biscay.

Kitted salmon

Whereas in 1774 all the salmon had been barrelled for export, there is evidence for a fairly rapid change in the curing method from the mid-1770s. Kitts were tubs containing 40 pounds of salmon, and the fish was pickled with vinegar as well as salt. By luck the

31

following recipe for kitted salmon has survived from the Commieston papers, datable to c.1772–80, the very period when kitting took over the trade:

> Boil your salmond with a strong pickle of salt as uswell and after it is boiled take it from the pickle, lett it stand till cold, scum all the fat from the pickle and boile it with Jamaica pepper [allspice] and a little black pepper, a few bay leaves, when it is cold take half the pickle and half vinegar and putt over your salmon. I have not one exact wight for the epecerie that is just as you would have it – it keeps long.

The commercial variant may have lacked the refinement of the 'epecerie' (spices). Kitted salmon, which seems to have largely replaced the barrelled variety by the mid-1780s, was in turn largely superseded ten years later by fresh salmon packed in ice.

Iced salmon

As early as 1765 the great innovator and radical laird George Dempster of Dunnichen seems to have had pits cut in Dunnichen Moss and the winter ice stored in specially constructed ice-houses for use throughout the summer. There is however no evidence for the commercial use of ice, in the Montrose area at least, until just after 1790. In 1792 in St Cyrus parish, which included the Warburton, Kirkside and Woodston fishings, the salmon was iced or vinegar pickled (kitted). A very elaborate ice-house is shown on Henrietta Auchterlony's lithographic view of Montrose of 1813. It was originally owned by a Mr Ridpath who in 1797 asked permission of the Council to cut ice from a pond on the Links. A number of surviving ice-houses on the Angus and Mearns coast, mostly dating from the 1820s to 1840s, also testify to this process, which was used until refrigeration was introduced. The salmon were packed in large oblong boxes with pounded ice between them and stored in the ice-houses until ready to go aboard the smacks for London.

From the mid-18th century merchant fish curers, by leasing the fishings or operating in partnership with the proprietors, controlled the whole trade, fishing, curing and shipping. Many of the prominent curers originated in Berwick, including Joseph Johnston, who came to Montrose in 1825 and whose family were to dominate curing and the fish trade in much of Angus and the Mearns.

© Bob Falconer

16 *Lobster*

Gazetteer

Torry [1]

Nigg NJ950050

The Barony of Nigg or Torry belonged to Arbroath Abbey from around 1190, probably from its foundation in 1178. A charter of 1233 mentions lands, pastures and mills but not fishings, although the community is likely to be a very early one. Salmon fishings were mentioned in leases from the early-16th century. In 1495 James IV created the *ville* (toun) of Torry a free burgh of barony, with rights to a weekly market. Although from early times under the influence of Aberdeen, Torry was effectively by-passed by the building of the Bridge of Dee upstream c.1500–25.

A small fishing community grew at a kink or bay on the south bank of the Dee, a mile west of its mouth at Girdleness. Upstream the Dee formed a wide estuary with up to seven channels separated by grass-covered inches on which were erected salmon fishers' huts; ebb tide revealed a maze of river channels and mud banks. In the 16th century large vessels bound for Aberdeen had to anchor off Torry to await the tide as Aberdeen harbour was so shallow. The subsequent growth of Torry is bound up with attempts to improve the harbour entrance.

In 1607 a long bulwark of stones and oak beams was built on the Torry side opposite Sandness. Three years later an obstructing rock called Craig Matellan or Knock Maitland was removed from the harbour mouth and in 1637 a great bed of sand, clay and stone was dug away to deepen the channel. Although it provided a footing for the capstans which pulled ships up-river during westerly winds and helped to scour out the river channel by narrowing it, the bulwark was considered to disturb the flow of water into the harbour and it was removed in 1810, when Aberdeen's North Pier was also extended. Subsequent improvements on the Torry side included the construction of the two south breakwaters, in 1815 and 1874 respectively, a new pier and in 1860 the leading lights. Part of the original Torry was lost when a new channel was cut for the Dee in 1869, but an area north of Sinclair Road and west of the pier was reclaimed and new houses were built for the fishers. These in turn were largely demolished in the 1970s when Torry Quay and the 19th-century harbour were reclaimed for a North Sea oil supply base, although some still remain in the area of Wood Street and Abbey Road known nowadays as Auld Torry.

From 1787 granite sets were being exported from the pier at Torry, and coal and lime imported. Salt panning and kelp burning took place on the shore. A whaling company

---

1 Compiled by editor from author's notes.

was established in the early-19th century with a boil house on the old pier. In the 1790s James Mann, shipbuilder in Torry, was building brigs, ketches and sloops. In the mid-19th century, in the heyday of the clippers, two ferry-loads of ship's carpenters crossed daily from Torry to the ship-building yards of Aberdeen but the industry also continued in Torry itself into the 20th century with both John Duthie's and John Lewis's shipyards, the latter specialising in trawler construction.

17 *Monument to a shipbuilder*

The fishing community

Gordon and Pont (1641x1650) show three groups of buildings at Nether Torry opposite Pockraw. Garden's 1774 survey has two rows of cottages near the shore. By 1791 there were six boats plus yauls hence around 45 fishers, who also served as pilots. In 1838 Torry was described as having a tolerable harbour and a pier for small vessels. Its fishermen carried haddocks and other fish to the fish market of Aberdeen but were now 'fewer than formerly', with only three to four boats. Three boats with five or six men went to the herring fishing in mid-July, but it was regarded as generally unprofitable. By the 1841 census the number of fishermen was down to 17 and white-fishing was stated to be less important than at Cove. Lewis however in 1847 lists catches of cod, haddock, ling, turbot and shellfish which were sold at Aberdeen market, while salmon were sent to London. Three boats of 14 ton burden with crews of six went to the herring fishing on the north coast. At this time the population of 295 included both fishers and tradesmen. In 1855 there were 30 fishermen and boys and a total of 14 boats but by 1858 this had risen to 20 boats and 80 fishers.

By the 1880s, with the building of Victoria Bridge in 1881 to replace the Wellington Suspension Bridge of 1830, Torry was simply a suburb of Aberdeen. New Torry expanded rapidly and new industries developed, including stone polishing yards, a provisions factory, a brick and tile works, a foundry, and other industries more closely linked to fishing, such as fish-box manufacturing and coopering. Even before this Torry had sucked in fishers from outlying areas, especially Portlethen, but from the 1880s there was the attraction of new tenement housing. With the invention of steam trawling Torry became the home of a fisher proletariat with no share in the boats. By the 1930s most of the 2800 fishermen of Aberdeen lived in Torry.

Salmon fishing

In the 16th century salmon fishers' huts were noted on the inches which separated the channels of the Dee. A rental agreement in the Arbroath Abbey register for two nets at Lagart, two at Powdown and half a net at Furdis, made with Walter Sinclair and his son Robert in 1510, includes 16 barrels of sweet red salmon of the common measure of Aberdeen. In 1527 the barony of Torry included the mill, alehouse, croft, ferryboats and salmon fishings.

By 1838 salmon fishing took place in the Dee, at Nigg Bay and all along the coast. Cobles and sweep nets were used in the Dee, bag-nets (recently introduced) at the river mouth and in inlets along the coast, and stake-nets on the beach. The 1841 census lists 11 salmon fishers.

Fisher names

Nigg parish records from the 17th century include Messon (Masson), Naper (Napier), Smith, Baxter, Bran(d), Fouler (Fowler), Forbes, Brydie/Brodie and Mitchell, all fisher names and all occurring later. All of these with the exception of Mitchell, and including Allan, are listed in 1813. The 1841 census shows no predominant name, the commonest being Morrice and Caie, also Allan, Robertson, Wood, Webster, Fowler and Mitchell. By 1881 there is an influx of new names, including: Jappy, Walker, Craig, Pert, Ritchie, Knowles, Leiper, Tait, Thomson, Main, Rennie, Neilson, Burnet, Carnegie and Freeland. They include settlers from the nearer Mearns fishertouns but also from Ferryden to Buchan. An influx of English trawlermen and their families c.1900–14 brought in further surnames.

Some variations of the place-name and spelling

Torry	1641x50, 1703, 1791, 1838, 1855 to date
Tory	1774, 1822
Torie	1822

Number of fishermen and boats

Year	Fishers	Boats	Type
1791	36 + 9 boys	10–12?	6 boats plus yauls
1813	c.65?	15	8 boats, 7 yauls
1838	c.18?	3–4	3 herring boats (10–14T burden) plus?
1855	30	14	2 large, 8 standard, 4 yauls
1881	156	79	all sizes

The 1928 Boat Account includes Torry under Aberdeen.

Altens   Nigg NJ962024

This short-lived fishertoun lay only 400 yards north of Burnbanks, between Altens farm
and Altens haven. The haven is accessible under a railway bridge off the back road
between Nigg Bay and Cove. On the north side of the track leading to the haven are the
forlorn ruins of several houses which appear to be relics of this hamlet which probably
only functioned as a white-fishertoun for 19 years at most. The haven itself is a rocky
sloch similar to that at Burnbanks, but it has a beach of large pebbles, more space to
draw up boats, and is accessible by a cart track.

The origins of Altens fishertoun must have lain in the improvements being made to
the estate of Altens from the late-18th century by the owner David Morice, an Aberdeen
advocate. From 1787 granite sets were being quarried and exported via Torry pier, two
miles away, by which lime for the fields was also imported. It was said in 1791 that there
were several 'indented hollows' where a vessel could be landed along the coast between
Cove and Torry (then the only fishertouns in the parish), and that one had recently been
fitted up with a pier. Altens haven is the most likely place referred to, as it alone had
suitable access by a cart track. There are no signs of a pier apparent today, however.

Map 1 *Altens and Burnbanks in the 19th century*

The community

The fishertoun was clearly founded just around 1800, certainly between 1794 and 1807, but it had a very short existence. The first actual record in the Nigg parish registers of fishers being resident at 'Altens' is from 1807 and the last in 1813. In that period about five couples had children baptised and their surnames, together with the fact that some of the witnesses were Cove fishers, show that the settlers all came from Cove, unlike their close neighbours at Burnbanks who came from Portlethen. In 1813 there were two boats which seem to have had a crew of five each. This would imply a minimum of eight families, confirmed by the number of houses recorded later, a small but apparently viable community. But Altens seems to have been abandoned by the white-fishers soon afterwards. In 1838 it was stated that 'Altens Harbour' had formed a 'considerable settlement' by then wholly deserted by fishermen and that the houses were now occupied by crofters or used as farm outhouses.

It was suggested that the reason for abandonment by white-fishers was the unfitness of the 'harbour' and the want of suitable 'turf and moss' to cure haddock. Since the fishers of Cove and Burnbanks were able to get suitable peat to make finnans, which was the most valuable way to market the haddock catch, it is odd that those of Altens could not. Altens haven is also more easily accessible from the land than Burnbanks haven, and since Altens was a far more flourishing fishing community in 1813 than Burnbanks it is strange that it was abandoned so soon while the latter continued to flourish into the 1880s. Nineteen years was then a regular term of lease for land, houses etc. and it may be that whatever problems the Altens white-fishers had, they may have returned to Cove, or otherwise abandoned the place, after their initial leases ran out.

Salmon fishing

No salmon fishers seem to have been resident in 1838. The 1841 census, however, apart from Altens Farm, records the residents of 'Easter Croft of Altens', where there were then eight houses inhabited by farm workers, a cow feeder (dairyman) and three salmon fishers. The Ordnance Survey of 1865 shows that there were once houses on both sides of the track leading to the haven. From 1849–50 the railway embankment seems to have done away with one or two of the houses. The remains of a salmon bothy lie above the haven, along with an ice-house which existed in the mid-19th century but which was disused by the 1920s. It seems to have been converted to wartime use as a lookout around 1939–40 while the remains of an army hut and gun emplacement lie by the path at the head of the haven. Salmon fishing continued until the mid-1960s when the gaffer was killed trying to secure a winch cable in a violent storm, which resulted in its abandonment.

Fisher names

All the white-fisher folk, male and female, recorded 1807–13 were called Guyon, Brand or Robertson, a set of surnames only otherwise found at Cove.

Some variations of the place-name and spelling

Altens	1807–13
Altens Harbour	1838
Easter-Croft of Altens	1841

Number of fishermen and boats

Year	Fishers	Boats	Type
1813	10	2	under 25ft

Burnbanks Nigg NJ957020

The site of this hamlet lies about three-quarters of a mile north of the centre of the old fishertoun of Cove and only a few hundred yards north of its modern extensions, west of the road leading to Torry via Nigg Bay. The fisher dwellings consisted of two rows of cottages in a line running north–south, another at right angles to the north, while to the east another three short rows completed an irregular three-side square. After a gap a few more straggled southward. The latter have long disappeared but the ruins of others could be seen until around 1990. The community was tiny before the 1830s and at its largest around 1881. Each cottage originally had a small garden or kailyard. Across the road from the cottages a track leads by a bridge across the railway, which has separated them from the shore since 1849, to a rocky inlet about 150 yards eastwards. The shore can only be reached by scrambling down a very steep path to a rocky shelf and pebble beach which formed the landing place. The small fishing boats must have been pulled up onto the grassy slopes above high water mark as there is little space around the head of the rocky creek. This was surely one of several inlets on the coast between Torry and Cove considered in 1791 where, it was said, a boat could be landed safely. Burnbanks must have been founded only shortly before 1802 when the Nigg parish registers first record baptisms of children of resident fisher families. The origin of the name is a mystery as there is no burn to be seen, at least in summer; perhaps a small trickle down the bank above the shore in wet winters gave the creek its name. The hamlet itself was recorded as 'Burnbanks haven' in 1813 although this normally referred to the creek rather than the settlement. The Fishery Board records it as 'Burnbank' but elsewhere it is invariably 'Burnbanks'. The particular set of surnames of the Burnbanks fisherfolk found throughout its existence as a fisher community show beyond doubt that the settlers all came from Portlethen, five or six miles to the south, rather than nearby Cove or Torry in the same parish.

The community

This was originally tiny. Only four families are recorded around 1802–04, implying only a single boat's crew, and in 1813 there was only a single yaul manned by a weak crew of three. But the community survived and by the 1830s had expanded considerably. In 1838 there were two large and three standard boats but the 1841 census records only eight fishermen aged from 23 to 65 and one aged 90. So it seems that the herring crews must have been augmented by hired men from elsewhere, as each boat needed a crew of five. By 1855 there were 14 fishermen and boys and a total working population of 42 persons assisting with baiting, gutting and vending. There were eight boats, two over 30 feet, three standard and three yauls. By 1881 there were 11 boats of various sizes worked by 23 fishers according to the Fishery Board creek returns; but only 17 are recorded in the census (though 18 fisher households), so herring crews must have included seasonal men as earlier. There were also two farm workers resident, making 20 inhabited houses in all. Shortly afterwards virtually the whole fisher population decanted to Torry and by 1891 only Janet Main, 'fisherwoman', remained, with ten other houses inhabited by salmon fishers, farmworkers, quarriers and railwaymen with their families.

18 *Burnbanks, with salmon coble and 'blondin' (winch) on top of the cliff*

39

The start of herring fishing shortly before 1838 must have been responsible for the sudden growth of the community and for its viability up to the 1880s. The larger herring boats had to be kept in the Dee near Torry in the winter while the boom in white-fish marketing in Aberdeen from 1882 must have encouraged the Burnbankers to land their white fish there, and the ultimate logic was to take up residence in Torry, Aberdeen's expanding fisher suburb. Most of the haddock landed at Burnbanks had been made into finnans, which were said, like those at Cove, to be comparable to the real thing from Findon itself. The houses are said to have had the Findon-type fireplaces to smoke haddock. Having been settled by Portlethen folk the method of smoking would have been identical to that in Findon and its neighbours but the local peat or turf must have differed from that of Portlethen Moss which gave the true finnan cure its particular flavour.

A few of the houses continued to be inhabited into the 1950s when one old wifie sold lemonade and crisps from her porch to passing walkers. Some time after Burnbanks became uninhabited Aberdeen City Council turned the houses into an agricultural museum for a time but it was semi-derelict by the 1980s. There were several plans to redevelop the cottages but this was only achieved from around 1990 when the entire square was rebuilt. The once neglected coast road from Cove to Torry was improved about the same time.

Salmon fishing

This probably began around 1840 and at time of writing a bag-net fishery was still carried out. The catches and gear were winched up the cliff by the 'blondin'.

Fisher names

The Nigg parish registers from 1802–04 record the names Leiper, Main, Craig and Wood, a set of names otherwise peculiar to Portlethen. In 1841 there were five Craigs, two Mains, one Leiper and one Wood. By 1881 Main was the commonest surname with fewer Craigs and Leipers.

Some variations of the place-name and spelling

Burnbanks	1802–04, 1838, 1841 to date
Burnbanks haven	1813
Burnbank	1838, 1855, 1881

Number of fishermen and boats

Year	Fishers	Boats	Type
1802–4	4?	1	yaul
1813	3	1	yaul
1838–41	8–9*	5	boats 23 to 30ft?
1855	14	8	2 large, 3 standard, 3 yauls
1881	23*	11	all sizes
1891	–	–	–

* including seasonal herring crews

Cove [1]

The area was part of the barony and parish of Nigg, which belonged to Arbroath Abbey from the late-12th to early-13th century as described under Torry. The earliest record of the name appears to be from 1527 when 'le Coyf' is listed among the lands comprising the barony of Nigg. In 1608 a charter of the Regality of Arbroath included 'Halymayns-coif' in the lands of Nigg or Torry. The Cove was listed as one of several 'little shores for fisher boats' in the Mearns in 1642 while about the same time Gordon's survey marks 'Coves' south of Aberdeen. In 1662 a retour of the superiority of the Regality of Arbroath lists 'Halymanes Coiff' with its manor place and gardens. 'Coves' was the name used on early 18th-century maps, later 'the Cove', and simply 'Cove' by the 19th century was the recognised form of the name. Except for its existence being noted on maps the only other documentation before 1790 is the record of fishers resident at the Cove in the parish registers from 1676 to 1819. However, with its sheltered natural harbour Cove is probably much older even than 1527 and it remained the most important fishing village in the area until the rise of Torry in the late-19th century.

The fishing village lies east of the railway and consists of a single street, which includes the hotel, the only original two-storey building, and other cottages in terraces. These face down the slope rather than across it as at Portlethen, Findon and Downies. A good road leads down to the shore. Just above the shore is a row of salmon fishers' houses.

The population of Cove declined between 1740 and 1786, principally due to the 'drain of men to the fleets'; 24 men were said to have been impressed or voluntarily entered the Navy. By 1791 the fishing population was recovering with 24 men in four boats besides 14 boys and old men in yauls. A number of fishers were reported to be having success with lobster creels (introduced in the 1780s) while women supplemented their incomes by gathering edible dulse. By 1838 the number of large boats had increased to nine, with six men to each, who were absent at the herring fishing for some six to eight weeks in the summer though this was not always a profitable business. At the same time the community was enjoying a considerable reputation for dried and smoked haddocks which were sold in Aberdeen and other places where they were regarded as equal to those of Findon itself. One fisherman was still smoking haddock in the 1960s but there are no signs now of any smoking houses.

In the 1880s ninety-six men were employed on a total of 30 boats. Cove also became something of a resort for visitors from Aberdeen, who would arrive by train and enjoy a partan tea or a poke of buckies. Thereafter, as fishing centred on Aberdeen, there was a steady decline, with only 12 fishermen and seven yauls by 1928.

---

1 Compiled by editor from author's notes.

Salmon fishing

Bag-net fishing was not mentioned in the 1790s but was being carried out with some success by 1838, thanks largely to the quick conveyance of fish in ice to London in steamboats. An ice-house was built on the slope halfway down the brae. In the 1990s Cove was still an active salmon station and bag-nets were still used.

Fisher names

The Nigg parish registers from 1676 to 1819 record the names Cowper, Allan, Fowler, Guyon, Donald, Paterson, Freeman, Kay/Caie, Robertson, Neilson, Brydie/Brodie, Webster, Morrice, Leiper, Craig and Thomson. By 1841 Morrice and Robertson predominate and Caie, Craig, Guyon, Allan, Neilson and Webster are still found along with Wood, Brand and Smith. In 1891 Caie and Webster are the commonest names, followed by Guyon, Robertson, Allan, Morrice, Craig and Neilson.

Some variations of the place-name and spelling

Le Coyf	1527
Halymayns-coif	1608, 1662
Coves	1641x50, 1703, 1747x55
The Cove	1642, 1774, 1791
Cove	1791, 1813, 1822, 1838, 1841 to date

Number of fishermen and boats

Year	Fishers	Boats	Type
1791	38*	7–8	4 boats, 3–4 yauls
1813	46	9	5 boats, 4 yauls
1838	54	9	boats (10–14T burden)
1855	71	30	12 herring, 14 standard, 4 yauls
1881	96	30	all sizes
1928	12	7	yauls

* including boys and old men

19 *A coastguard cottage in Cove*

20 *Nets drying at Cove*   21 *Boats drawn up on the beach at Cove*

Findon   Banchory-Devenick NO937975

The estate of Findon is first recorded in 1281 when a Justiciary Court was held on the Moor of Nigg to settle a boundary dispute between Philip de Fyndon with the Abbey of Arbroath, feudal superiors of the lands of Nigg, and Thomas, son of the thane of Cowie. Philip de Fyndon, along with most of the Scottish landed gentry, paid homage to King Edward I of England at Berwick in 1296. The estate seems to have been confiscated by King Robert Bruce and granted to John Crab, a Flemish engineer who had shown great skill in assisting the Scots at the siege of Berwick in 1319. The Crab family became burgesses of Aberdeen and held lands there commemorated by the name Craibston. The lands of Findon are recorded as a barony from 1359, and seem to have included the whole coastal and south-eastern part of Banchory-Devenick parish as far west as Cookston, Badentoy and Redmyre. In 1390 William Chalmers (sometime provost of Aberdeen between 1392 and 1420) secured an annuity on the lands of Findon from Robert Crab and by 1420 the barony belonged to Chalmers. Later in the 15th century the lands passed to Menzies of Pitfodels. But the earliest inference for a fishertoun is only from 1577 when the Crown confirmed a charter from the deceased Thomas Menzies of Pitfodels granting the liferent of the lands of Findon with its mill, fishings and other privileges to his wife Violet Forbes. In March 1622 the Crown confirmed a charter by Gilbert Menzies of Pitfodels to his son and heir of the lands of Findon with the mill, fishings and haven of Findon. In 1642 Findon was listed among the 'little shores for fisher boats' in the Mearns. In 1691 nine householders of Findon had to pay the full 14 shillings Hearth Tax.

The community

The fishertoun stands on a bleak exposed site from which the land slopes down to low cliffs and the small rocky inlet almost half a mile away. At the head of the inlet is St Ternan's Well, a once-sacred spring named after a Celtic holy man who also gave his name to Banchory-Ternan parish to the north-west. Like the neighbouring fishertouns the village consists of several rows of cottages parallel to the coast. But there are gaps in the rows of houses and they have mostly been modernized beyond recognition.

The fishertoun may have existed some time before 1577, although its landing place is a dangerous-looking rocky sloch unlike any other early fishertouns, which all had fairly sheltered beaches or were situated in estuaries. It may be that the Menzies or earlier lairds had founded the fishertoun in the late-middle ages. Despite its fame for smoked haddocks Findon is ill-recorded before the 1790s, although a reference to Findon haddocks in 1642 showed that the distinctive cure was already famous. Since there were apparently at least nine fisher households in 1691 there were presumably enough men and boys to crew two boats. A description of the parish in 1725 doesn't mention Findon but states, 'There are a great many white fish taken in this parish and those which are famous are commonly called Finnan Haddocks'. The Statistical Account of 1791 mentions that Findon gave its name to peat-dried split haddock which were already known and esteemed in most parts of Scotland. In 1818 Robert Southey had finnans for both breakfast and tea at Stonehaven, Thomas Telford having prevented him from sampling them farther south in case they were tainted. He referred to them as a 'dainty' of Aberdeen. By the 1840s or earlier the finnan cure was known and appreciated as far away as Edinburgh, although unheard of in Fife. This was reputedly the result of a Findon man having a brother who drove 'the Defiance', the stagecoach which connected Aberdeen and Edinburgh from 1829 to 1847. However, it seems they were known and consumed in Edinburgh at an even earlier date.

Despite the fame of its cure and the keen demand for finnans, in 1791 there were only two boats with six-man crews and three yauls with four-man crews, giving a total of 24 fishermen and boys. Great lines as well as sma' lines were used, since skate, ling, turbot and cod were caught as well as haddock, whiting and flounders. Crabs and lobsters were also caught, presumably using recently introduced creels. By 1813 there was an additional boat and so around 30 active fishers, but real expansion began with the introduction of herring fishing in the early 1830s. In 1838, totals for the parish suggest that Findon then had around ten boats, of which three or four were used at herring fishing, and probably around 30 to 40 active fishers. This increased to 21 boats in 1855 – eight herring boats, nine haddock boats and four yauls, manned by 50 fishers. Another 97 persons were employed in ancillary activities but there was no commercial curer: the making of finnans was purely a domestic industry and remained so in the place of origin until the community died out. The community had already begun to decline by 1881 when only 14 boats were manned by 39 fishers. Migration to Torry had started. The population was then 156 persons. By 1892 herring fishing may have ceased as there were only four boats and 24 active fishers. By the 1920s fishing was all but abandoned.

Salmon fishing

This is not mentioned in 1838 and no salmon fishers were resident in 1841. But fishing may have started soon afterwards with bag-nets. In 1890 the Findon fishery was worth £270 compared with £180 for Portlethen's.

Fisher names

In 1691 there were two residents called Leper (Leiper), a name which remained common until the demise of the fisher community. Other individuals were named Andersone, Tendell, Smithe, Coly, Walker, George and Martin, none of which are recorded later in Findon or its immediate neighbours although the first five were found in fishertouns down the coast in the 17th and early-18th centuries. So it appears that those paying Hearth Tax that year were mostly, if not all, fishermen, as appears to be the case at Portlethen. The surname Leiper is recorded in the parish registers (extant from 1711) from 1717 and Wood from 1737. The surname Knows is recorded in 1738, 1756 and 1764, as Knolls in 1765 and Knowles from 1772. In 1841 there were 15 active fishers called Wood, 11 called Leiper and four called Knowles. These three, Leiper, Knowles and Wood, remained the only fisher surnames in Findon until its abandonment by fishers in the 1920s.

Some variations of the place-name and spelling

Fyndon	1281, 1296
Findon	1390 to date
Finnan	1703, 1725
Finnin	1717, 1736
Fishertoun of Finnan	1738
Seatown of Finnan	1740
Finnen	1747x55
Locally pronounced Finnan	

Number of fishermen and boats

Year	Fishers	Boats	Type
1691	9 + 2–3 boys?	2?	under 25ft
1791	24	5	2 under 25ft, three yauls
1813	27–30	6	3 under 25ft, three yauls?
1819	27–31	7	3 under 25ft, four yauls
1838	30–40?	c.10?	4 large, 6 under 25ft?
1841	30	6–7?	boats and yauls
1855	50	21	8 over 30 feet, 9 standard, 4 yauls
1881	39	14	all sizes
1892	24	4	boats and yauls?
1928	–	–	–

Portlethen

Portlethen was originally the name of a barony which took its name from the Gaelic *port leathainn* (broad haven), which refers to the 'muckle shore' of Portlethen about half a mile north of the 'little shore' where the fishertoun developed. The lands of Portlethen were originally part of the barony of Findon, consisting of 720 acres separated from Findon in the north by the deep ravine of the Findon Burn. In the early-15th century the estate belonged to David Menzies, a wealthy burgess of Aberdeen. The earliest evidence for a fishertoun is from 1557 when John Vaus, spouse of Elizabeth Menzies, sold Gilbert Menzies, burgess of Aberdeen, two parts of the toun and land of Portlethen except the Fischerland with its buildings, boat and fishings occupied by his fishers. By 1608 Portlethen belonged to William Forbes of Monymusk who granted his son and heir the lands of Portlethen and its main market place, the mill with its lands, the rights to wrack and ware washed up on the shore within the barony and the haven and anchorage with its white-fishings. In 1625 Forbes resigned the same into the hands of Robert Buchan, burgess of Aberdeen. The haven and harbour of Portlethen were mentioned again in 1637 when Buchan sold the barony to George Rickart, burgess of Aberdeen, while 'Port Leviathan' was listed among the 'little shores for fisher boats' in the Mearns in 1642.

22 *At Portlethen*

The community

Although there is only evidence for a fisher community from 1557, when there was a single boat and crew, Portlethen has an excellent little shore facing south-east, well sheltered by rocks and having a shingle shore and ample room to draw up boats. So it seems likely that a fishing community may have developed by the early-middle ages. The Fischerlands mentioned here, as at some other fishertouns, show that they were not entirely dependent on the sea, but had some arable for subsistence. In 1691 the Hearth Tax record suggests that there were then six fishers who could only have crewed a single boat. In 1791, however, there were three boats, each with a crew of six, and a yaul with a crew of four. A total of 22 fishermen and boys suggests that there were around 18 to 20 families and a total fisher population of about 100, a thriving little community. The disappearance of some surnames and the introduction of two new ones in the period 1771 to 1816 suggest some seizures by the press gangs and subsequent immigration. There was also emigration as Portlethen fishermen colonised the new-founded fishertouns of Downies from the 1770s, Burnbanks around 1800 and Stranathro from 1814. In 1813 there were three boats and four yauls worked by 33 fishermen and boys. Rentals of boats by the landlords in 1816 show that two of the boats had a crew of five men and a boy, the other a crew of five while the yauls had crews of four. In 1838 the total boats for the parish suggests that there were five or six herring boats and probably seven haddock boats with crews of five, so a minimum of 35 fishermen. The 1841 census records 46 active fishers so the community was growing rapidly and by 1855 there were 27 boats manned by 68 fishers, 13 large, 12 standard and two yauls. Expansion continued and in 1881 there were 37 boats of all sizes crewed by 89 fishers. In 1890 fifty Portlethen fishermen petitioned the Fishery Board to improve Stonehaven harbour from where they worked 11 large boats. Herring fishing probably ceased by 1914 at the latest, as at other small creeks, and a few old men would have carried on inshore fishing with yauls. By 1928 there were two sailing yauls each with a crew of four. This declined to a single motor yaul by 1939 and two fishermen who may have fished into the 1940s but by 1946 there were no boats. By 1953, however, there were two boats and four fishermen. Full-time fishing may have carried on for a few years after but latterly part-time creel fishing is more likely to have been the only activity.

Salmon fishing

This was carried out at the muckle shore of Portlethen, which is unsuitable for launching and landing keeled boats as the beach slopes very gently into the sea at any state of the tide. The fishing was worth £180 in 1890. At time of writing the salmon station[1] had only recently been abandoned; some of the old winches were still used by part-time creel boats. There is a salmon store dated 1953.

---

1 Based at the little shore of Portlethen (ed.).

Fisher names

The Hearth Tax returns of 1691 record six persons in Portlethen paying the full 14 shillings; three were called Craigie, the others Blaiber, Couper and Neilson, who may all have been fishermen. The surname Craigie is recorded in other Mearns fishertouns in the same decade. Blaiber or Bleber occurs in Portlethen and elsewhere from early in the following century while the last two names occur at Cove in 1676 and 1677. The parish registers, extant from 1711, record residents of Seato(u)n or Seatown of Portlethen between 1713 and 1819. The surnames Craig and Main are predominant. Dunn is recorded only once, in 1713; Bleber occurs in 1716, 1739 and 1766 but no later while Leiper only appears from 1771. Estate rentals of 1816 record 32 fishermen and a boy; 18 bore the name Craig, seven Wood, four Main, two Leiper and one Will. In 1841, of 46 active fishers, there were 26 called Craig, eight Wood, five Main, four Leiper, two Robertson and one Alan. In 1890 out of 50 fishermen who petitioned the Fishery Board regarding Stonehaven harbour there were 27 called Craig, nine Wood, eight Leiper and six called Main.

Some variations of the place-name and spelling

Portletthin	1641x50
Port Leviathan	1642
Port Lethim	1703
Seato(u)n/Seatown of Portlethen	1713–1819, 1822
Port Lethem	1747x55
Portlethen	1774 to date

Number of fishermen and boats

Year	Fishers	Boats	Type
1557	6?	1	under 25ft?
1691	6	1	under 25ft?
1791	22	4	3 boats under 25ft, 1 yaul
1813–16	33	7	3 boats under 25ft, 4 yauls
1838	35?	12?	5–6 over 30ft, 6–7 standard
1841	46	16?	7–8 over 30ft?, 8–9 standard?
1855	68	27	13 large, 12 standard, 2 yauls
1881	89	37	all sizes
1890	c.90?	20+	11 large and others
1914	?	?	yauls?
1928	8	2	yauls (sail)
1939	2	1	yaul (motor)
1946	–	–	–
1953	4*	2	motor yauls

* part-timers?

Downies Banchory-Devenick NO923951

This fishertoun was on Clashfarquhar estate, once an integral part of the barony of Portlethen. Clashfarquhar, apparently a third part of the lands of Portlethen, was acquired around 1773 by Andrew Thomson, advocate in Aberdeen and a member of the same family which had owned the whole barony since 1699. His son, aged only seven, succeeded on his death in 1781 and his trustees are unlikely to have founded a new fishertoun by 1790, when 'the Downnies' is first recorded in the Banchory-Devenick parish registers; so it appears likely that Thomson senior founded the new fishertoun, probably soon after he acquired Clashfarquhar. Moreover, a William Main and his wife Margaret Masson 'in Clashfarquhar' had a son, William, baptised in 1777 and another, George, in 1780. Main and Masson were common fisher names in the area. In 1809 a William Main 'in Downies' had a son baptised as did George Main, also there, in 1811. If these were the sons of the earlier William Main and his wife their ages, 32 and 31, would fit. On the pattern of other fishertouns the name Seatoun of Clashfarquhar might have been chosen. In 1809 the form 'Seaton of Downies' occurred, although there is no record of a farm called Downies. The name probably derives from a coastal feature since there are several on the Mearns coast ultimately deriving from Gaelic *dun*, meaning a small fort but extended to natural outcrops of rock: Downie Point just south of Stonehaven; another Downie Point between the old shore of Muchalls and Stranathro; and Downie/Dounie Hill and Doonies Yawn near Nigg Bay. The present usual pronunciation (down-) is an example of creeping Anglicisation since in Scots 'ow', 'ou' and 'oo' sound the same, as the various spellings illustrate. Doonies was the local pronunciation and it is still sometimes referred to as 'the Doonies' by local folk.

The community

As implied above Downies was founded around 1775 while the surnames of the first settlers indicate their origins in Portlethen with a few from Findon later. Since the shore of Downies is not exactly an ideal place to land a boat some inducement such as the provision of housing or several years' free rent may have been given. There is only a rocky inlet with a shelf of flat rock for a landing place. In rough weather the boats must have run for Skateraw or Portlethen. Planks had to be bolted to the rock shelf in order to enable the launching and landing of boats. There is little space behind for boats, which had to be hauled up a steep grassy slope where a couple of rusting windlasses can still be seen. In 1791 there was only a single yaul which would have had a maximum crew of four. By 1813 however there were two boats each crewed by six fishers. Herring fishing began in the early 1830s and by 1838 the total number of boats for the three fishertouns in the parish suggests there were probably eight boats in Downies then, of which three were used in herring fishing. This estimate is confirmed by the 1841 census which records about 25 active fishers from 21 households and a total population of 122.

There were only fisherfolk resident in the village at that time. In 1855 there were 18 boats crewed by 45 fishermen and boys, six large, eight standard boats and four yauls. Sixty-one others were in ancillary employment. The community was remarkably stable, since in 1881 there was only one less boat crewed by the same number of fishers. However, whereas in 1841 there had been 21 households and a total population of 122, in 1871 there were 42 households and 243 persons resident, so the number of boats, fishermen and population probably reached a peak in the 1870s and the number of occupied houses and the population slowly declined afterwards.

In the peak years of the later-19th century there was an occasional shoemaker, tailor and shopkeeper resident, otherwise Downies was entirely a fisher community. By 1865 there was a square and five rows of houses parallel to the coast. Up to 1871 all the houses had been thatched but they were all slated by the following decade. The number of boats remained the same until 1881 with four or five being herring boats. From the later 1880s some of the young fishers began to migrate to Torry, but the decline was very slow in contrast to some other places. In 1890 16 Downies fishermen petitioned the Fishery Board to support improvements to Stonehaven harbour from where they worked six herring boats. In the following few years the number of boats dropped to 12 or 13 crewed by 25 to 27 fishers. In 1898 there were 15 boats and 33 fishers but by 1900 only ten boats, the decline being in the smaller boats while there were still three herring boats. In the period 1902–14 there were around eight or nine boats and 28 active fishers so it seems herring fishing and perhaps great lining continued up to 1914. By 1921 however there was only inshore sma' lining and creel fishing with three haddock boats and a yaul, which ranged from nine to two tons burden, crewed by nine fishers. Later there were only three or four yauls and eight fishers up to 1928. A few old men continued to use creels and handlines in good weather into the 1950s.

As late as 1928, and probably later, all the boats relied on sail. Later there were two tiny motor yauls. Downies is only one mile south of Portlethen station and thus from 1850 the fishers had easy access to the Aberdeen market, so fresh, smoked and dried haddock were hawked around the suburbs of Aberdeen. As the population declined and some houses became derelict gaps were created in the orderly rows of cottages giving a scattered layout to the village as it is today. Aberdeen University owned the village from around 1875 to 1945 after which it sold off the remaining houses to the occupiers.

Salmon fishing

This seems to have begun from 1851, using bag-nets, when John Yeats, then owner of Clashfarquhar and Portlethen, leased the rights from the Crown. They were valued at £10 annually but rose to £50 by 1882, a fraction of the worth of those at Portlethen and Findon. The fishing was probably worked in conjunction with Portlethen salmon station by salmon fishers from there since none seem to have been resident in Downies.

Fisher names

The surname Main is recorded from 1777 and remained the commonest one in the community. There was at least one Leiper from 1803 and it also remained a common surname thereafter. The first Wood is recorded from 1835. Main was previously only found in Portlethen, while Wood and Leiper occur previously in both Portlethen and Findon. By chance few called Craig, which was an overwhelmingly common name in Portlethen, migrated to Downies. Knowles, a surname originally peculiar to the Findon fishers, is only recorded from 1841. The surnames of women recorded in the parish registers 1777–1835 show that most also came from Portlethen and Findon although they showed more variety and at least one, a Masson, possibly came from Skateraw. In 1871 seven fisher householders bore the name Main, while there were five Leipers, four Woods and two Knowles. By 1881 thirteen fishermen were called Main, 11 Wood and five Leiper. In 1890 there were 16 called Main, seven Wood and seven Leiper. Only an occasional transient fisherman in other years bore any other name.

Some variations of the place-name and spelling

(the) Down(n)ies	1790–1811
Dounies	1791
Downies	1803, 1838, 1841 to date
Seaton of Downies	1809
Dunnies	1822
Doonies	1855
Dunies	1868
Locally (the) Doonies	

Number of fishermen and boats

Year	Fishers	Boats	Type
1791	4	1	yaul
1813	12	2	boats under 25ft
1838	c.25	8?	boats 23–30ft
1855	45	18	6 large, 8 standard, 4 yauls
1881	45	17	all sizes
1898	33	15	all sizes
1900	33	10	3 large, 7 others
1910	28	8	2–3 large, 5–6 others
1921	9	4	3 boats and 1 yaul
1928	8	3	yauls
1939–45	2	1	yaul (motor)
1948	2	2	yauls (motor)
1953	3	2	yauls (motor)

Elsick took its name from the barony of that name to which it belonged. It was quite distinct from its near neighbour Skateraw, which lay in the same barony, and with which it shared the use of the same small haven known as Elsick Shore or Skateraw Harbour. No village called Elsick appears on any of the early maps but there was a tradition handed down among the Skateraw fishers that there was once a village 'abuin the cave' on the braehead to the north of the haven and the Burn of Elsick, near the footpath to Downies. Although there was no recollection of the name or nature of this village there can be little doubt that this was a folk memory of the fishertoun of Elsick. Although there is no record of Elsick before 1636 it is quite probable that it is medieval in origin since it had such a fine natural haven. The Court Book of the Barony of Urie in 1636, in reference to Cowie, indicated Elsick and 'Muchallis' as also being fishertouns but made no reference to Skateraw. This may infer that Elsick was the earlier or the more important of the two fishertouns in the barony of Elsick at that time. The Court Book also stated that the fishermen of Cowie were to pay for the use of boats as those of Elsick and Muchalls did. This tradition could well refer back to a period before 1387 when the large barony of Cowie, which once comprised most of the parish of Fetteresso and contained the three villages, began to be broken up. Shore of Elsick was listed as a fishertoun along with Skateraw in 1642, and in 1722 both Elsick and Skateraw were mentioned as fishing villages, by which, it was said, the estate of Elsick was well provided with fish. The above

23 The salmon fishery at Elsick Shore

© The Estate of Colin Gibson

are the only three references to the fishertoun of Elsick. The parish registers of Fetteresso, extant from 1716, unfortunately record no residents of a Seaton of Elsick, which might be expected. The surname Masson is recorded in 1737 in Netherton of Elsick. But this common local fisher surname was not then exclusive to fisherfolk and also occurred among the landward population of the parish, so Netherton may have been a lost farm name. It seems, therefore, that Elsick may have been in decline by the early-18th century, contrary to the general pattern of events, and there may only ever have been a single boat. It is unlikely that the involvement of the last Bannerman laird of Elsick in the 1745–46 Jacobite Rebellion and subsequent sale of the barony had hastened the decline of the fishertoun. Sir Alexander Bannerman of Elsick certainly raised forces from among his tenants and some may have come to grief, but the fishertoun of Elsick may have been defunct or in terminal decline before these events; the truth may never be known. The village was certainly long defunct and forgotten by 1790. Garden's map of Kincardine-shire of 1774, normally very detailed and accurate, shows no sign of a settlement either by name or by indicating cottages and names the haven Skateraw Harbour, as do two other maps of 1822. The New Statistical Account of 1842 and the Ordnance Survey of 1860–65, however, both name it Elsick Shore, but this was more than likely derived from the name of the estate, rather than the long-lost fishertoun of that name.

Some variations of the place-name and spelling

Elsick	1636, 1722
Shore of Elsick	1642

Skateraw   Fetteresso NO912933

The earliest record of Skateraw is only from 1642, but with its fine natural haven (which it shared with Elsick) it is likely to be much older. At Cowie in 1636 the laird laid down that his fishers must pay a boat's share every time boats from Muchalls and Elsick went to sea but made no mention of Skateraw, though this may simply indicate that Elsick was the more important of the two at that time. Skateraw is included as a fishertoun along with Shore of Elsick in 1642 and with Elsick in 1722. This is the final reference to the latter, which had disappeared and been long forgotten by 1790 while Skateraw grew.

In 1747 an inventory of the effects of Sir Alexander Bannerman, a Jacobite exiled after the 1745–46 rebellion, included five fishing boats at Skateraw; these were all embargoed and carried to Stonehaven or Aberdeen. The four skippers named were all called Chrystie – Alexander, William, Thomas and John. This implies about 20 to 24 fishermen and so a population of about 100 to 150 people.

In 1790 there were seven boats at Skateraw, each manned by six fishers catching ling, cod, turbot, skate, haddock and other fish. The fish was consumed by the people in the adjacent countryside. In 1813 there were only four boats and two smaller yauls, so about 28 to 30 fishermen and boys. By 1842 however the number of boats and presumably the population had grown, in addition to seven line boats there were six herring boats. In 1855 Skateraw had a total of 26 boats, 11 over 30 feet and probably herring boats, nine between 30 and 18 feet and six under 18 feet (yauls).

Herring fishing was not the only factor which led to growth. The Findon or Finnan cure, already famous locally in the 1730s, had become sought after in Edinburgh and Glasgow by the 1830s and 40s and all the northern Mearns villages began to make finnans. Cod and ling fishing had declined by the 1840s, those caught were partly dried on the rocks like the haddock speldings and partly salt-pickled in barrels for distant markets. Some haddock was sold fresh locally in addition to those made into speldings and finnans. The coming of the railway in 1850 made distribution easier as well as the acquisition of mussel bait from far afield. The population peaked in the early 1880s and then dropped as in all the small fishertouns due to migration to places with harbours large enough to operate the larger herring boats, particularly Aberdeen and Stonehaven.

Salmon fishing

A salmon station operated from 'Elsick Shore'.

Fisher names

As well as Chrystie, names found in the 18th century included Breddie/Brodie, Lipper, Freeman, Blebber, Taylor, Masson and, from 1809, Main. Stiven occurs in 1732, Stephen and Craig from 1738 and Lees from 1786. In the mid-19th century the commonest name was still Christie, followed by Masson, and there were also Stephens and Lees.

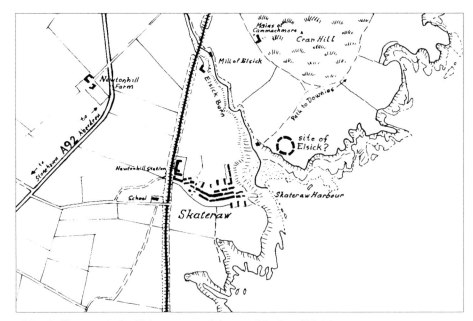

Map 2 *Skateraw in the 19th century and the possible site of Elsick*

Some variations of the place-name and spelling

Skateraw	1642, 1722, 1774, 1813, 1841, 1855, 1881, 1900, 1928 to date
Sketrow	1720
Skaterow	1722, 1822, 1871
Skettraw	1723–24
Sketraw	1732, 1765, 1767, 1785–86, 1790, 1814, 1842
Skeatraw	1768
Scateraw	1813
Skatraw	1875

Locally Sketra/Skaitra

Number of fishermen and boats

Date	Fishers	Boats	Type
1747	20–24	5	under 25 ft
1790	42	7	under 25 ft
1813	c.30	6	under 25 ft
1842	35?	13	6 boats 25–30ft, 7 others
1855	48/50*	26	11 over 30ft, 9 18–30ft, 6 yauls
1881	72	39	all sizes
1928	6	6	under 30ft, 1 motor, 5 sail

* extra men taken on in herring season

Stranathro   Fetteresso NO903922

This was originally the name of a farm on Muchalls estate recorded from 1606 and shown on maps of around 1650, 1750 and 1774. Stranathro was not included in lists of fishertouns in the area of 1642 and 1722, in the Statistical Account of 1790 or by Robertson in 1813. However, part of Muchalls estate, 'East Muchalls', was sold off in 1814, and in the very same year the Fetteresso parish registers begin to record fisherfolk resident at Stranathro. So it seems that the new proprietor must have founded the fishertoun in that year. It was comprised mainly of three parallel rows of cottages adjacent to the farmstead of Stranathro: Front Row (now called Stranathro Terrace), Mid Row and Back Row (now forming Monduff Road), and a few at right angles (Dunnyfell Road). These all lie at the northern end of the settlement now called Muchalls. The main shore lay 500 yards to the south of the fisher houses, past the former site of the hotel (now replaced by houses) and since 1850 reached under the railway embankment. By then it was known as 'Muchalls Shore' rather than Stranathro Shore, while the haven once used by the fishers of Seaton of Muchalls (q.v.) came to be referred to as the 'Old Shore of Muchalls'. The broad shingle haven could be reached by a broad sloping cart track, since blocked by wartime anti-tank blocks. There is another shore much nearer to the fisher houses called the Ritchie Shore, a small shingle beach reached by a very steep path. It may have been used by the smaller boats at one time; although nearer it was less convenient of access.

The fisher hamlet became part of a larger community. The adjacent Muchalls Coastguard Station was probably established in the 1830s. In 1850 the Aberdeen Railway was completed and Muchalls station opened. The origins of the hotel may go no further back than the coming of the railway. In 1856 'Muchalls Inn' and its croft were advertised to let as having the convenience of a white-fishing and salmon station nearby and also a weekly market by the railway station. The inn was later enlarged or rebuilt at least twice to become the Marine Hotel. The road leading past the coastguard station towards the railway, once Station Road, became Marine Terrace, after the hotel, when the station closed. A new Muchalls Episcopal Church, St Ternan's, opened in 1868 and an Episcopal school at Stranathro, taught by Eppie Wishart up to 1874 when she retired aged 80 (she had earlier taught at Skateraw). This shows the confusion over the name of the combined settlement by the 1860s, by then consisting of the farm, fishertoun and school to the north, the coastguard station in the middle and the station, hotel, church, parsonage and one or two villas to the south. Muchalls came to be promoted as a health resort as there was a popular spring near the hotel. Towards 1900 more private houses were built and Aberdeen business folk travelled to work from, or retired to, Muchalls, as the whole settlement has become known since the fisherfolk abandoned Stranathro and their houses were bought up. A Muchalls Trust renovated the vacant Stranathro cottages and around 1902 the only residents there were labourers, fish dealers and retired and professional folk from Aberdeen. Nearby coastal features, especially the natural arch Grim Brigs, were popular with visitors and residents but several people fell to their deaths, and after one accident in 1892 the arch was rendered impassable. The railway station has now closed, but new houses and a pub have been built around the Stranathro end of the village although the hotel closed in the early 1990s and the site is now occupied by houses.

The community

Some commentators have assumed that the Seaton of Muchalls fishers resettled at Stranathro but this was not the case since the former was abandoned a generation or more before the other was founded and the surnames of the inhabitants also disprove this assumption. The evidence from the parish registers clearly suggests that a single boat and its crew with their families moved here from Portlethen in 1814 and up to 1819 or somewhat later there was only a single boat. The landlord may have built the cottages and offered low rents as an inducement. Sometime before 1841 other settlers came from Skateraw. In 1841 the population of Stranathro, including five coastguards and their families, was 126, so there must have been nearly 20 fisher families by then. The majority seem to have been episcopalians, obviously influenced by the incomers from Skateraw, who were particularly staunch episcopalians, since Portlethen was mainly presbyterian. In 1842 there were four boats at 'Shanathro' (*sic*, clearly a copying error). Each had a crew of five and two or three of them were also used in herring fishing. In 1855 there were 14 boats, five over 30 feet, five standard and four yauls operated by 31 fishermen and boys. No curers, gutters or packers were resident but 47 others were active in ancillary activities. In 1871 the total population of Stranathro proper was 118 so the fisher population was only a little larger than in 1841. In 1879 however there was a sudden mass exodus to Stonehaven, leaving only five boats and eight fishermen in 1881. An ageing fisher population soon declined and by 1893 there were no active fishers resident. Even the proximity of a railway station does not seem to have outweighed the advantage of moving to Stonehaven, which had a built harbour, an organised market for white fish and was also a herring-curing station.

Muchalls Coastguard Station

This was one of the few stations purpose-built by the coastguard service and was apparently established in the 1830s, certainly before 1841. It consists of a two-storey block which provided a lookout, office and accommodation for the five coastguards and their families. A photograph survives from 1890 of the 'Muchalls Champion Rocket Detachment', apparently all coastguards though some fishers may earlier have taken part. Their place was taken by Skateraw fishers from the later 1920s up to about the 1940s. On one occasion between the wars they rescued the crew of a German ship which had run aground and took them into their homes to warm up. The station seems to have closed sometime after 1925 when the service was transferred to the Board of Trade. The building survives as private housing.

Salmon fishing

Salmon fishing probably began by about 1840 using bag-nets at the same shore used by the white-fishers, one of 'several' salmon stations flourishing in the parish of Fetteresso in 1842. The fishing was certainly functioning in 1856 and presumably somewhat later but no salmon fishers seem to have been resident by around 1900.

Fisher names

The prevalent surnames show that Stranathro was originally colonised by Portlethen fishers, later by others from Skateraw. In the period 1814–19 the names Main, Craig and Leiper were recorded but in 1841 and 1871 Christie was the commonest name, while other common names were Main, Leiper and Law. Other names occurring in 1841 were Greig and Brown.

Some variations of the place-name and spelling

Stranathro	1606, 1641x50, 1814–19, 1841–71, 1902 to date
Strathnathrey	c.1750
Stranathraw	1760
'Shanathro'	1842
Stranathra	1855, 1868, 1881

Number of fishermen and boats

Year	Fishers	Boats	Type
1814	5–6?	1	under 25ft
1842	20	4	boats 23–30ft?
1855	31	14	5 large, 5 standard, 4 yauls
1881	8	5	boats and yauls?

Muchalls

24 *The Old Man of Muchalls*

© *The Estate of Colin Gibson*

The exact location of this village is unknown, but it was probably on the high ground above the Old Shore of Muchalls with a view of the sea. This was immediately south of the Mill of Muchalls. Access to the shore is through a field and via a notch in the ridge overlooking the bay from where the Old Man of Muchalls can be seen: a cliff stack resembling the craggy profile of an old fisherman. On the north side of the bay, above a grassy bank, is a deep cave with graffiti on the walls dating back to the 18th century. To the south is a cave only accessible at very low tide, which was once believed to reach to Muchalls Castle and to have a phantom piper, as did a cave in the cliffs north of Arbroath.

The earliest record of the existence of a fishertoun at Old Shore of Muchalls is from 1606 when Alexander Burnet of Leys bought the lands of Muchalls from Francis Hay, Earl of Errol and Baron of Cowie, of which barony the lands were originally a part. In 1606 the property consisted of: the lands, toun and manor place of Muchalls, with the lands or farms of Pettyet, Contlawhills, Blackbuttis, Montgatheid, Stranathro, Stralathin, Dennabuck, Quartennis and Greenheids (most of which are identifiable today), together with the fishings, fish boats and fisherlands and the mill and mill-lands of Muchalls. A new manor house of Muchalls was built in 1619, the present Muchalls 'Castle', but the Burnets' main residence was at Crathes Castle near Banchory. The Burnets later sold the lands of Muchalls but seem to have retained the feudal superiority until 1824. In 1636 Muchallis was recorded as a place with fishing boats and in 1642 Shore of Muchalls was included in a list of 'little shores for fisher boats' in the Mearns. On 31 August 1663 the Crown confirmed Robert Burnet of Culney in possesion of the manor place Muchels, including the plough, or mains, of Muchalls called Hillhead, Blackbutts, and the sea-town of Muchaells with fishings, fishing boats and roods of land pertaining to it, as granted to him by the deceased Alexander Burnet of Leys.

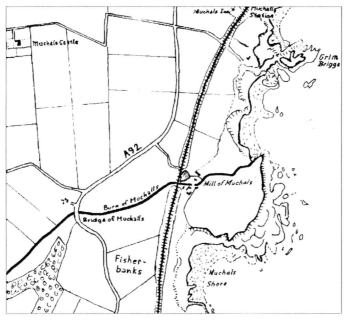

Map 3 *Muchalls*

Muchalls Shore is indicated on Adair's map of the east coast of 1703 but no settlement is shown. However, Muchalls is listed as one of four fishertouns in Fetteresso parish in 1722, while the same source states that Muchalls estate was well accommodated with a fishing village. The *Aberdeen Journal* of 8 April 1760 published an advertisement for the roup of Muchalls estate, including the manor, Milltown, Stranathraw, Dennabuck and the fishertoun and lands tenanted by the fishers. It was also stated that there was lately made out, at a very considerable charge, a harbour or pier for the convenience of bringing lime by sea to the tenants. The estate was bought by Fullerton of Gallery but in August 1760 was re-sold to Aberdeen Town Council, who sold it to a Mr Silver of Netherly in 1801.

The community in early times

Although only recorded from 1606 it seems likely that Muchalls was medieval in origin, along with Elsick and Cowie one of the three original fishing communities in the barony of Cowie and possibly dating to before 1387 when the barony became divided. The bay, protected by a high headland to the south and rocky banks to the north, has a shingle beach only accessible from the sea at high tide. At low or half-tide there is a large expanse of flat rock between the water and the beach. In the centre is a narrow inlet or creek about six feet wide and having three or four feet of water at half-tide, adequate to accommodate the type of small boats used on this coast before 1800. It is uncertain if this channel in the rock is purely natural or if it was improved in connection with the pier built before April 1760, of which no vestige otherwise remains. However, trading sloops were too large to have used the channel and could only have landed or sailed away at high tide. Coal may not have been landed here since the area had extensive peat-beds, enough to supply a surplus to Aberdeen.

The few inferences of a community from 1606 to the 1760s suggest a small but stable community up to the mid-18th century. The mention of boats in 1606 and 1663 clearly implies at least two in a period when Cowie only had one. By 1749 there seem to have been at least three boats. Three would imply 15 to 18 active fishermen and boys, ten to 12 families and perhaps 50 to 60 inhabitants in all. Inhabitants of Seaton or Seatown of Muchalls are recorded in the parish registers of Fetteresso from the time these begin in 1716 up to 1764, when children were still being baptised. Virtually all the surnames can also be found in Cowie and Skateraw in the same period, and it is likely that none except fishers resided in the Seatoun of Muchalls. The fishers had arable land beside the village (although by the 18th century it may have been sub-let to others to cultivate) and they could graze a cow on the Muir of Muchalls. The fisherlands of Muchalls are mentioned in 1606, the roods of lands pertaining in 1663 and the lands tenanted by the fishers in 1760, while as late as about 1918 fields between the main road and the railway were called North and South Fisherbanks.

The full name of the settlement was Seatoun of Muchalls (occasionally anglicised to Seatown), while Shore of Muchalls strictly referred to the inlet and landing place rather than the settlement.

The demise of Muchalls

In the Statistical Account of the Parish of Fetteresso of 1790, the minister (who had arrived in 1763) stated that 30 years earlier two boats belonging to Muchalls had been lost in a storm with the loss of their crews. This was an oversimplification of events. On 5 February 1749 the Kirk Session of Fetteresso recorded that a boat's crew belonging to Seatoun of Muchalls had perished in a storm. According to traditions collected from their descendants over a century later, a boat had been cast up at the Skatie Shore north of Cowie but it was allowed to fall apart as no-one would reclaim it, even for firewood, for fear of bad luck. Nine years after this loss, disaster struck the small community again. The *Aberdeen Journal* of 13 December 1758 reported that a crew of six was lost as their boat was overset while entering the 'harbour' at Muchalls. The community must have been seriously or even mortally wounded but it was not yet dead since baptisms of fisher children, each witnessed by two adult male residents of the Seatoun, are recorded in 1754, 1762 and 1764. The sale notice of 1760 also implies an active boat's crew after 1758, and gravestone inscriptions in Cowie kirkyard, the usual burial place of the local fisherfolk, show that the community existed well into the 1760s. Other evidence however suggests that it was probably defunct and the village all but abandoned by about 1770, although in 1790 it was not actually stated that the place was totally deserted, only that there were no boats.

A gravestone in Cowie kirkyard commemorates John Nepar seaman in Muchall who died on 28 March 1768 aged 90 and his wife Jean Nepar in Seatoun of Muchels who died aged 30 in 1717. Another monument records James Caddonhead sea-man in Muchall who died in 1738 aged 46, his wife Elspet Calder who died in 1777 aged 74, their sons John and Robert who died abroad, and other descendants. Even with the loss of two boats' crews the community might have survived but it seems that another factor, always present in the later-18th century, was probably the final nail in the coffin of Muchalls. Traditions gathered by James Donald in 1918 relate that the fishers were plagued by visitations from the press gangs, who first began to operate on the local coast around 1758–65. On one occasion the fishers bought immunity, on another occasion one man was seized but a willing substitute was procured. However, others may not have been so lucky. The two sons of the above James Caddonhead who died abroad are likely to have been pressed into the Navy. It seems likely that the single boat's crew left after 1758 was so weakened by the seizure of men in the 1760s that the remaining community decided to move. Garden's map of Kincardineshire of 1774 marks the haven as Shore of Muchalls but indicates no settlement nearby. Some migrants went to Stonehaven; Alex Taylor, born at Muchalls in 1750, became a fisherman at Cowie, his son David migrated to Catterline and his descendants to Gourdon. Others took to landward occupations in the vicinity: John Leiper, born in 1756 the son of a fisherman became the smith at nearby Bridge of Muchalls; William Kilgour born in 1751 became a weaver at Glithnow for 62 years and died aged 86 in 1837 (he was also a mechanical genius who made clockwork machinery from wood); two sons of Muchalls even became farmers, Alexander Cadenhead, an orphan, and John Taylor, who became grieve at Montgaithead and then tenant at Uras.

Salmon fishing

This did not take place at Old Shore of Muchalls but around 400 yards to the north at the mouth of the Burn of Muchalls with the introduction of bag-nets around 1840. The burn shows signs of having been quarried out into a pond from which ice must have been collected in midwinter to be kept in the nearby ice-house. There are also the remains of a bothy and the station may have been worked into the 20th century.

Fisher names

The parish registers begin in 1716 and the last reference to Muchalls residents is in 1764. Most of the common names were also found in Cowie in the same period. The names occurring throughout most of this period were: Kermack/Cormack, Taylor, Cadenhead and Leiper. Watt, Masson, Caddel, Cobban/Gibbon and Brodie also occurred before 1740, Brebner and Grey only in 1764. Kilgour (see above) seems to be unique.

Some variations of the place-name and spelling

Muchalls	1606, 1722, 1760 to date
Muchallis	1636
(Shore of) Muchels	1642, 1663
Sea-town of Muchaells	1663
Seaton/Seatown of Muchalls	1716–64
Seatoun of Muchels	1717
Muchall	1738, 1768
Shore of Muchalls	1774

Number of fishermen and boats

Year	Fishers	Boats	Type
1606	10–12	2 min.	under 25ft
1663	10–12	2 min.	under 25ft
1749	15–18	3	under 25ft
1758	10–12	2	under 25ft
1760s	5–6?	1	under 25ft

Cowie [1]   Fetteresso NO877867

The fishertoun of Cowie lies at the mouth of the river Cowie, which falls into a bay of the same name forming a 'small and commodious harbour'. The community was probably medieval in origin. The Barony of Colly is recorded in the time of Robert I (1306–29) as belonging to Alexander Fraser. On 27 December 1375 Robert III granted the barony to Robert Keith, son of Sir William de Keith, Earl Marischal. In 1430 William Hay of Errol, Constable of Scotland, held the Barony of Cowie, confirmed in 1450. On 28 December 1502/03 the Crown confirmed to William Hay of Ury certain crofts *in villam de* [toun of] *Cowy*. These included Langcroft alias Brounisland, le Batehalch, Maldiscroft, Smiddycroft of Cowy and Abbotiscroft. 'Batehalch' is Boathaugh, perhaps the landing place at Cowie fishertoun. In 1540/41 Cowie, like Kincardine and Durris, was created a free burgh with the rights to a market cross, a weekly market on Sunday and an annual fair on the feast of St Nathalan (8 January). In 1645 Cowie was plundered by Montrose's army. By the end of the 17th century the market was defunct, having moved to Stonehaven. The ancient burgh is believed to have been on higher ground in the neighbourhood of the castle.

There is no definite evidence for white-fishers until the early-17th century. The boats, fishertoun and fishings are first mentioned in 1606 and 1609. In 1642 Cowie was listed as one of the 'little shores for fisher boats' in the Mearns and in 1722 was one of four fishing villages in Fetteresso parish. It was described as an estate with a fishing village in 1725. According to the Court Book of the Barony of Urie (1604–1747) the skipper of the land's boat came mid-way between a husbandman and a cottar in superiority of

1 Compiled by editor from author's notes.

tenure. He held the fisher crofts directly of the proprietor and was responsible for the rents of the members of the crew. The fishermen also had to cart peats and assist at harvest and to all intents were *bona fide* tillers of the soil, but this was subsidiary to fishing. The proprietor had considerable control over the crew and could compel them to go to sea in fine weather on pain of a fine of 'an boits pairt of fisches for ilk day thay ly on land, quhen thay may convenientlie go to sie'. The boat and hwill (small rowing boat) were the laird's property. Fishers paid a money rent for their share in the boat and surrendered a 'boat's part' or boat's deal – the same percentage of the catch as received by the crew members. A yearly custom of 100 haddocks or three large cod 'to the lady' with a pint of fish liver oil from each man completed the payments.

The Court Book for 1607 implies a single boat and from 1627–36 the crew of five are named as Law, Leiper/Leaper, Smyth, Robertson and Fouler (once Falconer). George Caddel, fisher in Cowie, is named in the Court Book in 1721. In 1722 Cowie, along with Muchalls, Elsick and Skateraw supplied not only the whole parish but 20 or 30 miles south and westward, 'besides a great quantity to be salted for exportation'. In 1790 Mr Innes of Cowie was proprietor of the white-fishings and there were three boats, catching ling, cod, turbot, skate, haddock etc., mostly consumed in the neighbourhood. By 1842 the population was 174 and included around 40 fishers with eight boats, catching mainly haddock. Some of this was consumed fresh but the rest was dried on the beach as speldings or smoked at home over peat as finnans or over wood in purpose-built smoke-houses. Cod was largely dried or pickled. Processing was mostly in the hands of curers who forwarded large quantities, particularly finnans, by cadger to Angus and Perthshire, by coach and sea to Edinburgh and Glasgow, and by steam vessel from Aberdeen to London. Almost all those employed in fishing also went in the herring season to Peterhead and Fraserburgh, though several were reported to have had success at the Stonehaven fishery, then recently established. A total of 15 boats of 20 to 30 tons burden were recorded for the parish as going to the herring, which must have included six or seven from Cowie. In 1855 there were 62 fishers and 23 boats, including nine large herring boats. In 1864 however the village suffered an outbreak of cholera as a result of taking in rescued Swedish sailors; 20 to 30 men, women and children became ill, although some recovered. By 1871 the number of fishers had dropped to 31. In 1890 nineteen Cowie fishermen petitioned the Fishery Board regarding improvements to Stonehaven harbour. After 1900 the community declined and from 1905 onwards the only boats were a few sailing yauls. In the 1930s a handful of men fished from a single motor yaul.

Salmon fishing

On 22 April 1525 the Crown confirmed to William Keith, son and heir of Robert Keith and nephew and heir of William Keith, Earl Marischal, the baronies of Dunnottar, Fetteresso and Garvock and the sheriffdom and constableship of Kincardine with the fishings in the Waters of Bervie and Cowie. Fifteen years later William Keith Earl Marischal was confirmed as proprietor of the salmon fishings within the tide between the outflows (*fontes*) of the Cowie and Downyheid (Downie Point, south of Stonehaven). In the early-18th century it was said that 'a very pretty salmond fishing' took place at the mouths of the Carron (Stonehaven) and Cowie Waters. The Cowie was also renowned for sea trout, '100 dozen in one day having been taken with a small drag net'. In 1790 the salmon fishing in Stonehaven Bay was the property of Mr Barclay and by 1842 cobles, stake-nets and the new bag-nets were all employed. The bay was the principal salmon fishing in the parish, most of the catch being sent to London. An old salmon fishers' bothy still exists at Cowie and an ice-house at the Skatie Shore to the north. At time of writing salmon fishing still took place as part of the bag-net fishings between Cowie and Newtonhill.

Fisher names

Between 1618 and 1636 the names Leiper, Smyth, Robertson, Fouler/Falconer and Law are recorded. This is a different set of names from those occurring in the 18th century, which are Masson, Cadenhead, Caddel, Watt, Cormack (all also recorded at Muchalls) and Main, Burnett, Gibbon, Mitchell, Craig, Adam, and Lees. Alex Taylor (1750–1814) was one of the Muchalls orphans, as possibly was Moses Cadenhead whose house could still be traced in 1919 about 100 yards south of Dennabuck and who used a small creek called Cadenhead Shore, later Black Loch. By 1841 the names found are mainly Taylor, Lees, Adam, Masson, Brodie and Christie, plus Neilson, Williamson and Blair. By 1871, out of 31 fishers, Taylor and Masson are the predominant names. The names of the fishers' wives indicate that some of them came from Crawton and Skateraw. In 1890 seven fishermen bore the name Taylor, four Masson and Adam, two Lees, one Fairweather and one Christie.

Some variations of the place-name and spelling

Cowy	1641x50, 1642
Cowie	1700 to present. Nearly every source from 1700 to the present day consistently spells the name as Cowie
Fishtown (of Cowie)	1822

Number of fishermen and boats

Year	Fishers	Boats	Type
1606	5–6	1	under 25ft?
1790	15–18	3	under 25ft?
1813	30–36	6	under 25ft?
1842	40	8–9	5/6 over 30ft, 3 others
1855	62	23	9 large, 11 standard, 3 yauls
1871	31	?	all sizes
1881	35	17	all sizes
1890	19	6+	6 large plus others

Year	Fishers	Boats	Type
1900	22	10	boats and yauls?
1905	17	6	yauls (sail)
1910	9	3	yauls (sail)
1915	4	3	yauls (sail)
1920	9	8	yauls (sail)
1925	4	4	yauls (sail)
1928	4	2	yauls (sail)
1930	4 (2 part-time)	1	yaul (motor)
1935	4	1	yaul (motor)
1938	2	1	yaul (motor)

Stonehaven [1]   Dunnottar NO876854

On 20 December 1506 the Crown confirmed to the merchants and burgesses of Montrose a monopoly of the export of wool, hides, leather, salmon and salt cod within the burgh's liberties (from the Findon Burn to the Dighty Water near Broughty Ferry), since the Crown had been defrauded of Customs payments by the 'paking and peling' (packing and exporting) of these commodities at ports on the Mearns coast, including Stanhiffe. In 1587 George Keith Earl Marischal was confirmed *in villam de Stanehyve cum libero portu et lie havin sylver at parvis custums, anchorages* (with the liberty of a harbour and the rights to 'haven silver' (harbour dues), petty customs and anchorages), along with all the privileges of a burgh of barony including a weekly market. These privileges were renewed in 1592 and a further charter of 1612 confirmed William Keith, son of George, in the fishings in fresh and salt water from Cratoun-ness to Carrown de Cowy. In 1600 Stonehaven replaced Kincardine as the county town.

The original harbour was a small natural bay to the south of the Carron, sheltered on the south-east by Downie Point and protected by Craig-ma-cair, which gave the haven its name. The first man-made harbour, erected at the beginning of the 17th century, was demolished in a storm and in 1642 the Rev Mr Keyth, sometime minister of Dunnottar, declared the haven would be 'as serviceable and ready as any 'twixt the two Firths' (i.e. the Moray Firth and the Forth) if the pier were re-erected. A quay was constructed on the north side in 1688. There is no mention of Stonehaven among the 'little shores for fisher boats' in the Mearns; however in 1715 there were stated to be five boats; if these were fishing boats it appears that Stonehaven had more fishers than either Muchalls or Cowie at this period. In 1792–93 there were three six-man boats and a yaul in the parish; all but one of these were probably at Stonehaven as Crawton (the only other fishertoun) may have had only a single boat at this time. The fishing was stated to be 'much declined', no doubt due to the dearth of haddock in the late 1780s, but the quality was excellent. Cod, ling, haddock, whiting and flounders were caught, besides crabs and

---

* Compiled by editor from author's notes.

lobsters which were mostly consumed locally. By 1842 there were stated to be five or six boats, implying 25 to 30 fishers. In 1826 Robert Stevenson blew up Craig-ma-cair and constructed an enlarged harbour five acres in extent which was further improved by the addition of a pier to form an inner basin.

Herring fishing began in 1814 and first results were not always promising, although by 1842 it was stated that the fishery was now 'prosecuted with enterprise' and that curing establishments had been formed. In 1855 fifty-five herring boats landed at Stonehaven, including boats from Fife and England, and there were eight curers in the town. The fishery continued to expand, with 100 to 200 boats landing by the 1860s, considerably more than Montrose and Gourdon with 40 to 60 each, Arbroath with 30 to 40 and Aberdeen with only ten to 20 at this period. By the 1870s it was not uncommon for the pier to be filled to capacity, with barrels lining the High Street and the gutters working through the night. By 1928 Stonehaven had its own fishery district[1], which included Shieldhill, Catterline, Crawton, Cowie, Cove and Skateraw. Some 50 to 60 line boats also operated from Stonehaven, most of the haddocks being sold fresh. The old pier was extended in 1877 but in 1890 fishers from Portlethen to Catterline, who often ran for shelter to Stonehaven, petitioned the Fishery Board for further improvements as the outer harbour was inadequate and the entrance so shallow that boats often had to lie out awaiting the tide, with a consequent loss of the value of their catch. Despite this the outer breakwater was only finished in 1908–09, when the peak of the herring trade was past. The advent of steam trawlers, too large for the harbour, meant that by the early-20th century white-fishing too was much reduced. By 1915 there were still 18 large and 19 to 20 medium and small boats but the herring boats were laid up at the end of the 1913 season and never re-used. Motors were at first distrusted but were adapted for line fishing as they made it safer to go long distances. One hundred men were still employed around 1920 but by 1928, when there were still 47 boats, the 78 fishermen were all either middle aged or elderly. Many fishers migrated to Torry (Craig, Christie and Masson, today thought of as Torry names, really originated in Stonehaven).

Salmon fishing

The renewal of Montrose's burgh charter in 1506 specifically forbade 'Stanhiffe, Gowrdone' and other places within Montrose's precinct from packing and exporting salmon and other fish. In 1540/41 the Crown confirmed William Keith Earl Marischal in the salmon fishings 'within the tide between the outflows of the Cowy Water and Downyheid' (Downie Point, south of Stonehaven) and a renewal of this charter to William Keith's grandson (also William) in 1612 includes fishings in fresh and salt water

---

1 A fishery office had previously been set up in Stonehaven in 1820, the year the Fishery Board first paid bounties on cured cod and ling as well as herring. The office moved for a time to Montrose but from 1850 the whole area north of Gourdon was subsumed in Peterhead District (ed.).

from Crawton-ness to Carroun of Cowy. Salmon fishing took place at the mouth of the Carron in 1792. In 1842 it was stated that no salmon fishing took place in the parish of Dunnottar (i.e. south of the Carron) although in Stonehaven Bay the process was conducted by cobles and stake- and bag-nets. Most of the catch was sent to London but the quantity procured was said to be 'not great'.

Fisher names

The earliest names recorded, between 1672 and 1698, are Ritchie, Bridgefoord, Gowan, Christie, Watson, Masson and Law. Those recorded throughout the 18th and early-19th centuries include Brown, Leiper, Ritchie, Craig, Brebner, Blair, Lees and Stephen. In 1841 four fishers bore the name Adam, three Lees, and two each Mackie, Brown and Stephen. By 1861 Lees was predominant but by this time the majority were incomers, mainly from Cowie and Fetteresso parish but also from as far north as Banchory-Devenick (e.g. Wood and Main) or from Gourdon to the south (Lownie). By 1881, at the height of the herring boom when the Boat Account lists 211 fishers, many fishers had migrated from other Mearns villages. Lees was still common along with Adam, Christie, Leiper, Wood and Craig. Further incomers include Noble (Burnhaven near Peterhead), Moncrieff and Meldrum (Cellardyke), McKechnie (Easdale in Argyll) and even a Jamieson from the Isle of Man.

Some variations of the place-name and spelling

Stanhiffe   1506
Stanehyve   1587
Stone-Hyve   1641x50
Stonhive   1703
Stonhaven   1747x55
Stonehaven*   1774, 1792–93, 1813, 1822, 1842, 1855 to present
* Locally pronounced Steenhive

Number of fishermen and boats

Year	Fishers	Boats	Type
1715	25?	5	under 25ft
1792–3	15?	3	2 boats under 25ft, 1 yaul
1813	15–18?	3	boats
1841	18	?	boats and yauls?
1842	c.25?	5–6	'boats' (including herring boats)
1855	17	11	2 large, 3 standard, 6 yauls
1881	211	88	all sizes
1899	280	101	all sizes
1900	265	96	all sizes
1905	205	69	all sizes
1910	176	53	all sizes
1914	c.170?	65	25 large, 32 standard, 8 yauls
1915	132	38	all sizes

Year	Fishers	Boats	Type
1920	100	60	some motor boats(?), many sailing yauls
1925	87	59	some motor boats, many sailing yauls (10 part-time)
1928	78*	47	8 motor (30ft plus), 6 small motor, 33 sailing yauls
1930	62	40	all types as above? (12 part-time)
1935	55	29	all types as above?
1938	37	23	1 motor (30ft plus), 4 motor (under 30ft), 18 sail
1948	68	48	5 motor (30ft plus), 19 motor (under 30ft), 24 sail

* all aged over 50

Crawton   Dunnottar NO878797

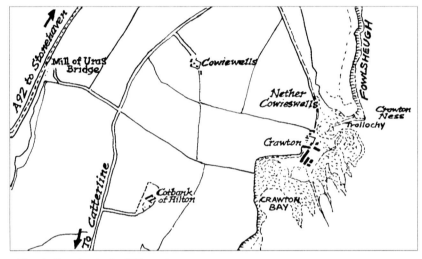

Map 4 *Crawton in the 19th century*

The lands of Crawton were part of the barony of Uras, first recorded in 1370. In 1371 half of the barony with its fishings was resigned to the Crown by Mathew Eychles but by 1390 it belonged to Thomas Rait. A Walter Ogilvie of Owres is mentioned in 1478 but in 1491 the lands of Crawtoun and Mill of Owres passed to William Keith, Earl Marischal, who already owned most of the land around, including Dunnottar, Stonehaven and Cowie. In 1554 and 1574 one merk (13 shillings and fourpence) was paid out of the lands of Crawtoun and Owres to the Irvines of Drum. In 1592 the Crown confirmed George Keith, Earl Marischal and his son William in the lands and barony of Owres including Cratoun with its white-fishings in the sea and salt waters. Craton was listed in 1642 as one of the many 'little shores for fisher boats' in the Mearns. A description of Dunnottar parish from around the same date fails to mention Crawton but recounts that the Earl Marischal had a man who, by means of helpers, was lowered twice daily by rope down the cliffs at Fowlsheugh to collect eggs and young kittiwakes between May and August. These were considered a 'delicious meat' and were sold by the collectors in the country around. The men who did this were of course the Crawton fishermen. In 1792 more detail was given: five men assisted in lowering a sixth – i.e. a fishing boat's crew – down the cliffs. A rent of £2 10s was paid to the Earl for the privilege of being allowed to do this! The feathers and down as well as the flesh of the kittiwakes were said to be in great demand.

The community

Although Crawton was originally the name of a farm immediately adjacent to the fisher houses, a fishing community must have existed by the 1370s and probably much earlier; since the only fishings at Crawton were white-fishings this implies a permanent community resident near the haven, probably partly employed on the land and partly at white-fishing in early times. The name is simply Middle English or Scots *craw tun*, crow farm. The haven is wide and sheltered, facing southwards. The shore is formed by large pebbles with the advantage of a cart track reaching down to it. The rocks form a natural pier at some states of the tide so it is an excellent natural haven, likely to have been settled at a very early period. There are no indications of the size of the community in early times, but like many other such places there may only have been a single boat, five or six fisher families or households, and a maximum population of about 20 to 30. Residents of Seaton of Crawton are recorded from 1698 and throughout the 18th century in the Dunnottar parish registers. About 15 adult males are named in the decade 1700–10. Only seven adult fishermen are named in the 1720s and as many in the 1740s, fewer in later decades. So it appears possible that there may have been two boats' crews in the early-18th century, declining to one later due to the activities of the press gangs or being lost at sea. As at Catterline the surnames formerly predominating all disappear entirely around 1775, which suggests a sudden loss of men. In 1792 there were three white-fishing boats and one smaller yaul in Dunnottar parish. It seems very likely that Crawton had only one boat at this time while the others were at Stonehaven, since in 1813 there was only a single boat with a crew of six at Crawton. Population growth was probably quite rapid thereafter, to some extent due to an influx of newcomers as four new surnames appear from the 1820s.

In 1842 it was said that white-fishing in the sea was the sole occupation of the villagers of Crawton but the number of boats was not given. However the 1841 census shows that there were 15 households and a total population of 77, with about 16 men and boys over the age of 14, enough to crew three boats, so the community had expanded rapidly. Stonehaven had become a herring station by 1842, but the Crawton fishers were apparently not involved in herring fishing until sometime shortly afterwards. Salmon fishing, even with the adoption of the bag-net at many places in the district by 1840, never seems to have been introduced here and only white-fishing existed, as in earlier times. By 1855 there were no less than 11 boats: four of over 30 feet, four standard and three yauls. There were 21 fishermen and boys and a further 30 persons involved in fish selling, processing, etc. There was also a fish curer and cooper who employed five gutter/packers, presumably pickling cod and ling for the London market. There was still a resident curer in 1881 and probably somewhat later. By 1881 there were 13 boats of all types but only 17 fishermen from 12 fisher families resident. In 1890 fourteen Crawton fishermen petitioned the Fishery Board to support improvements to Stonehaven Harbour, from where they worked three large boats. Since only larger decked herring boats gave viable returns by the 1880s it became advantageous to move to Stonehaven, near where the herring boats were kept in winter. There was also an organised white-fish market there, so most of the families migrated to Stonehaven just before 1914, although a few moved to Catterline and Gourdon while others went to Torry where the men took jobs on board trawlers working out of Aberdeen. Fishing then ceased as no boats or active fishers were recorded in 1915, 1920 or 1925. The deserted houses became ruinous although the last family only migrated to Stonehaven in 1927. An old photograph in their possession, taken early last century, shows that the Crawton houses latterly had red pantiled roofs. The Gourdon fishers regarded the Crawton folk as 'heugh-heid pleengs' (cliffhead seagulls) who danced and fiddled the whole time away in winter, and why not?

Fisher names

The Dunnottar parish registers, extant from 1672, record the names Muffart, Cant, Lumsden and Taylor at 'Crawton' up to the 1690s, but that could have referred to the farm as well. From 1698 they record residents of Seaton of Crawton as 'seamen'. From then up to 1775, after which they disappear, the names Barclay and Brigfuird/Bridgefo(o)rd were by far the commonest fisher names, while Watt and Walker occurred more than once. From 1775 folk bearing the name Davidson first appeared, and remained in the community thereafter, although not initially numerous. Moncur occurred first in 1800 and Wylie and Clark from the later 1820s. Dunbar and Hogg occurred only once in 1828. In the early-19th century there was no predominating set of surnames but the names Wylie, Clark and Freeman were borne by more than one family in 1841, while other fisher surnames in the village were: Davidson, Moncur, Watt, Andrew, Mason and Inglis. The majority of these names originate in other Mearns fishertouns, mainly in Fetteresso parish to the north. In 1881 out of 12 fisher households, five families were called Davidson, two Wyllie and the others were called Clark, Webster, Brodie, Noble and Buchan. By 1891 there were ten working fishers called Davidson, six called Wyllie and one called Masson. The last resident fisher family in the 1920s were Davidsons who migrated to Stonehaven before 1928.

Some variations of the place-name and spelling

Crawtoun	1491, 1554, 1574
Cratoun	1592
Kratown	1641x50
Craton	1642
Seatoun of Crawton	1698–1828
Crawston	1747x55
Cratown	1774, 1822
Crawton*	1792, 1842 to date

* Locally pronounced Cratton or Cra'in (glottal stop)

Number of fishermen and boats

Year	Fishers	Boats	Type
1792–93	6	1	under 25ft
1813	6	1	under 25ft
1841–42	16	3?	2 boats under 30ft, 1 yaul?
1855	21	11	4 large, 4 standard, 3 yauls
1881	17	13	all types
1890–91	14?	?	3 large, plus standard and yauls
1900	14	8	1 boat, 7 yauls?
1910	8	6	yauls
1928	–	–	

Catterline Catterline & Kinneff NO868782

The church of Caterlyn with its lands, teinds and offerings was granted to Arbroath Abbey by its founder King William I at or soon after its foundation in 1178. Around 1206 William, son of Bernard, the owner of at least part of the lands of Katerlyn, granted two oxgangs of land called Rath, with the use of the mill of Katerlyn, to Arbroath Abbey. Around 1222x40 he confirmed the earlier gift and also granted 19 acres by the sea called Tregles with its (unspecified) rights and pertinents. Both gifts were witnessed by the donor's son and heir Bernard 'within the farm of Tregles'. Around 1211x14 John de Montford granted to the abbey the lands called Glaskeler which lay between his lands of Catterline and the Catterline Burn, with the use of the mill dam of Catterline; also with the stipulation that all men on his half of Catterline called Lungyrg were to pay their mill dues to the abbey. Few of these names can be identified with any certainty. Rath was presumably the

© The Estate of Colin Gibson

25 *Catterline pier*

Reath, the ridge of high land to the south of the village, between the sea and the steep den of the Catterline Burn. Lungyrg sounds somewhat like Lumgair to the north but it is in Dunnottar parish and seems too far away. Perhaps Tregles, by the sea, was an old name for part of Hilton, which is next to Trelong bay. In 1371 the Crown granted Thomas Rait the barony of Uras with its fishings (at Crawton), Cloak, Hilton and other lands to the north, and Katerlyne with rights over the haven of old owing and customary. This does not necessarily mean that Rait was the actual occupier of the lands and haven of Catterline, he may have only held the feudal superiority.

A few leases of the abbey's lands have survived. In 1483 Arbroath Abbey leased their lands and toun of Katirlyng with its mill to Duncan Spark and his wife for £10 annual rent, with the right to have co-tenants and subtenants. In 1526 the lands and mill were leased for 19 years to Andrew Moncur of Mains, near Dundee, and his wife Janet Graham for an annual rent of two chalders of barley, two chalders of flour and ten multures from the mill. But by 1542 the lands and mill of Catterline were leased to David Wood of Craig, near Montrose. Wood leased other lands with salmon fishings from the abbey, on the South and North Esk estuaries near Montrose and at Torry on the Dee, but no fishings of any kind are mentioned in connection with the abbey's lands at Catterline.

The lands belonging to Arbroath Abbey, Rath, Glaskeler, Tregles and the church's lands, were not necessarily in a compact block but some were around the church and mill. There is not a hint as late as 1542 that the abbey owned the haven, so when it acquired such rights is a mystery. However, after the abbey was secularised at the Reformation in 1560 it appears that by then it also owned the haven since charters of the superiority of the Regality lands of Arbroath Abbey of 1608, 1641 and 1662 list Catterline with its harbour and fishings.

The community before 1800

There may have been a small fisher community, their cottages perched on the heugh-heid of Catterline, from very early times, since there is a shingle shore within a small sheltered bay, ideal for landing and launching small boats. The bay is protected by a headland to the south and rocks to the north, although northerly and easterly storms can sweep over an underwater reef, which normally gives added protection at the entrance to the haven, making for dangerous conditions to land a boat. At other times it is safe to land and launch small boats and there is ample space to draw them clear of the highest tides. Rights over the haven of Catterline, old-established in 1371, would seem to suggest that a fishertoun existed by the 14th century, if not earlier. Although no fishings are mentioned, the existence of trade is highly unlikely at such a date, and rights to charge rent for fishing would seem much more likely. The haven is only mentioned again from 1608. There may only have been a single boat's crew in these early times. In 1627 Thomas Watt and John Findlay were recorded as dwellers in Heughhead of Catterline.

The name Watt was still the commonest fisher name in the parish in the 18th century while Findlay was later a common fisher name at Ferryden. In 1642 Heuchhead was listed among the 'little shores for fisher boats' in the Mearns. Gourdon folk in recent times referred to the Catterline fishers as 'heughheiders', an apt description of their place of residence on top of the heugh, or cliff, overlooking the bay.

The Catterline and Kinneff parish registers, extant only from 1730, record fisher residents of Seatown of Catterline. In 1772 Arbroath Town Council was arranging to pay the removal costs of a boat's crew of five men and a boy, with their families, from 'Hacterland near Bervie'. Four of them bore the distinctive surname Bridgefoord, the other two Alexander, which proves beyond doubt that this referred to Catterline. But it appears that they never made the move to Arbroath as neither surname is recorded there later. In 1792 there were two boats at Catterline, each with a crew of six, so there must have been about ten to 12 fisher families and a possible maximum population of around 50 persons of all ages. It was said then that the fishers were giving up fishing due to the haddock dearth (c.1783–93), the checking of smuggling by the vigilance of Customs cruisers, and the seizing of fishermen by press gangs. The surnames predominant in the earlier-18th century disappear by the 1770s and incomers from Stonehaven, Cowie or further north began to settle in Catterline. This suggests that quite a few men had been seized by the press.

The community since 1800

By 1813 there was only a single boat and crew so the decline noted in 1792 had not been reversed despite some immigration. But by the 1840s, and probably somewhat earlier, the community had recovered, largely due to another influx of newcomers. The New Statistical Account of 1842 states that there were two boats and crews, implying around 12 fishermen and boys, but the 1841 census in fact shows that there were 13 fishermen aged between 20 and 45, two aged 70 and 80 and two or three boys of 15 so enough to man a yaul as well. There were 15 houses inhabited by fisher families and one by Helen Christie, spirit seller, so the inn had been established by then. The coastguard station was probably established from around 1830. It is adjacent to the fishers' houses and consists of a two-storey house for the officer, four cottages for the men and their families and an office of similar size to the fishers' cottages. The station seems to have been built by Lord Arbuthnott for lease to the service, a common arrangement, and seems to have been one of those closed in 1905. There appears to be no record of a rocket life-saving team as found elsewhere, although there may have been one. The watch-house perched on the edge of a cliff above the harbour was probably manned during the 1939–45 war. Lord Arbuthnott may also have set up the dram-shop or inn. It was suggested in 1792 that a pier be built for the convenience of coasting sloops which brought in coal from the Forth or Tyne, and occasionally lime for the fields. A pier was built by Lord

Arbuthnott shortly before 1842. In more recent times, up to about 1930, a wooden-hulled steamer brought in coal once a year.

By 1855 there were nine boats: three over 30 feet, four standard haddock boats and two yauls manned by 22 fishers, and by 1881 no less than 28 boats of all types manned by 30 resident fishers. In 1890 thirty-four Catterline fishermen petitioned the Fishery Board to improve Stonehaven harbour from where they worked seven large boats. Herring fishing probably ceased by 1914. Decline was very slow but by 1928 there were only eight yauls, three with motors, manned by 20 fishermen. By the 1940s only one yaul out of the eight in use relied on sail. Most had been built before 1914. After the war there were still six or seven motor yauls under 20 feet long. The last two fished up to 1955. From 1962 three, later only two, former salmon fishers went sma' line and creel fishing in a 21-foot former ship's lifeboat. From 1985 only summer creel fishing was carried out.

Salmon fishing

There were four or five salmon fishers resident in 1841, most with white-fisher surnames. There are no early indications of salmon fishing in the parish and it presumably started with the introduction of bag-nets shortly before. The bothy sits behind the former coastguard boat shed near the pier. Salmon fishing seems to have ceased in 1950. Latterly it was operated by Johnston's of Montrose. There was another fishing and a bothy at Trelong Bay which seems to have ceased before 1900. In recent times the salmon fishers here mostly worked on the local farms tattie-dressing in winter.

Fisher names

In 1627 the names Watt and Findlay were recorded. From 1732 the parish registers show that the surname Bridgefoord was predominant in Catterline up to 1776, after which none are recorded. Other names in the 18th century were Largie in 1734, Watt in 1750, Cormack in 1755 and Alexander in 1772. The name Stephen first appeared in 1785 and became predominant after 1800. Other surnames from Stonehaven and Skateraw, such as Christie and Freeman, appeared soon after 1800. In 1841 around 17 out of 30 heads of families were called Stephen and 14 out of 30 fishermen in 1881. Other names in the 19th century were Taylor, Davidson and Noble. A MacKay was a native of Caithness. In 1890 sixteen fishermen bore the name Stephen; three Noble, Taylor and McBay; two Gove, Davidson and Brodie while two individuals were called Adam and Melvin. A family of Watts migrated from Shieldhill in 1919.

Some variations of the place-name and spelling

Caterlyn	1178x98
Katerlyn	1206, 1211x14, 1222x40
Katerlyne	1371
Katirlyng	1483, 1526
Catterline*	1542, 1606, 1642, 1662, 1732–1814, 1792, 1842 to date
Catterling	1608
Heughhead (of Catterline)	1627, 1641–50, 1642,
Caterlyne	1641
Catarline	1684
Cartalin	1703
Seatoun/Seatown of Catterline	1732–1814
Ketterline	1747x55
'Hacterland'	1772
Katerline	1774, 1813
Caterline	1792
Katterline	1822

* Locally pronounced Ketterlin or Ke'erlin (glottal stop)

Number of fishermen and boats

Year	Fishers	Boats	Type
1792	12	2	under 25ft
1813	6?	1	under 25ft
1841–42	13–16	2–3?	2 boats, 1 yaul?
1855	22	9	3 large, 4 standard, 2 yauls
1881	30	28	8 large, 12 standard, 8 yauls
1890	34	29	7 large plus others
1900	35	18	boats and yauls
1910	27	17	boats and yauls
1920	17	11	yauls?
1928	20	8	yauls (3 motor)
1935	14	5	yauls (some motor)
1938	10	5	yauls (some motor)
1940	20	8	yauls (7 motor, 1 sail)
1945	15–16?	6 or 7	motor yauls under 20 feet
1955	8	2	motor yauls under 20 feet
1962–90	2	1	motor yaul 21 feet

This village has left no trace. It was situated about quarter of a mile south-west of Braidon Bay immediately north of Hallhill farm. Access to the broad sheltered bay was by a path off the road to Todhead, ploughed up in 1986. Access to the bay can still be got by a very rough track past Millhill near Fernyflatt. There is some level land behind Braidon Bay recently used to grow tatties on. The farmer of Hallhill on whose ground the village was situated claims never to have ploughed up any signs of occupation, although James Crabb Watt, author of *The Mearns of Old* (1914) knew of the lost settlement of 'Gapple' and found a bottle in the area. Gawpol must have been the Fischertoun in the barony of Kinneff recorded around 1400 and again from the 1540s. On 22 July 1545 the Crown confirmed Walter Bisset, son of James Bisset of Kinneff, in half the barony of Kinneff, which consisted of the lands of: Overton, Fischeartoun, Glisland, Batisland, Largiesland and half of Blacklaws, not all of which can be identified today. In 1571 the Crown confirmed Jean Bisset, elder sister and quarter heiress of Walter Bisset, in a quarter of the above half of the barony of Kinneff including Fischeartoun. In 1589 Margaret Bisset, heir to Walter, resigned to Andrew Graham of Morphie a quarter of the barony of Easter Kinneff or Fernyflatt consisting of a quarter of the lands of: Mains of Fernyflatt, Hallhill or Bodisland, Braidlie or Fyschartoun, Blacklaws, Overton, Glasland and Largiesland. In December 1625 William Graham of Fernyflatt granted to Patrick Lichtoun of Dunninald: Ovirton, Fischertoun alias Gawpule alias Braidlie, as well as half of Blacklaws, Beatislandis or Hallhill, Glaslandis, Weitlandis alias Mains of Fernyflatt, Largie, the mill and mill lands etc. and the fishing boats in the barony of Fernyflatt or Easter Kinneff.

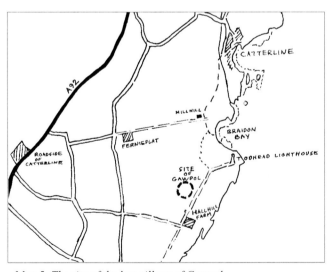

Map 5 *The site of the lost village of Gawpol*

The name Braidlie is 'broad lea'. Nearby the Braidon Burn runs into Braidon Bay. By 1625 the name Gawpule appears as an alternative. Gaw is old Scots for a drainage ditch or patch of boggy ground, pule or poll means pool. In various spellings it was later the only name for the settlement. Gappall was listed among the 'little shores for fisher boats' in the Mearns in 1642. The parish registers record persons resident at Seaton of Gap(p)al in the 1730s but from the 1750s to 1790 at Gaphill. It is shown on General Roy's survey of around 1747x55 as Gaphill and as Gap-hill in the Statistical Account of 1792, though Garden's map of Kincardineshire of 1774 has Gawpol. The transformation of the name to 'Gaphill' was presumably because the village stood on the head of a rise just north of Hallhill's cottar house to the north of the road to Todhead lighthouse.

The community

Little is recorded except intermittent mentions of the settlement from around 1400 to 1792. The excellent sheltered shingle bay is far superior to many others settled at an early period. In the 18th and early-19th centuries small barks or sloops landed coal at Braidon Bay since there was easy access for farmers' carts to get down to the shore. Fernyflatt farm has a chimney for a stream-driven threshing mill (horse- or water-power was more common in the mid-19th century), so coal may have been landed well into the 19th century. The lands of Fischertoun are mentioned in the 16th century so the fishers, as at some other places, had some arable lands or crofts to work. The name Seaton of Gappal, used in the early-18th century, would seem to imply a separate farm of the same name, as found at Usan, Crawton etc. but none is recorded. At least two boats are implied in

1625, any more are unlikely as there were only two in the mid-18th century, a period of likely expansion. This would imply ten or 12 fishers, about eight to ten families and a total fisher population of around 40 to 50 in the 17th and mid-18th centuries. In the 18th century at least there were a few others forby fishers resident. A gravestone in Kinneff kirkyard commemorates Robert Pithie, shoemaker in Gaphile, who died in 1779 aged 64, his wife Elspeth Goodfellow who died in 1778 aged 67 and three of their children who died in childhood. Another daughter is recorded in the parish register married to a fisherman.

Sma' line and great line fishing were carried out around 1792 since ling, cod and skate were

26 *Robert Pithie, 'sometime shoemaker in Gaphile'*

caught as well as haddock. As elsewhere on the coast there was a dearth of the main catch, haddock, from around 1783 to 1793. Smuggling, which had been rife in the district earlier in the 18th century due to the distance from any Customs station, had fallen off after the 1760s. This, and the loss at sea by accident or activity of the press gangs from the 1760s had reduced Gawpol from two boats to one by 1792. The last entry in the parish register concerning the inhabitants of the village was in 1790 so it seems soon after 1792 the loss of the last boat and crew must have forced the dependent women and children to abandon the village entirely, a similar fate to that of Seaton of Muchalls. Gawpol is not mentioned by Robertson in 1813 nor in the New Statistical Account in 1842. By the time of the 1865 Ordnance Survey not a trace of its location remained on the ground. The Catterline fishers have no traditions of its existence but call Braidon Bay Gapple Shore. A tradition from Gourdon was that 'Gapol' was destroyed by a storm and a north-west wind. Since the village was so far above the sea this is impossible and it would seem more likely that the last boat's crew was probably lost at sea in a storm.

Salmon fishing

There was once easy access to a landing place just below Hallhill farm, recorded otherwise as Bodislands (boat's lands). In recent times this was known as Powden but may be the Ha' Door referred to in the ditty quoted under Shieldhill. No salmon fishing seems to have been carried out in living memory although it was known by the Gourdon fishers to have been a coble fishing at one time.

Fisher names

From 1731 to 1790, when inhabitants were recorded in the parish registers, the name Watt predominated, borne by about half of the men and many of the women. Other surnames borne by men were Cormack, Law, Hog, Thom and Donald.

Some variations of the place-name and spelling

Fische(a)rtoun (of Kinneff)	c.1400, 1545, 1571
Braidlie or Fyschartoun	1589
Fischertoun alias Gawpule alias Braidlie	1625
Gappall	1642
Gawpoll or Braidlie	1644
Seatoun of Gap(p)al	1731–47
Gaphill	1747x55, 1750s–90
Gawpol	1774
Gaphile	1779
Gap-hill	1792

The Catterline fishers know Braidon Bay as the Gapple Shore.

Number of fishermen and boats

Year	Fishers	Boats	Type
1625	10–12?	2	under 25ft?
c.1750	10–12?	2	under 25ft?
1792	5–6	1	under 25ft?

Shieldhill   Catterline & Kinneff NO857747

The remains of this small fishing hamlet lie perched near the edge of a cliff more than 50 feet above the sea. Immediately below is a rocky sloch but a narrow path winds down to a small sheltered bay to the south, known as Kinneff Haven or Crooked Haven. This was the main landing place. The bay has a shingle beach ideal for landing and launching small boats. The Kinneff Burn runs to the sea through the bay past the ruins of two abandoned salmon bothies. Although only 200 yards east of the glebe steading of the famous Kinneff kirk, the location of this erstwhile hamlet is scarcely known outside the immediate area as the path is overgrown in summer and not obvious to the uninitiated visitor. There was a Fischertoun in the barony of Kinneff recorded from around 1400 which was undoubtedly Gawpol. It seems that Shieldhill did not exist until much later and it is surely significant that it was not included among the 'little shores for fisher boats' in the Mearns listed in 1642, whereas all the other known fishertouns were included. However, on 26 February 1678, Robert, Viscount Arbuthnott leased to David Carmack and Thomas Phatt (Watt) at Newhaven of Kyneff from Whitsunday that year for the space of a year:

> all and haill that fisherland with houses, bigings, yards, tofts, crofts, pertainents, appendices, grasing, shore right and privilage of fishing at the said Newhaven of Kyneff.

The rent was 80 merks (£53 6s 8d Scots; about £4 8s Stg.) along with 'ane disson of killing (large cod) and ane disson of skait yearly' between them. A very brief description of Catterline and Kinneff parish of around 1725 only stated that seals sheltered in the caves on the coast and fails to mention any of the fishertouns or refer to any fishing in the parish. The parish registers, however, only extant from around 1730, record residents of Shieldhill with the familiar fisher surname Watt from 1732. The hamlet by then took its name from the nearby outcrop of rock called Shield Hill just to the north which has the shape of a medieval shield when seen from the sea. A very old ditty remembered in Gourdon records four coastal features within the original parish of Kinneff, bounded on the north by the burn running past Fernyflatt and Millhill:

> The Pintle Beach, the Ha' Door, the Muckle Shield and the Gapple Shore.

The Pintle is a spindle of rock near Grange; the Muckle Shield is Shield Hill; the Ha' (hall) Door may be the inlet below Hallhill, more recently called Powden; while the Gapple Shore is Braidon Bay, site of the lost village of Gawpol.

The community

In 1678 the two fishermen who took a lease were already resident so it seems that Lord Arbuthnott must have founded the fishertoun some years earlier, also providing some arable ground and grazing. The settlers probably came from nearby Gawpol and Catterline in the same parish, which also belonged to Viscount Arbuthnott and where both their surnames occurred by the 18th century. It is uncertain if the above lessees worked a single boat with the help of sons or if each had a boat with subtenants to crew them. In the first half of the 18th century the names of only five fishermen are recorded and it would appear that by then there was only a single boat's crew. The keiling and skate stipulated as part of the rent in 1678 are proof that great line fishing was carried out in mid-summer. The hamlet is indicated by only three buildings, and is un-named, on Garden's map of Kincardineshire of 1774. So it appears that there were only three households then, just enough men and boys to man a boat or yaul. The hamlet is not mentioned along with Gawpol and Catterline in the Statistical Account of 1792. Possibly there were not enough hands to crew a boat then. In 1813, however, there was an active boat's crew. The New Statistical Account of 1842 states that the single boat then was 'weakly manned' although the 1841 census records six fishermen in their prime, aged from 21 to 48. Three of these were from a single family, and there were only three families resident. This surely makes Shieldhill the smallest fisher hamlet ever to have existed! Several others had only a single boat before the 1830s but usually had at least five families.

Sometime between 1841 and 1851 it appears that Lord Arbuthnott re-developed Shieldhill, building five new slate-roofed stone and lime cottages in rows of three and two facing the sea, the ruins of which can be seen today. The original three, to the other side of the path, may have been of clay and thatch. In 1851 eight fisher families were resident, there were nine fishermen and boys and a total population of over 30. The re-development had attracted an influx from Ferryden although there were two native families resident. The Ferrydenners had gone by 1861, replaced by other transients from the Mearns then and in later years. The 1855 creek return lists four boats: one over 30 feet, two standard boats and a yaul under 18 feet; 12 fishermen and boys and a total of 31 persons involved in fishing and ancillary activities, including a cooper or curer and two gutter/packers who would have packed cod and ling late in the year for the London market. This was Shieldhill at its peak of population and activity as a fishing community. The population declined very slowly thereafter, with only seven households and seven or eight fishermen in the 1870s. By 1881 there were only three fisher households out of seven occupied houses, the others being salmon fishers and farmworkers. There were five fishermen and boys and yet still four boats. There was probably a herring boat among the four, perhaps extra hands were hired to operate the herring boat in summer. This large boat, used for herring and great line fishing, could not have operated out of the small

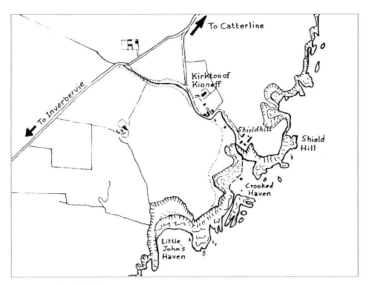

Map 6 *Shieldhill*

bay at Shieldhill, possibly out of Catterline, and in winter may have been kept at either Gourdon or Trelong Bay. The mid-1880s probably saw an end to herring and great line fishing, and three or four fishers probably operated a boat or yaul at sma' lines and creels thereafter.

Around 1900 there were still six houses occupied, and four or five in the early 1920s. But by 1925 there were only two fishermen working creels in summer. They landed at the rocky sloch north of the shingle haven and had to put the partans, which then fetched sixpence each, in barrels, which they had to carry up the steep track on their backs. They were taken to Bervie station by pony and trap. In 1926 Shieldhill became deserted when the last fisher family moved to Stonehaven. The 1928 creek returns list no boats and full-time fishing had ceased, but in fact one man continued to fish occasionally with creels for lobsters and partans and with handlines for white fish using a small coble or rowing boat up to about 1950, when he was in his 80s, shortly before he died. He is also said to have had a pet seagull which sometimes accompanied him. This was 'Eleckie Forret' as he was remembered by the Gourdon folk, correctly Alexander Forrest, who was recorded as a boy in the 1881 census, the stepson of George Christie, fisherman. He latterly lived in Kirk Cottage at Kirkton of Kinneff with his step-sister and for 60 years was kirk beadle and gravedigger, looking after both Kinneff and Catterline kirkyards. Until the 1970s Gourdon women used to visit Shieldhill to pull sea-grass to line their wicker sculls in which baited lines were laid. An occasional small creel boat sometimes still lands here.

Salmon fishing

There are no early references so this may only have begun when bag-nets were introduced to the area shortly before 1840, and fishing seems to have ceased by the 1960s. The remains of two salmon bothies, in which the men would have lived during the salmon season, are below the cliff, behind the little bay. According to local tradition a salmon fishing once operated from Little John's Haven, a small shingle bay a few hundred yards to the south, but no bothy is shown here by the Ordnance Surveys of 1865, 1904 or 1925 so it was presumably worked by the Shieldhill salmon fishers.

27 *Deserted houses at Shieldhill*

28 *The shore and old salmon bothies*

Fisher names

The name Carmack recorded in the 1678 lease is found at other fishertouns in the area in various spellings such as Cormack and Kermack. The surname Phatt, clearly written so thrice in the same document, can only be a peculiar rendering of the name Watt which was very common among the fishers of the parish. From 1732 up to the 1841 census, Watt was almost the only surname borne by the men of the hamlet, although a Mearns was recorded in 1749, and a Moir in 1789. The names Durward, Cormack, Gowan and Falt, as well as Watt, were borne by women. These occur as fisher names elsewhere on the southern Mearns coast. Between 1841 and 1851, when five new houses were provided, two families of Perts, two Coulls, a West and a Smith, all from Ferryden, moved in, but were gone again by 1861. In that year there were still two families called Watt and new incomers, called Cormack, Gilbert, Cruickshank and Davidson, from elsewhere in the Mearns, and a widow Smith were resident. By 1871 there was a single family of Watts resident and another set of incomers: Walkers, Christies and Carnegies from Gourdon and a McLean from Banffshire. In 1881 the Walkers and Christies (with a stepson Alexander Forrest) were still resident as was William Watt and his family. One family of Watts moved to Catterline in 1919, the last about 1926 to Stonehaven.

Some variations of the place-name and spelling

Newhaven of Kyneff	1678
Shieldhill	1732 to date
Locally pronounced Shiel'hill	

Number of fishermen and boats

Year	Fishers	Boats	Type
1678	4–5?	1?	boat or yaul
c.1750	5?	1	boat or yaul
1792	0?	0?	
1813	5–6?	1	under 25ft
1841–42	6	1	under 30ft
1855	12	4	1 large, 2 standard, 1 yaul
1881	5	4	all sizes
1900	8	5	yauls
1905	7	6	yauls
1910	6	5	yauls
1915	5	3	yauls
1922	4	3	yauls
1928	–	–	–

Inverbervie   Inverbervie NO830725

There is evidence for a settlement here of some kind from the 12th century but it was only created a royal burgh in 1341. On 2 June 1341, on returning from exile in France, King David II made landfall here at Craig David, just to the north, under which is a flat rock called the King's Step. Burghal status had little or no effect on the growth of Inverbervie and in fact it seems to have stagnated, partially because it lacked a convenient harbour. The fact that its trading precinct was undefined and lay within the precinct of the old-established and relatively important burgh of Montrose was an added disadvantage. It was also dominated by neighbouring landowners, who owned much of the assets of the burgh such as its lands, mills and fishings. A Carmelite Friary was established some time before the Reformation of 1560 but nothing is known of its foundation. Six Carmelite friaries were founded in Scotland before 1400, another five,

© The Estate of Colin Gibson

29 Bervie bay

including Bervie's, before 1560. In 1355 Philip Arbuthnott, ninth laird of that Ilk, granted three shillings and four pence annually from his estates to the Carmelite friars of Aberdeen. So it would appear that the Inverbervie friary probably didn't exist then. In 1567 the friary building was sacked by the Earl of Moray and its property granted to the Hospital Fund of Montrose. In 1587 it was granted to David Lindsay, minister of Leith, but by 1599 was acquired by the lairds of Arbuthnott. It seems to have been on the north-west corner of the square near the bridge, commemorated by the name Friar's Dubs. The square, just off the coast road to Aberdeen, seems to be the oldest part of Inverbervie. David Street, down nearer the shore, originally called Fishgait or Fishergait, was where the salmon fishers once lived. Despite the plainly daft local tradition that ships once sailed up the Bervie water as far as the bridge, the stream is far too shallow for anything but a flat-bottomed salmon coble to float in. The steeply sloping shingle beach is likewise unsuitable to land or launch any boat except a coble. It was only with the growth of the linen industry from the late-18th century that the population of Inverbervie rose to over 500; by 1813 it was around 600 and by 1837 had risen to 757. In the parish then, and mostly in the burgh of Bervie, were eight shopkeepers, several shoemakers and tailors, building tradesmen, cartwrights, blacksmiths, a saddler and a clock- and watchmaker.

White-fishing

The evidence for this is to say the least somewhat equivocal. 'Other fishings' in the bay, mentioned in 1588, are no proof, since the same is often stated of coastal salmon fishings, probably to allow the occasional netting of other species such as sea trout. The charters of 1600 and 1602 quoted below appear somewhat suspect since they suggest there were white-fishings in the Bervie water as well as in the bay, an impossibility. But this was just a matter of inaccurate phrasing or a determination to miss out no potential asset. In 1642 'Bervy' was listed among the 'little shores for fisher boats' along with all the other known white-fisher touns in the Mearns. In 1793 it was said that lines, hooks and shells (from bait) had been found when digging in different parts of the burgh 'but beyond memory of man there have been no professional (white) fishermen' and it was thought that they had removed to Gourdon which was more suitable for such fishings. So it may be that the configuration of the watermouth and shingle beach around 1600 and into the mid-17th century was more suited for using white-fish boats than it has been in more recent times. As at many small creeks at that time, there may only have been a single boat and crew. From the documents quoted below, it seems that if white-fishing was ever carried out at Inverbervie, it ceased sometime after 1642 and before 1724, when only salmon fishing is mentioned.

Salmon fishing

This may have been carried out from time immemorial but there appear to be no very early references. Both the Bervie water and the shingle-lined bay were long important salmon fisheries. The stream widens into a shallow pool, the Tidal Basin, just before it enters the sea. In 1474 the Crown granted Alexander Straton of Knox of Benholm and his heirs the salmon fishings at the mouth of the Bervie water to recompense him for building the first recorded bridge. In 1582 Andrew Arbuthnott was confirmed by the Crown in possession of the barony of Arbuthnott along with other property including: the two-ninth part of Inverbervie called Halgrene, the two-ninths called Brouislands with a third part of its mill, and fishings in the Bervie water. In 1588 his successor Robert Arbuthnott was confirmed by the Crown in possession of the same parts of Inverbervie with salmon and other fishings belonging to the burgh in the Bervie Water in fresh water and salt at the 'watter mouth' and the 'sey-schoir' as far as Hallgreen, with the right to have a coble and nets. This was again confirmed in 1591. In 1600 the Crown confirmed Andrew Arbuthnott with his wife Margaret and heir Robert in possession of Gourdon with its fishings etc. along with white and salmon fishings in the Water of Bervie in sweet and salt water. But the Arbuthnotts seem to have sub-infeued this to William Rait of Hallgreen and his son and heir David, who were granted a Crown charter in 1602 of property which included Gourdon with its fishings and the two-ninths of Inverbervie called 'Celiflat' (Sillyflatt) with white and salmon fishings in the Bervie water, in fresh water and salt, from the manor of Allardyce to the sea with the right to have cruives. They were also granted white and salmon fishings in the sea from the watermouth of Bervie to the burnmouth of 'Halgrene'. In 1622 a later William Rait, son of the above David Rait, was granted a charter of the same fishings along with 'Celliflat' and the mill and mill land of Inverbervie, with the right to have cruives in the *aquaducta* (mill lade) of Inverbervie, together with Johnshaven, its haven and fishings, and other property. In 1649 William Rait, son of the above, was confirmed by the Crown in possession of Johnshaven, Gourdon and the Bervie fishings as described in 1622.

In 1724 a brief mention only states: 'Bervy; here is salmon fishing'. By 1793 part of the salmon fishings belonged to Viscount Arbuthnott and part to Barclay of Ury, who owned nearby Allardice. They were worked by the salmon fishers of Inverbervie and were worth £120 in rent. Colin Gibson lists 19 picturesquely named salmon pools in the Bervie water from its mouth to the Peattie Burn below Allardice Castle. Latterly only used by anglers, these were originally sweep-net fishings belonging to the burgh, although most of the names don't appear to be much older than 1800. In the Tidal Basin was Donald's Hole, between the footbridge and road bridge the Rousie, Lintie Shotts and Jubilee Pot. Between the bridges and the Peattie Burn opposite Allardice Castle were the Upper Bridge Pot, the Bridie, the Little Dam, the Rockie, Water Pipe Pool, the Lade Pool, Clay Brae Pool, Guthrie's Dam, Roughside Pot, Little Pot, Long Pool, the Saughs, Castle Pot, Upper Castle Pot and Gean Tree Pot.

Stake-nets were probably introduced soon after 1800 while bag-nets were also in use by 1837, when it was stated that there were stake-nets near the watermouth and 'floating nets' in the bay. The whole emphasis of salmon fishing had shifted, as elsewhere, from upstream to the coast. The rent, however, had only risen to £130. The season was from 2 February to 14 September. Some of the salmon fishers may have turned to handloom weaving in winter since the textile industry became so important in the burgh in the 18th century.

Some variations of the place-name and spelling

The only variety of spelling other than Inverbervie was Inverbervy, often contracted to Bervie or Bervy. Locally it is usually referred to as Bervie.

Number of fishermen and boats

Year	Fishers	Boats	Type
c.1600–50?	5–6?	1?	under 25ft

Gourdon [1]   Inverbervie NO825707

According to James Crabb Watt in *The Mearns of Old* (1914) there was a mention of Gourdon as a farm and fishertoun in 1315 but no evidence for this statement can be found. The earliest undoubted evidence for the existence of the place as a fishertoun and port is from 20 December 1506, when King James IV granted a new charter to the merchants and burgesses of Montrose, confirming their monopoly between the Dighty Water and the Findon Burn of the export of wool, hides, leather, salmon and salt cod; this was necessary as the Crown was being defrauded of Customs duty by the 'paking and peling' of such goods at ports such as Stanhiffe, Gowrdone and others, contrary to earlier charters. On 5 March 1587/88 the Crown confirmed to Robert Arbuthnott of that Ilk the barony of Arbuthnott which included two-ninths of the lands of Inverbervie called Hallgreen with salmon fishings and with fishings of quhyte fische in the haven of Gordoun with the right to have boats and all the other privileges of a port. The same was confirmed on 16 November 1591.

On 26 June 1600 the Crown granted to Andrew Arbuthnott of that Ilk, his wife Margaret Hoppingall and their son Robert Arbuthnott the *portum, stationem et navale hospitium* (port, haven and landing place) in the sea and shore of Gourdon to safeguard ships and other vessels which used it, with petty customs, tolls, anchorage dues, sysisbollis (assize bolls, a levy on grain exports), wrack, ware, waif (flotsam, seaweed,

---

* Parts of this chapter are incomplete (ed.).

jetsam) and other proceeds of the said port, with right to have a free port with fortifications and defences to protect ships from storms, and victuall-housis (granaries) with rights to the inhabitants to buy and sell victual etc.

On 18 September 1602 however the Crown granted William Rait of Hallgreen and his heir David Rait the barony of Drumnagair with Sillyflatt, fishings in Bervie Water, the port of Gourdon in sea and shore etc. (as in 1600) and access to the common muir of Inverbervie. On 31 January 1622 the Raits of Hallgreen were given Johnshaven and various lands and the landing place of Gourdon with right to receive barks, creans etc. with petty customs, tolls etc. as granted to Arbuthnott in 1600, with bulwarkis, victual houses, the right to deal in grain and with fishings within sight and near the said haven.

So it would appear that although there is no documentary evidence as early as 1315 Gourdon was important enough as a trading port to offend the Montrose merchants' monopoly of foreign trade within the Mearns by 1506. It seems even at that early date that it may have been the port of the Royal Burgh of Inverbervie but from the later evidence it was never within the burgh boundaries but only in the hands of the Arbuthnott and Rait (and later Farquhar) proprietors of Hallgreen and Sillyflatt into the late-19th century.

The community

The apparent importance of Gourdon in the 16th and 17th centuries does not mean that it had a large population, the traders and shipowners were probably burgesses of Inverbervie in the main with white-fishers probably being the bulk of the residents. The salmon exported in 1506 would mainly have been caught in the Bervie Water and Bay and perhaps packed by coopers resident there also, although exported from Gourdon with other goods from inland and salt-dried cod produced by the white-fishers of Gourdon itself. Gourdon was listed among Mearns fishertouns in 1642 and a description of the parish in 1724 merely says: 'Village of Gourdon 1 mile south of Bervy on the sea coast'. The parish register, extent from 1698, records many residents throughout the 18th century with familiar fisher names found later and it seems there must have been a few who crewed barks or sloops in summer; but there would be few residents other than fishers, who numbered 30-odd by the 1760s with three large boats and several smaller yauls. Despite the apparent importance of grain exports this would not have generated much of a workforce apart from a few seasonal mariners. The 'Bervie' cure, which probably came from Gourdon and consisted of haddock smoked over very recent, mossy peat, was once well-known (Forfar town councillors consumed bervies at their meetings in the mid-18th century) but fell off in popularity as the making of finnans spread. In 1793 there were only 42 habitable houses and a total population of 188; a similar decline in the fishing community seems to have occurred as at Johnshaven and elsewhere, and there were said to be only four small yauls manned by 12 decrepit old men eking out a miserable existence.

Gourdon in the 19th century

By 1831 the population had risen to 238 and by the late 1830s the place was booming due to the expansion of the fishing fleet and the trade in coal, lime and grain. The rise in population had been fairly recent: it seems there were the same number of fishermen in 1813 as in 1793 but by 1837 this had leapt from 12 to 50. Ten large boats went to the herring fishing from mid-July for six to eight weeks and throughout the rest of the year the cod and ling fishing was kept up by a curer who engaged the fishermen and employed a gutter to dress and salt the cod for the London market. The same person dried cod in summer for home consumption.

By 1855 the number of fishers had more than doubled while by 1871 the population at large had also more than doubled mainly due to the continued expansion of fishing and a modicum of trade. The population rose another third to over 900 and more gradually to over 1000 by 1891. In 1881 there were 108 boats and 165 fishermen and boys; three sizes of boat were kept, all sail: herring boats, great line boats and winter boats. Herring fishing remained important throughout the 19th century. The fishing fleet grew far more rapidly than that at Johnshaven, and Gourdon was more purely a fishing and seafaring community than its similarly situated neighbour. A few flax spinners and weavers were resident in the mid-19th century, a mason and wright or two since the place was expanding, and a tailor. There were three spirit dealers in 1841 and at least one inn throughout the 19th century if not earlier. Those fishers interested enough attended Bervie Parish Church but the North-East Coast Mission set up a preaching station from 1859 and by 1868 the Gourdon Mission Hall was erected by public subscription; in 1887 Gourdon Public Hall was erected on the same basis. Revival meetings were conducted by James McKendrick, a noted Brethren preacher. In 1872 the Victoria Lodge of the

30 *The Gourdon Debating Society*

Independent Order of Good Templars was established, and in 1889 the Court of Hallgreen Ancient Order of Foresters. A Post Office was set up around 1860 and in 1865 the Montrose–Bervie Railway opened. There may have been a school of some sort in earlier times but in 1847 no less than three teachers were resident. In 1868 a day-school opened in the Mission Hall and two years after the 1873 Education Act the school board built a new school and schoolhouse. Gourdon otherwise had fewer shops and services than its more cosmopolitan neighbour Johnshaven, since Bervie was nearby. A visitor to Johnshaven from Gourdon in the 19th century is said to have been amazed at the range of shops there and to have remarked, "We hae only ae merchant in Gurdon and he's a wifie!".

In the 1980s Gourdon had 280 houses and just over 600 inhabitants.

© *The Estate of Colin Gibson*

31 *Gourdon harbour*

The harbour

Gourdon must have originated as a port and fishertoun because it had a natural haven among the rocks, which small medieval trading vessels of 20 tons could reach, and a beach on which they could be drawn up. It is uncertain if there were any artificial harbour works by 1600 but the wording of the Latin charter to the Arbuthnotts might be construed as suggesting this, particularly since the anchorage dues and tolls of goods may have been levied towards the upkeep of such works; certainly, if not already built, harbour defences were intended. The 1602 charter to the Raits granted rights to build defences from the sea and the new charter to William Rait in 1622 mentions bulwarks, as does a later charter of 1649. So it would seem that the earliest breakwaters or piers were probably constructed between 1600 and 1622, presumably in the area of the 'Old Harbour'. There is no indication of any further development and in 1793 it was said that there was a harbour but that it was neither safe nor commodious, being difficult of entry, and much exposed to the violence of south-east winds. In 1819 however a new harbour was built to the design of Thomas Telford. In 1842 the laird, James Farquhar of Hallgreen, extended and rebuilt the harbour to encourage white- and herring fishing and in 1859 built the New or 'Guttie' Harbour. It was a hundred years before any further harbour improvements were made, when Kincardineshire County Council erected a new breakwater. A report of 1983 records the depth of water at mean high water at four-and-a-half metres with a tidal range of four metres, and the main Old Harbour as half a hectare. In rough weather when all the boats are in harbour a gate protects the inner harbour from the sea, breaking up the force of the waves.

The last of the long-line fishermen[*]

Today Gourdon is famous for its line-caught haddock and codling, the former supplying mainly a local market of fish and chip shops and delivery vans, the latter going to the English market. Unlike fish caught by trawl and seine net the catch is undamaged and must be lively to take the mussel bait, and so commands a premium. Yet the line fishing is in decline. The reasons given for this by Alex Welsh senior, ex-fisherman and retired harbourmaster, are education and the motor car: in other words other opportunities, and the ability to live in Gourdon and work elsewhere. The reasons are however diffuse. Line fishing is not an occupation but a way of life. The lines have 1200 hooks, each of which has to be baited with two mussels. The mussels are supplied commercially from Montrose Basin, delivered by lorry. The mussels have to be sheiled first and the process of sheiling and putting 2400 mussels on hooks could take one woman nine hours; usually several members of the family help sheil, and although one woman usually baits the line unaided (in about five hours), sometimes two sit side by side baiting alternate hooks. Since the boats go to sea before 5am the women also get up at the back of 4am and start sheiling and baiting for the next day's fishing. This task is completed and the boats have returned usually by mid-morning.

This is a way of life going back centuries although it has eased considerably in recent times. Early last century, with large families to support, toddlers of three learned to help with the mussels and pick limpets for bait. Before fish curers were established in Gourdon about 170 years ago, the fisherwomen would have had to gut and salt dry most of the fish themselves. Until the 1880s, when steam trawlers were first introduced at Aberdeen, white fish were hardly ever caught at all off Scottish coasts except by line.

---

[*] Written mostly in the 1980s. Long-line fishing is no longer practised at Gourdon (ed.).

Between the wars Gourdon, in contrast to most other fishertouns of its size on the Angus and Mearns coast, saw a remarkable resurgence of line fishing. They were even leaving the local jute mill to join the boats and several cases of men leaving the plough and marrying into fisher families to become fishermen occurred. Contrary to the usual belief that fisher lassies had to be born and bred to the tasks of sheiling mussels and baiting lines I am told that several girls married Gourdon lads 'even from Glasgow!' and learned to rise before dawn summer and winter to sheil and bait lines. At one time when most of the women were busy at these tasks in the kitchen in winter and at the door of the house in summer young children were a problem to keep an eye on. Nowadays with so few women involved in baiting there are always others to look after the youngsters and families are much smaller. Even so a young man tells me his mum used to stick him in a basket to keep him from wandering. Between the wars these activities moved from the house to sheds and outhouses and electricity came in 1937 to improve life.

In the 1980s the Gourdon fleet comprised two seine netters (25 to 54 feet) and two trawlers (50 feet), which sometimes landed at Montrose, as well as five or six 36-foot liners. The liners fish about three miles out. The twice-daily fish sale, at 11.30am and 3.30pm, is conducted by the Fishermen's Association. Shellfish and crabs are also sold, and in 1992 there were 12 boats fishing with creels in spring and summer.

Fisher names

The parish registers (extant from 1698) record 14 surnames of which the commonest are Criggie, Gowan and Blewis/Blews, the others being Dickie, Hampton, Falt, Muffart, Allan, Watt, Milne, Ritchie, Freeman, Jamie and Gove. By 1841 out of 45 fishers Ritchie and Criggie were predominant, followed by Gowans, Walker, Freeman and Stuart/Stewart. In 1861 out of 65 fishers and 19 names, Ritchie and Criggie were still the most numerous and by 1891, out of 113 fishers with 35 names, no less than 27 were called Ritchie; also frequent are Smith (8), Criggie (7) and Moncur (from Dunnottar) and Mowat (6 each), with several instances each of Gowans, Gove, Lownie and Coull (a Ferryden name). Other names indicate probable settlement from Aberdeen or the northern Mearns (Guyon) and Benholm parish (Middleton). The Welshes came in the 1920s.

Some variations of the place-name and spelling

Gowrdone	1506
Gordoun	1587/88
Gourdoun	1600
Gourden	1600, 1822
Gurdon	1641x50, 1774, 1793, 1822
Gourdon	1642, 1703, 1724, 1747x55, 1793, 1813, 1837 to date
Locally pronounced Gurden	

Number of fishermen and boats

Year	Fishers	Boats	Type
1760	c.30	3-plus	3 boats, several yauls
1793	c.12 old men	4	yauls
1837	c.50	17	10 large herring, 7 medium
1855	118	47	22 over 30ft, 20 standard, 5 yauls
1881	165	108	all sizes
1891	113	?	all sizes
1928	146	39	22 motor (30ft+), 11 small motor, 6 sail
1938	107	32	17 motor (30ft+), 12 small motor, 3 sail
1948	99	33	14 motor (30ft+), 19 small motor
1951	?	22	seine netters and liners
1980s	?	9	2 seine netters, 2 trawlers, 5 liners

Johnshaven   Benholm NO795670

If there was a fishing community established here before 1506 it was not important enough, unlike Gourdon and Stonehaven, to be specifically mentioned in a new Montrose burgh charter issued in that year, which forbade country markets and the packing and export of fish from coastal places in the Mearns within its trading monopoly, which extended to the Findon Burn. The earliest record of the existence of Johnshaven is from 19 December 1611 when the Crown confirmed the sale by Robert Falconer of Balandro to William Rait of Hallgreen and his son David Rait of the lands of Balandro and Whitfield and the lands and toun of Johnishevin with its haven and white-fishings belonging, together with Bank of Johnshaven. In 1622 this was confirmed to the Raits along with Gourdon and Sillyflatt and other lands. In 1642 Johnshaven was listed as one of the 'little shores for fisher boats' in the Mearns. In 1649 the same lands and properties were confirmed in the possession of William Rait, son of William Rait. Before 1700 however Johnshaven belonged to the Scotts of Brotherton in whose hands it continued until recent times.

According to one local tradition, Johnshaven was colonised by fisherfolk from Peterhead, brought in by the laird in the late 1500s, but there is no evidence for this and the surnames recorded among the fishers do not support the tradition. The existence of a natural haven on the low rocky shore could have attracted settlement from a very early period. It is notable that the lands of Johnshaven are mentioned in 1611 and later. Several other fishertouns have the same name as neighbouring farms and there is some evidence to suggest that the fishers were once part-agricultural tenants although by the 16th and 17th centuries they had few obligations on the land though they may have held crofts. Most seem to have been full-time fishermen by that time, by the 18th and 19th centuries few seem to have cultivated as much as a garden. From the early-18th century there is ample evidence not only for a flourishing fishing community but for merchants, weavers

Photographs courtesy of Tom Valentine

32 *Johnshaven – a fishing community at work*

93

33 *Mending herring nets by Johnshaven harbour, c.1910*

34 *Repairing cod nets at Johnshaven, c.1944*

Photographs courtesy of Tom Valentine

and other textile workers. Although described in 1744, 1875 and on other occasions as a fishing village it was always much more than that, unlike Ferryden for instance where fishing was the only activity.

The fishing community, its rise and fall

From 1684, when the parish registers begin, there is ample evidence for a flourishing fishing community from the frequency with which the familiar fisher surnames of later times occur. In the early-18th century Johnshaven had one of the largest fishing communities on the east coast, with 26 boats of two sizes and a minimum of 130 active fishermen and boys in 1722. The larger boats with a crew of ten were used in summer, the smaller, with a crew of eight, in winter, there being 13 of each type. Robertson however, writing in 1813, states that there were once 234 fishermen, which is just possible if the smaller boats were also used for inshore fishing in the summer, but this huge figure may well be an error; the Statistical Account for Benholm parish of 1793, referring to this earlier time, certainly implies no more than 130. Even so, this was still a phenomenal number of boats and men when most fishing places had two to six boats and a maximum of 30 to 35 fishermen and boys. It may have been in the early-18th century when the flourishing state of fishing inspired the verse:

> Quo' the haddie tae the fluke,
> "Fat gars yer mouie crook?"
> "Ma mouie's no been aven
> Sin' I cam by Johnshaven."

Two boats were lost at sea with their crews in 1743. The drastic decline of this impressive fishing fleet however was due to the activity of naval press gangs from the time of the Seven Years War (1755–63). In 1756 they impressed the best men from three of the boats at sea. Soon afterwards the government demanded every fifth seafaring man for the Navy. The fishermen could serve themselves or pay a willing substitute. By the end of that war in 1763 the fishers could only fit out and man eight large and eight small boats. The press gangs were active again from 1768 and demanded a new levy or payment of £10 to £12 per man. This caused many of the fittest young men to abandon fishing and to bind themselves to coal boats in order to escape naval service. The result was that the surviving boats were poorly manned and only went to sea in good weather. Because of poverty boats were not replaced as they fell to pieces and by 1776 there were only five left. The American War of 1775–83 created a new demand for seamen and press gang tenders pursued men at sea and on land. Oral traditions have preserved a memory of the time when the old folk patrolled the shore to warn of the approach of the press gangs while the young men hid.

Some men raised, with some difficulty, the £15 for a protection certificate but despite this one skipper was seized at sea with his certificate in his pocket and died aboard HMS

Salisbury on the way to the West Indies. So by 1793 the fishing community was at a very low ebb with only one large boat manned while four or five inshore yauls were used by old men and boys 'scarce fit to man an oar'. The French Wars of 1794–1815 must have made new demands but few can have been recruited from Johnshaven. The compiler of the 1793 Statistical Account of Benholm gives the most vivid and damning account of the iniquitous system of impressment for the Navy. Johnshaven, having been such a large seafaring community, must have been a prime target; there is some evidence that other such communities were reduced but not so drastically.

Another result of men being pressed for the Navy was that some of the more fortunate returned with wages saved and a share of prize money and bought small trading vessels of 50 to 150 tons burden, but since the haven was unusable by these in winter, 15 skippers with their families had moved to Montrose by 1793. As many remained in Johnshaven but had to berth their vessels at Montrose for about half the year. At Montrose and Ferryden some crews of coasting sloops took up haddock fishing in winter, the same may have been true at Johnshaven.

The 1837 Statistical Account gives no numbers but the 1841 census accounts for 39 fishermen and boys. Johnshaven was slower to recover and grow after 1815 than comparable places. Gourdon had leapt from four boats and 12 fishers in 1813 to 17 boats and 50 fishers by 1837 and in the period 1855–81 it had half again as many boats and men as Johnshaven; a better harbour may have been an important factor. The fishing fleet did grow, however, like others in the period, due to involvement in herring fishing as well as a growing market for white fish. By 1855 there were 27 boats manned by 68 men and boys: 14 over 30 feet and used for great line fishing as well as herring, eight haddock boats around 23 feet and five yauls of 17 feet. A total of 147 persons were employed in all, with curers, coopers, gutters, packers and vendors. By 1881 the number of boats peaked at 59 and the number of fishermen and boys at 120. The proportion of large, medium and small boats may have been similar to that of 1855.

In 1891 there were 54 boats, a slight decline. Johnshaven, with a reasonable harbour by 1884, could accommodate the larger herring boats. Small havens declined rapidly from the mid-1880s when falling returns and the need for larger herring boats squeezed them out. Most of the 14 herring boats which landed fish in Johnshaven in 1890 may have belonged to the port. By 1915 the total number of boats had fallen to 16, manned by 50 men and boys. Five were herring boats and three worked great lines. By the 1920s herring fishing had been abandoned but the introduction of motor boats and the seine-net stabilised the decline and in 1928 there were 23 boats and 48 fishers. Half of the boats were sma' line boats, the others great line boats also used for seining in winter. By the 1930s most of the boats were motor vessels, only one or two wee inshore yauls still had a sail only. From the 1930s to the 1950s about half the fishermen were seasonal or part-timers. The number of boats and men fell to 13 and 44 by 1935. The war must have seen some reduction but in 1948 there were 15 boats and 43 men, declining to 13 boats in 1953. By the 1960s however there were only six or seven small boats and some Johnshaven men fished out of Gourdon.

Boats

Johnshaven was very unusual in the early-18th century not only for the large number of boats and fishermen but for the size of the boats in use. Half were of eight to ten tons burden with a crew of ten, used only in summer for deep-sea great line fishing and laid up in winter. The others were of five or six tons burden with a crew of eight, used in inshore sma' line fishing. According to local traditions the larger boats were 30 to 35 feet and were also used at Milton of Mathers. The Johnshaven boats could well have been of that size but the evidence from the mid-18th century and earlier from Milton is for six-man boats, possibly seven in the 16th century. The usual size of boat used on the Angus and Mearns coast in the 18th century was 23 feet and under six tons burden; these had a crew of five or six and were used for all types of fishing, although some places had smaller yauls of 17 feet and two or three tons burden manned by a crew of four or less for inshore fishing. The boats at Johnshaven in the 18th century were probably built there since several 'carpenters', i.e. shipcarpenters or boatbuilders, are recorded from 1720. The laird loaned 100 merks Scots (about £5 12s Stg.) to three of the crew known as skippers who were also responsible for paying the £2 10s annual rent. In recompense the skippers, in addition to their own share of the catch, got every fifth fish to enable them to pay the laird. This system may have come to an end by the late-18th century.

By the 17th century Scottish fishing boats usually had two masts rigged with lugsails (in medieval times all ships and boats had a single mast and square sail). A carving on a lost gravestone from Bervie cemetery, which commemorated a Gourdon skipper who died in 1811, showed a large boat with a mainmast and lugsail in the centre with a smaller mast and lugsail forward, while there was a small accompanying boat. There were only four small yauls at Gourdon in the period 1793–1813, so the carving must represent a larger type of boat used somewhat earlier and it seems may have been similar to the large boats used at Johnshaven in the 18th century. By around 1800 the large boats had all gone and only from the 1840s did the fishing community and fleet begin to recover.

Trading vessels

There is some evidence to suggest that trading vessels called, or that at least one was based here, from 1730. These would have been clinker-built barks of only 20 tons burden with a single mast and fore-and-aft (gaff) sail and a single jibsail on a bowsprit. There were 12 trading sloops of just under 40 tons burden belonging to Johnshaven around 1790. Sloops were single-masted with a gaff mainsail and topsail and several triangular jibsails. They were manned by the skipper, two men and a boy, used mainly in coasting but capable of crossing the sea to Norway. The trade of Johnshaven is unlikely to have needed so many vessels and they had to be kept at Montrose in winter and probably carried goods for other ports. The main seaborne trade of Johnshaven was the bringing in of coal from Sunderland and the Forth and occasional cargoes of lime for agricultural use probably from the 1770s. Sometime shortly before 1793 two merchants of Johnshaven began a trade in malted barley, shipping 3000 to 4000 bolls annually to the Forth and Norway. Previously Montrose merchants had bought up all the barley for miles around.

By 1837 however there were only three sloops of 50 tons burden belonging to Johnshaven, carrying coal in and an occasional cargo of grain out. One sloop came annually with a cargo of 'Scotch' coal for industrial use. In 1875 it was said some coasting vessels used the harbour and in 1891 a shipmaster and at least one seaman were resident, so possibly there was one vessel belonging to the place. Others may have called up to around the 1914–18 war or later.

The harbour

The natural haven, a break in the low rocky shore backed by a sandy beach, was adequate for early fishing boats. A small 'pier' or wharf was built shortly before 1793 by which trading vessels could load or unload at any state of the tide in favourable weather. But it was said it could never become a place of safety until a 'bulwark' (breakwater) was raised to break the force of the sea. The sloops could not enter it safely in winter and had to be kept at Montrose. An architect had surveyed the haven in 1754 and estimated the cost of an adequate harbour at under £900. It was said in 1793: 'Nature has indeed laid the foundation, and likewise furnished the materials for building a proper harbour'. On the east was a ledge of freestone rock about 30 yards broad, exposed at all states of the tide and seldom overflowed except in severe storms. On the west, flat rocks ran out from the beach south-south-west into the open sea, close by there were six to eight fathoms of water. The seaward end was covered at half tide when small trading vessels could enter but they could not reach the wharf until high tide. The depth of water at ordinary high tides was ten to 12 feet but it was said it could easily be deepened as the bottom was soft marly rock. In 1793 it was said the expense of a safe harbour could be justified if it served the southern part of the county and not the Johnshaven area alone, and that it could remove obstacles to the growth of manufacturing.

It was Gourdon however that was first to have its harbour improved, in 1819, although it had a bulwark of some sort by the 16th century when grain was exported. In 1837 it was only said that Johnshaven's harbour was 'very small' and that if it were improved trade might increase. It was not until 1870 that the east or main harbour was built, enclosing the area naturally protected by rocks. It must have been for the benefit of fishing boats, presumably by the laird although possibly with some assistance from the

Fishery Board. As the fishing fleet grew to a peak of 59 boats with about 30 large boats of 40 feet or more, the dock or west harbour was built by the laird, Scott of Brotherton, at a cost of £4000 in 1884. The entrance remained somewhat narrow and somewhat dangerous during onshore winds.

The community at large before 1800

Johnshaven may have existed as a farming and fishing community long before it happened to be recorded in 1611. The fishing folk would seem to have been the major element in the 17th century and into the mid-18th. In 1753, fishermen and their families constituted a third of the parish population of 1351, hence about 450 souls out of Johnshaven's population of 753 at that time, and probably about 90 families. By 1793 fisherfolk had declined to a sixth of the parish population, and were probably much poorer with possibly only about 30 active fishermen out of around 250 fisherfolk, so a higher proportion of dependents, especially old folk. Many other sorts of people lived in Johnshaven by the 18th century. Connected with the sea and fishing, several 'carpenters' are recorded, one called Mowat in 1720, William Dickie in 1730, James Gibbon in 1740, and three were resident in 1793. A family of Dickies descended from a Johnshaven skipper are mentioned in Montrose from 1727. From the 1770s they were self-employed boat and shipbuilders, recorded there and in Arbroath into the 1840s; one was recorded as a member of St John's Lodge of Freemasons, Johnshaven in 1811. Coopers are recorded from 1740 and may have been packing cod for Montrose merchants although there were brewers later. A 'seaman' is recorded in 1730, perhaps suggesting there was a trading bark in the early part of the century, sailors from the 1770s. Several 'skippers' recorded from 1720 have fisher names and so were fishing skippers. A Customs officer in 1741 also suggests that some seaborne trade took place from the early part of the century, even though no vessel was actually based at Johnshaven.

Weavers are recorded in Johnshaven from 1720 and persons employed in the domestic textile industry were probably the biggest section of the community next to the fisherfolk and may have outnumbered them by the 1770s. Montrose, Dundee and Aberdeen 'manufacturers', as linen merchants were called, gave out dressed flax for spinning, which was done by the women of Johnshaven, and then delivered it to handloom weavers who then sold the finished web back to the manufacturer. Flaxdressers only happen to be recorded from 1770 but show that the first stage in processing was taking place in Johnshaven. By the end of the century some local manufacturers appeared, such as John and George Baxter in the 1790s. Other trades serving the community at large from the 1720s include shoemakers, stonemasons and blacksmiths but wrights (or house carpenters) are only recorded from the 1770s. There must have been a tailor or two but only one recorded in the early-18th century. John Bleber, brewer, is recorded in 1754, and in 1800 William Allan. The remains of a circular kiln in Castle Street may date from the late-18th century: the house opposite was reputedly a grain store and could have been connected either with an early brewery or the trade in malted barley started by two local merchants before 1793 – or with both as they may also have been brewers. R. Mitchell, vintner, in 1776 was an innkeeper or spirit seller. Two merchants, David Pirie and George Milne, are recorded in 1730, John Crombie from 1736–38, and William Lyall before 1768 by which time he had removed to Ferryden as an innkeeper. Altogether Johnshaven was a flourishing community attracting settlement, with several streets by the 1770s and a variety of occupations and services despite the near destruction of the fishing community.

Fisher names

Unlike some villages a wide variety of fisher surnames are recorded from 1684, when the Benholm parish register begins. Only in the later-19th century do some names predominate.

Craig, Criggie or Craigie, Mearns, Blews or Blues, Largie, Robertson, and Carmuck or Kermack all occur before 1700 and throughout the 18th century. Watt, Law, Ritchie, Trail, Adam, Cruickshank, Kemlo and Alexander all occur throughout the period 1700–1840. McBey/McBay is only recorded from about 1830 after they had migrated from Tangleha' and Milton. The 1841 census records 39 fishers sharing 24 surnames so no name was predominant but there were four Ritchies, three Craigies, three Blues, three Alexanders, two McBays, two Mearns, two Weirs, two Trails, two Largies and two Murrays. The 1891 census lists 54 heads of fisher families sharing 20 surnames of which three – McBey (10), Ritchie (7) and Souter (7) – accounted for nearly half; others were Alexander, Walker, Blues and Simpson (3 each), and two each of Duncan, Gibb, Shepherd and Coull.

Some variations of the place-name and spelling

Johnishevin	1611
Johnsheugh, Jhonsheugh	1641x50, c.1645
Johnshaven	1642, 1774, 1793, 1813, 1822, 1837, 1841 to date
Johnsheavin	1649
John's Haven	1703, 1744, 1747x55
Johnnies Haven	1819

Often referred to as Johnner by the natives in modern times.

Number of fishermen and boats

Date	Fishers	Boats	Type
1722	130	26	13 large, 13 medium
1744	120	24	both types
1757	105?	21	both types
1763	80	16	8 large, 8 small
1776	25–30?	5	?
1793	15?	5 or 6	1 large, 4 or 5 yauls
1813	10	5	5 yauls

Date	Fishers	Boats	Type
1841	39	6–7?	medium and yauls?
1855	68	27	14 large, 8 standard, 5 yauls
1881	120	59	all types
1891	?	54	all types
1915	50	16	5 herring, 3 great liners (motor and sail)
1928	48	23	12 motor, 11 sailing yauls
1935	44	13	mostly motor
1948	43	15	14 motor, 1 sailing yaul
1953	35?	13	motor
1960	10–12?	6 or 7	small motor
1990	5	3	small motor (full-time)

Milton and Tangleha'   St Cyrus NO773655, NO770650

Milton and Tangleha' were situated by a small shingle bay just to the north of Milton Ness and were both mixed communities of white-fishers and others. The nearby hamlets of Seagreens and Burnmouth were also close to the shore but housed no white-fishers. Originally all were in the barony of Lauriston, long owned by the Stratons of Straton near Edinburgh. The earliest record of Milton appears to be from 21 April 1553 when George Straton of that Ilk granted his son and heir Alexander Straton and his spouse Agnes Arbuthnott the barony of Lowrenstoun, which included the lands of Mathers with the lands and toun of Myltoun of Matheris, the mill, its land and multures, excepting four acres of land and seven houses with their gardens for seven fisher inhabitants, with a boat worked by them but without any pasture. In 1585 the same Alexander Straton sold the barony of Lauriston to his heir of the same name, including its tower, lands, woods, mills, fishings and boats. In 1609 John Straton of Straton inherited the barony of Lauriston with its tower, lands etc. including the Mill of Mathers with its fishings and boats. Nothing more seems to be recorded until 1642 when Mill of Mathers was listed among the 'little shores for fisher boats' in the Mearns.

Milton before 1800

The evidence from 1553 implies at least one boat with a crew of seven, but there may have been more, as in 1585 and 1609 at least two are implied. The evidence from 1553 suggests that they were full-time fishers with little more than large kailyards to cultivate. In 1695 Miltonhaven was created a burgh of barony for a new proprietor, Falconer of Phesdo. It was to have a weekly market on Fridays and two annual fairs in May and October, each to last four days. Like many such burghs, these legal rights made little difference to the place. The parish registers of Ecclesgreig, extant from 1696, distinguish residents of Milltone from those of Seatoun up to about 1740, and it is in the latter that the familiar fisher surnames, known later, are recorded. Later only Milton or Miltonhaven is recorded, so the two settlements must have merged into one. There is a modern farmstead called Milton of Mathers on the higher ground inland from the mill but it may only date from around 1800. In earlier times Milton of Mathers probably referred to the settlement around the actual mill of Mathers on the raised beach below, close by the Lauriston Burn near where it enters the sea. Nearby, on the shingle bank overlooking the bay, were the fisher houses.

From the 1740s the occupations of the inhabitants are recorded and besides skippers and white-fishers we find salmon fishers, quarriers, weavers and agricultural labourers. There was at least one merchant or shopkeeper, Robert Scott, resident around 1775–94. The Montrose burgh records reveal some trade with, and migration to, Montrose in the later-18th century. By then Milton was the largest settlement in the parish. In 1781 there were 46 families and 170 persons. The population was still increasing in 1792 although the fisher population had declined. In the 1760s there had been three boats manned by 18 fishers so there may have been around 15 fisher families and 60 to 70 persons in all, comprising about half the population of Milton before the press gangs apparently reduced the number of active fishers to a single boat's crew by 1792. However not only haddock, whiting and flukes were caught then, but also cod, ling, halibut and turbot, which could only be caught with great lines some distance out to sea.

Milton is shown on Garden's map of Kincardineshire of 1774 as two short rows of cottages on the north-east, towards the mill, with a single row of buildings strung along the shore, extending southwards as far as the estate boundary, marked today by a field boundary. There was once a sheltered lagoon of water created by an outcrop of limestone rock but from around 1792 this was allowed to be quarried away, despite forebodings, by the greed of others, a continuation of the limeworkings begun at Seagreens in the 1760s. A wall was built in anticipation of erosion by the sea but disaster struck in 1795 when the sea, no longer broken by the reef, swept 150 yards inland, inundating the village. It was partially abandoned immediately but was not deserted until much later and in fact a declining population remained until the 1860s.

Milton and Tangleha' from 1800

A new hamlet of Tangleha' was developed after the inundation only about 100 yards to the south-east on a neighbouring estate. Tangleha' was recorded as early as 1720 as the residence of at least one family; it may originally have been a croft or a salmon station. By 1804 Tangleha' was the residence of at least two re-settled white-fisher families from Milton, recorded there into the 1820s. In 1813 there was a single boat at Milton but the boat must have been manned by fishers from both settlements. In 1841 a single boat supported two or three families and the combined population of Milton and Tangleha' was 50. Milton in 1841 had ten inhabited houses and 34 inhabitants. Only two seem to have been white-fishers, the others were four salmon fishers, stone quarriers, farm workers and aged paupers. Tangleha' had eight houses and 19 inhabitants. There was only a single white-fisher family consisting of a man aged 60, his wife and two sons aged 14 and 15, old enough to go to sea full-time. Others were a fishwife, two salmon fishers, stone quarriers, farm workers and an 85-year-old pauper, a very similar mix to Milton. So there was still a viable boat's crew of three men and two boys. In 1846 Milton was said to consist of several parallel rows of cottages with gardens and bleaching greens but by that time it was in terminal decline and no boats were recorded by the time of the 1855 boat account. The Ordnance Survey of 1864 (surveyed in 1858) shows only a few scattered houses at the north end of Milton, one in the centre and empty shells of others towards the southern end. The 1861 census reveals only four inhabited houses at Tangleha' with no white-fishers resident, while at Milton there were seven inhabited houses and only a single white-fisher aged 50 with a son aged 17, who can only have manned a small inshore yaul at most.

By 1875 Milton was referred to in the past tense and the 1881 census proves that it was by then uninhabited. There seems to be a low dyke along the shore where Milton used to be. Local folk believe that the site of the houses has been eroded away, but the site today, with the old two-storey salmon bothy at the point, seems to be very similar to the Ordnance Survey of 1864. In contrast Tangleha' in 1881 had seven inhabited houses, three occupied by white-fisher families. The single family of Charles Coull and his four sons aged 14 to 22 made up five active fishers out of eight, including one aged 73, who manned four boats. For the first time since the mid-18th century there was more than one small inshore boat and at least one was apparently a herring/great line boat belonging to the Coulls. But these incomers moved on, and after 1900 there were only

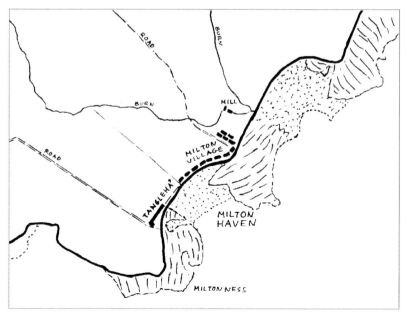

Map 7 *Tangleha' and the site of Milton village*

a couple of white-fishers operating one yaul. By the 1920s there was only a single white-fisher resident. Although no boats are recorded in the 1928 boat account, in fact the last full-time white-fisher worked on into the 1940s. Only one of the original fisher houses at Tangleha' has survived to be restored in recent times, and the shell of another. As the houses were abandoned they were allowed to decay but four new cottar houses were built to the south of the road in the 1920s or 30s. Some part-time creel fishing is still carried out from the little rocky creek at Tangleha'. An old hand-winch can be seen nearby. From Tangleha' it is a short walk northwards along the bay to the site of erstwhile Milton and the remains of the salmon bothy.

Burnmouth and Seagreens

To the north of Milton and parallel to the Burn of Finella another small hamlet called Burnmouth was built by 1800. It housed half a dozen salmon fishers and farm workers in 1841 but by 1891 only one house was inhabited and it disappeared thereafter. A bridge over the burn gives access to Seagreens, about 250 yards to the north-east of Milton. It is first recorded in 1757 when it may have been a croft or salmon station, but was probably redeveloped after 1768 when lime quarrying began on an industrial scale in the area. A pier was built and a small creek enlarged to enable the 'smallest class' of coal ships (sloops) to land, but it was said to be too exposed to easterly gales to be safe in all seasons. In 1841, just after limeworking had ceased, there were ten inhabited houses which housed three salmon fishers, farm workers and stone quarriers. Two rows of cottages and the pier are shown on the 1864 Ordnance Survey. By 1881 there were only three farm workers resident, and by the 1920s the pier had disappeared. An ice-house is built into the brae behind so it seems Seagreens was a salmon station of some importance around 1840 but abandoned later in the 19th century. By the 1990s there was only one permanent resident and one holiday home.

Lime and stone quarrying

This not only employed many men resident in the area in the 18th and 19th centuries but lime quarrying crucially affected the eventual abandonment of Milton, which might otherwise have grown in the 19th century to become at least as important as Usan or Catterline. An outcrop of limestone at Seagreens had been worked by the farmer at East Mathers for building stone and was burnt to make lime for plastering. From 1768, however, George Carnegie of Pitarrow leased East Mathers, including Seagreens, from Lord Arbuthnott. Carnegie applied much greater resources to exploit the outcrop on an industrial scale. Culm (coal dust) from the Forth was used to burn the lime. The stone was loosened with gunpowder. The best, which was like marble, was used for building and the rest was burnt to lime the fields and was carted over Garvock Hill to the Howe of the Mearns and the Grampians. The outcrop at Seagreens was 12 to 14 feet deep, sloping to 25 feet below the surface, cleared of water by a horse-powered pump. A mining expert from East Lothian was brought in and before 1792 the outcrop near Milton began to be worked by Carnegie. Prior to 1746 it had been leased by Robert Scott of Dunninald because of the limestone there; he was among the first to use lime on the fields and his successor David Scott built the huge lime-kiln at Boddin in 1771. But the workings became uneconomic and were abandoned in 1836. There were once several lime-kilns in the area. In the 1770s there was a large one between Seagreens and Milton but all sign of it had gone by 1864. The remains of another lie about 500 yards north of Seagreens and those of a smaller one behind Tangleha'. Some think the small rocky creek at Tangleha' was enlarged to allow coal sloops to land there but in 1841 it was stated that Seagreens was the only place sloops could land. Brown freestone was quarried near Lauriston Castle and was much used for building in Montrose as well as the Mearns, so some of it may have been shipped out at Seagreens.

Salmon fishing

Due to the importance of this in St Cyrus Bay and the North Esk estuary this part of the parish was ignored in the accounts but in the 18th century there were salmon fishers resident at Milton, if not Tangleha' and Seagreens. By the 1840s, due to the introduction of bag-nets, the number of stations increased, possibly to three or four, and salmon fishers were resident at Tangleha', Milton, Burnmouth and Seagreens in 1841. The remains of a large two-storey salmon bothy at Milton show that salmon fishing was very important in the mid-19th century although by 1881 there were very few salmon fishers resident in the area, so some of the stations may have been abandoned by then and the few salmon fishers recorded later at Tangleha' may have worked at nearby Rockhall.

Fisher names

Up to 1820 the commonest names were similar to those of Johnshaven, less so thereafter when there was a more transient fisher population. The commonest name found at Milton in the 18th century was Blewis (1706–40s), Blews (1740s–60s) or Blues (1770s–1820s) and it seems that there were always at least two families of that name at Milton and later at Tangleha' up to the 1820s. Goave was the name of one or two families from 1696, when the registers begin, later spelt Gove and recorded up to the 1780s. In the 18th century there were families called Law and Allan. Other names occurring more than once were Watson, Murray and Clark. The name Sutar occurs in the mid-18th century, probably a white-fisher name as it was at Johnshaven, later spelt Souter. Women called Ritchie were married to men called Blues and McBey. McBey or McBay occurs from the 1770s at Milton and up to the 1820s at Tangleha'. After 1800 a William Rae married to a Margaret McBey had several children baptised. By the time of the 1841 census only Ritchie of the old names is found. Others were named White and Anderson. At Milton in 1861 the single fisher family was called Dixon. Members of this family later moved to Johnshaven, where their Dickson descendants became well-known fish merchants. A Donaldson was resident in 1881 and a family called Coull from Ferryden moved into Tangleha' before 1881 but were gone by 1900. After 1900 the last few resident fishers were called Moir, Mowat, Walker, Pert and Beattie, the very last Freeman. Most were from Johnshaven or places to the north.

Some variations of the place-name and spelling

Myltoun of Matheris	1553
Mill of Mathers	1609, 1642, 1744
Milton(haven)	1695, 1744–1820
Milltone	1696
Seatoun (of Mathers)	1696–1744
Milton	1755, 1792, 1813, 1841, 1846, 1881
Milton of Mathers	1765, 1774, 1792, 1875
Milltownhaven	1777
Milton Village	1841, 1851, 1861

Number of fishermen and boats

Year	Fishers	Boats	Type
1553	7?	1?	boat under 25ft?
1585	12–14?	2?	boats under 25ft?
1609	12–14?	2?	boats under 25ft?
1760s	18	3	boats under 25ft?
1792	6?	1	boat under 25ft?
1813	4	1	yaul?
1841	5	1	boat under 25ft?
1855	–	–	
1861	2	1	yaul
1881	8	4	1 large, 1 standard, 2 yauls?
1905	2	1	yaul
1914	3	1	yaul
1921	1	1	yaul
1928	–	–	
1940	1	1	yaul

St Cyrus Bay and the North Esk salmon fishings

All these stations (except the Cruivestead), whether in the estuary or on the coast, were net and coble fishings until stake-nets were introduced by the 1820s and bag-nets by around 1840.[1]

© The Estate of Colin Gibson

35 *Stake-net on St Cyrus beach*

Rockhall   St Cyrus NO765649

This is situated at the north end of St Cyrus Bay. It was only founded as a bag-net station around 1840 and has consistently been one of the most productive fishings in the bay. An ice-house dated 1842 is perched above a low rocky cliff. Behind is the salmon gaffer's house and a disused bothy. A ramp across the cliff-face gives access to the shore.

Woodston   St Cyrus NO752643

This fishing is recorded from the 16th century but is undoubtedly much older. For most of its history it was a coastal fishing but from the later-18th century to around 1860 the North Esk entered the sea here and made it a more valuable estuary fishing. It has long been a stake-net fishing like most of the others in the bay. An ice-house and store are on the high ground above although the bothy is on the beach below. Access to the beach is by a path across the cliff face. Donkeys and then a pony were used for haulage until the 1950s, since when a tractor has been used.

---

1 North Esk coastal netting was suspended by the Esk District Salmon Fishery Board in 2008 in order to preserve fish stocks. A net and coble fishery is still (2010) carried out in the lower reaches of the North Esk at Kinnaber (ed).

Kirkside

This was a river fishing in the middle ages, when the North Esk entered the sea opposite the old kirkyard of Ecclesgreig or St Cyrus on the beach, which gave rise to the name Kirkside. The estate long belonged to the Straton family, members of which leased adjacent Warburton with its fishings in the 17th century. Later, when the rivermouth was at Kinnaber, Kirkside was a coastal fishing until just after 1749 when the river had changed its course to enter the sea to the north making it a more valuable estuary fishing again. The fishing had paid £30 annual rent in 1714 but rose in value to £50 in mid-century, to £600 by around 1780 and £800 by 1792. The increasing price of salmon due to new cures and a switch to the London market were elements in the rise in value, as well as the change to an estuary fishing which meant that more fish were caught. But by 1860 the river entered the sea near the centre of Kirkside's stretch and it is uncertain how it was fished, by sweep-net or stake-net. Since the winter of 1879, when the present channel broke through in a storm, the rivermouth has been near the southern limit of Kirkside so the fishings became totally coastal and exploited by stake-nets. The old channel, known as the Slunks, at times has flooded with every high tide so a wooden footbridge gives access from the bothy and store to the stake-nets on the seashore. At other times the channel has been entirely dry as the wind changes the low sand dunes from time to time.

The change of channel dispute

The course of the North Esk estuary has changed drastically several times in recorded history and geologists can distinguish 15 old river channels among the sands of St Cyrus Bay. The estuary winds its way to the sea on a raised beach below cliffs. The tidal limit is near the western extent of the lands of Kinnaber, which straddle the estuary, the name Kinnaber coming from Gaelic *ceann* + Pictish *aber*, head of the rivermouth. Thanks to the Montrose burgh records and the survival of the Commieston papers a great deal is recorded concerning the ownership and exploitation of the North Esk fishings as well as squabbles over the ownership of these prized assets, which arose largely from the changing course of the river. In late-medieval times the rivermouth swung northwards and entered the sea next to the old kirkyard, near the south-eastern boundary of the lands of Kirkside. By early modern times a change had occurred: Gordon's survey of the 1640s, Edward's map of Angus of 1678, Adair's survey of 1693, Herman Moll's map of Angus of 1725 and General Roy's survey, begun no earlier than 1747, all show the river flowing almost directly out to sea and making only a slight curve northwards. This is the line since followed by the Angus-Mearns boundary. Leases of Warburton's fishings in 1620 and 1645 made allowance for fishing 'within a bowshot' of this channel, so the change was still in people's minds and may have taken place within living memory or at most a few generations earlier. A new and drastic channel change in the mid-18th century meant that the river entered the sea even farther north than in the middle ages. The exact date of this change is a little uncertain but it appears to have been around 1747x49. By 1787 the channel extended northwards into Woodston's property and by 1790 the mouth was opposite the manse at St Cyrus village. A long sandbar had developed by then, shown on Ainslie's map of 1794, directing the rivermouth almost one-and-a-half miles northwards from Kinnaber. The result of this was that Kirkside and Woodston's fishings changed from coastal to include more valuable estuary fishings; moreover the former especially was in a prime position to take salmon as they entered the estuary from the sea. The spit gradually wore away; by 1860 the rivermouth was half-way down Kirkside's fishing and in a storm in 1879 it broke through the spit at Kirkside's southern boundary with Warburton, where it has remained since.

The mid-18th-century channel change was the cause of a dispute which arose in January 1749 between Scott of Commieston and Straton of Kirkside over the boundaries between their fishings. Later in the same year Fullarton of Kinnaber also began a dispute with Straton. Both had asked Montrose Town Council, as feudal superiors, to clarify the boundaries but the burgh charters were far too vague, so the matter was referred to the Court of Session. By July 1755 the Court of Session decided that Straton of Kirkside had the right to fish the new channel and that Scott and Fullerton had no rights north of a straight line drawn from the gate of Kirkside House and the Wynd Path to the sea. Scott and Fullerton appealed to the House of Lords, who in 1756 decided that neither had rights 'where the river could not be distinguished from the sea', implying that there it belonged to the Crown. Scott and Fullerton on the one hand, and Straton on the other, proceeded to make applications to the Crown for the fishing in the new channel. In 1758 Montrose Town Council was also seeking clarification from the Lords; the matter was submitted to the Treasury who referred it to the Exchequer in Edinburgh.

The Council were warned not to grant rights to anyone until a legal case had been put forward, and they were to confer with Scott and Fullerton's agent. By August 1759 a contract had been drawn up between the parties in which they agreed to cooperate to get recognition of the town's superiority over the new channel. If this were achieved, Scott and Fullerton could name the lessee who would be granted a tack of the fishings for five years on payment of £5 Sterling at Lammas. But if Scott and Fullerton were to pay £200 Sterling, and any legal expenses incurred, to the town, then the £5 would be payable to them and they would be granted all rights over the fishing. On 5 September 1759 a tack of the fishings was indeed issued by the Council, to James Dickson junior, merchant of Montrose, but soon afterwards he requested to give it up as his fishermen had been impeded in their fishing and he could no longer pay the rent. Presumably Straton was responsible for this. Nothing more is recorded but it seems the Town Council had been assuming rights it was never granted, and Straton's rights to the channel within the bounds of his land, as declared in 1755, must eventually have been recognised.

Scott of Commieston and Fullerton of Kinnaber are found in close co-operation later. In 1787 William Adam of Woodston and Joseph Straton of Kirkside made a complaint to Kinnaber and Commieston's legal agent concerning the illegality of a stone 'bulwark' built 18 years previously, which diverted the lower reaches of the North Esk. Some details of the building are recorded. David Jamie, mason, who had rebuilt Montrose's pier, received payment in 1775–76 for 'fencing the water off Commestouns fishous'. Fourteen men had been employed in the construction and another nine in carting. An 'injen', presumably a crane of some sort, was brought from Montrose to assist in the work, which took 37 days in all. There seems to be some sort of revetment on the north bank of the river near the site of Commieston's salmon boiling house, but exactly what form this stonework took is uncertain. The word bulwark was often used of sea walls and breakwaters, so some sort of dam may be implied. Unfortunately the outcome of Kirkside and Woodston's case seems unrecorded but no doubt the destruction of an illegal method of fishing must eventually have been ordered by the law.

The Cruivestead   St Cyrus NO710630

This was once the most valuable fishing in the area and originally belonged entirely to the burgh of Montrose. It consisted of a cruive dyke at Morphie and several coble fishings on the Mearns shore downstream to the tidal limit, or from 'northmyldam as far as the ebb and flow of the sea', where the road bridge is now. In 1455 the burgh of Montrose appointed a committee of seven to manage the burgh's salmon fishings, of which four formed a sub-committee to manage the Cruivestead. In 1460 the burgh's North Esk fishings were leased in half-nets, one individual paid £25 Scots for five half-nets, two others leased a half-net each. In February 1464 four tacksmen took a year's lease at nine merks (£6 Scots) each while two paid four-and-a-half merks (£3 Scots) each for a half-net. So a total of five nets was leased for 45 merks (£30 Scots). In 1466 the 'north water male' (rent) was only £13 so perhaps the rent was set according to the success or otherwise of the previous year's fishing, since it fluctuated so much. The lessees seem mainly to have been burgesses of Montrose who would have sub-let to, or employed, actual fishermen; hence it was possible to lease a half-net, the proceeds rather than the actual fishings being divided.

In 1381 Sir Gilbert Graham acquired the adjacent barony of Morphie, which originally included the lands of Commieston and Warburton, from a daughter of Lord Fleming. He destroyed the cruives due to some dispute with the burgh of Montrose over the fishings, for which the burgh was compensated out of the burgh ferme (a fixed duty) due to the Crown to the extent of £14 16s 8d Scots. In 1431 William Graham of Morphie junior married a daughter of Ogilvie of Inverquharity, and the marriage agreement stipulated that Graham senior should not alienate his lands and fishings of Morphie from any heirs begotten of the marriage. It seems that the Cruivestead had been feued to the

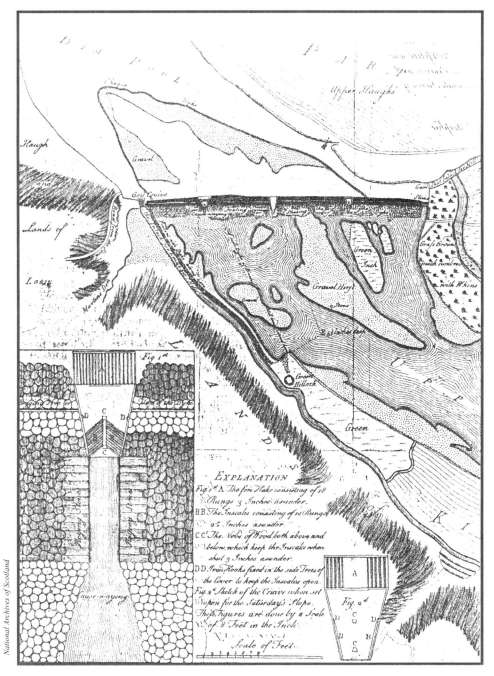

National Archives of Scotland

36 *Plan and section of the cruive at Morphie, 1768*

proprietors of Morphie by the 14th century. In the 1450s and 60s the burgh withheld
the feu for some reason and it was leased out instead. A further dispute over the North
Esk fishings must have been in progress in the period 1462–66 as commissioners for
the burgh of Montrose were appointed to appear before the King and Council at Stirling
and Linlithgow. The nature of this dispute is not recorded but was probably over feu

duty and entry fee with the proprietors of Morphie. In 1490 the burgh recognised Henry Graham, a minor, as heir to William Graham of Morphie in the 'crowis and crowstead' but refused to give sasine (feudal possession) either to him or his guardian, John Erskine Junior of Dun. In February 1491 the Crown issued a writ to allow the magistrates and community of Montrose to possess the fishing, as they had done for seven years previously, until the King's Council decided the matter, and commanded Graham and his guardian to desist from troubling the burgh. In April, however, possession of the 'croifsted' was granted to Erskine, on behalf of Graham, at the king's command. This was not the end of the dispute however. The following July, David, Earl of Crawford and Duke of Montrose, as superior of the burgh, issued a letter promising the community that he would see that a process brought against them by Graham and his guardian concerning the Cruivestead was withdrawn. In 1492 and 1493 Erskine terrorised the townsfolk, perhaps in connection with this but also over disputed possession of the mussel beds in the Back Sands. In 1502 a respite was granted to Dun and his associates for a felony against the magistrates of Montrose. The dispute went on until an agreement was signed at Edinburgh in February 1506 by the burgh's appointed commissioners and Henry Graham of Morphie, by that time of age. This stipulated that he should pay the burgh 45 merks (£30 Scots) for a year's lease of the cruives. Eventually in July 1507 the burgh issued a feu charter of the cruives to Graham, obliging him to pay 20 shillings annual feu duty. Thereafter the Cruivestead continued in possession of the Grahams of Morphie, Sir Robert Graham being recognised as heir in 1662.

From 1681 Stone of Morphie, to which the cruives and part of the Cruivestead were attached, belonged to the Scotts of Brotherton. Judicial proceedings concerning the cruives took place between them and neighbouring proprietors in 1684, 1702, 1746, 1762 and 1768. James Scott of Brotherton on the last two occasions had been ordered by the Lord Ordinary to desist from misuse of the cruive dyke. Brotherton had blocked some of the openings in the cruive dyke with boulders and brushwood, others were dry and above water. The inscales were fixed with iron to prevent them yielding to the fish so that not one salmon in ten managed upstream. He had also, contrary to an Act of 1696, fished the pool between the dyke and the barricade, or check dyke, upsteam, which fed mill lades on either side of the river. James Scott had succeeded his father Hercules Scott in January 1768 and paid Montrose Town Council £16 13s 4d (Scots) entry fee as their vassal in the cruive fishing. The following year he requested to buy the feudal superiority to the fishings from the burgh and agreed to pay the rate requested, which had been set at 30 years' feu duty, being £16 Scots annually, plus one and a half years' rent. In fact Scott had not rented the fishings out but had hired his own fishers, and he now claimed that although they yielded £130 Scots gross annually, £100 Scots had to be deducted for hiring men and for the upkeep of the dyke. He kept three men throughout the year, claiming that few winters did not see the destruction of a third of the dyke; this meant quarrying and carting stone which kept his servants and horses busy for two months. He therefore requested that the annual profit of £30 Scots be accepted as the equivalent of a year's rent. However nothing more is recorded and the agreement must have fallen through due to the destruction of the cruive dyke sometime before 1793 after litigation over its continuing misuse. Three 'pools', or coble fishings, were associated with the cruive dyke: Pondage Pool, Gatch Pool and John Alexander's Pool, all within the bounds of Stone of Morphie. In 1806 a nephew of James Scott succeeded him and requested recognition by the burgh as his heir in the North Esk salmon fishings with no mention of the cruives. The burgh retained the feudal superiority well into the 19th century.

Warburton   St Cyrus NO725623

In 1681 Warburton became part of the barony of Commieston created that year under Great Seal charter for John Scott. Commieston's fishings, attached to the lands of Warburton, consisted of three parts: one was held from the burgh of Montrose; another part was held of the Crown and had once belonged to John, Earl of Montrose; the third was the St Thomas Net, originally belonging to the Abbey of Arbroath. The part held of the burgh must originally have been part of the Cruivestead. It was feued in 16ths and multiples thereof in the 16th and 17th centuries. In 1638, for example, descendants of Andrew Beattie, a burgess of Montrose paid £6 3s Scots annual feu duty and double that as entry fee to 'a sixteenth part of a third part' of the burgh's North Esk fishings. This 'third part' recurs throughout the 18th and early-19th century when the Scotts and Fullertons were entered as heirs to it. It would seem that it was considered to be a third of the Cruivestead coble fishings. By 1735 one half belonged to Scott of Commieston, the other to Fullarton of Kinnaber for which a £4 Scots entry fee (on the succession of an heir) and £16 18s Scots (£1 8s 2d Stg.) annual feu duty had to be paid by each of them to the burgh.

The part held of the Crown seems to have been between the fishing held from the burgh and the St Thomas net. In 1440 John Ogilvie of Lintrathen was granted half the lands of Wardropestoun (Warburton) with fishings, which had belonged to Walter Ogilvie of Deskford. This passed to a son in 1483 and later to the Ogilvies of Airlie. The other half of the land and fishings of Warburton was acquired by John Wemyss in 1468 and in 1504 was sold to William Graham, Earl of Montrose. The earl also had a fishing on the south bank. In 1507 the burgh of Montrose had to answer to the King and Council on 1 June in Edinburgh in a cause raised by the earl charging them with interfering with his 'pretendit' (claimed) possession of a fishing in the North Esk by destroying the 'stuff and stainis' of a dam he had built through the said water. This may have been the illegal extension of a yair, or stone fish trap, the whole way across the river channel. The Lords of Council decided that the burgh authorities had done 'nae wrang' in destroying the dam. In 1591 James, Lord Ogilvie of Airlie sub-infeued his half of the Wardropestoun fishings to John Wishart of Pitarrow who was to render a nominal one penny annual feu duty. The Latin document refers in the vernacular to rights to 'cobillis' and 'landing places' as well as 'drawing of nettis, drying of nettis'.

The St Thomas net took its name from Thomas a Becket in whose honour the Abbey of Arbroath was founded by King William I in 1178. Among the properties granted to the abbey was 'a full net in the water of Northesk near Montrose'. This may have been leased at an early date but only one lease has survived. On 20 January 1532 it was let to David Wood of Craig and his son Andrew for 19 years from Andersmas (30 November) that year for three barrels of properly cured and packed salmon annually, to be delivered at Montrose at Michaelmas (29 September). No record seems to have survived of when the St Thomas net was sold to the proprietor of Warburton but by 1620 all of Warburton with its fishings belonged to Robert Graham of Morphie who leased it with the fishings between the bounds of Kinnaber and Kirkside to Andrew Straton of Kirkside. The rent included an annual render of grain as well as 60 barrels of properly cured salmon.

The Boynes   Montrose c.NO715617

On 26 May 1359 King David II granted temporarily to the burgh of Montrose the western part of a fishing on the south bank of the North Esk called the Boyne or Boynes which had been 'usurped' during his captivity in England (1346–57). A copy of the king's letter was made on 12 June 1445 on command of David Rukby, provost of Montrose. On 30 June Sir John Ogilvie of Lintrathen and Walter Tulloch were appointed to represent the burgh before the King's Council in Edinburgh concerning this fishing. Tulloch was a burgess and town councillor of Montrose while Ogilvie owned the fishings on the opposite bank. The fishing was upstream of, and may have been adjacent to, Kinnaber. It may have been held by the Earl of Montrose from 1504 as the papers concerning the dispute over his illegal dam in 1507 mention the 'ald fishing' as being granted by the Crown, although this could have applied to the burgh's other fishings. The burgh may have lost any claim over the fishing later since there appears to be no later mention of this fishing in the burgh records.

Kinnaber   Montrose NO723620

Kinnaber's fishing was on the south bank and in the tidal part of the river and was originally the Marynet or Net of the Virgin belonging to the Hospital of Montrose founded by King William I (1165–1214), probably around the same time as the fishing on the opposite bank, the St Thomas Net, was granted to Arbroath Abbey in or shortly after 1178. The feudal superiority of the Marynet belonged to the burgh of Montrose by 1571 but it seems to have been feued to the Fullartons of Kinnaber by 1602, so only feu duty and a fee on the entry of an heir rather than rent was payable to the burgh. The income was administered by the burgh's Hospitalmaster on behalf of the burgh poor.

In 1662 Fullerton of Kinnaber was due £16 Scots feu duty to the Hospitalmaster of Montrose, still unpaid in 1663. In 1774 however the annual feu duty was £12 Scots (£1 Stg). In 1796 Montrose Town Council refused a request by the Fullertons to buy the feudal superiority and it was feued by them into the 19th century, later feued by Joseph Johnston & Sons. The stores, bothy and ice-house are at Fisherhills.

© The Estate of Colin Gibson

37 *The railway viaduct over the North Esk at Kinnaber*

Montrose   Montrose NO7157

The shelter of one of the few navigable estuaries on the east coast and an ample supply of mussel bait in the South Esk estuary and the Back Sands or tidal basin provided ideal conditions for white-fishing here. Since the teind fish of the white-fish boats of Montrose belonged to the Hospital of Montrose, founded by the Crown sometime before 1245 and probably by King William I before 1200, it can be implied that there has indeed been a white-fishing community here from very early times. There may well have been some sea fishing before the inception of a burgh around 1130, the fishers emerging from a part-agricultural background on what was a royal estate. The establishment of a burgh with a population of several hundred by the 13th century must have created a ready market for fresh fish and exports of dried cod may have begun, but are only recorded after customs began to be levied on them from the 1420s. Exports of cod fluctuated but were around 10,000 annually in the later-15th century, dropping to 3000 around 1500 and to only 1500 around 1550. So Montrose must have had a vigorous white-fishing community in the middle ages and the decline in cod exports does not necessarily mean that the fishing community declined at a proportionate rate, other fishings or markets may have been pursued. More than a dozen small outlying fishertouns must also have contributed to the above totals, as they could legally only export fish through Montrose,

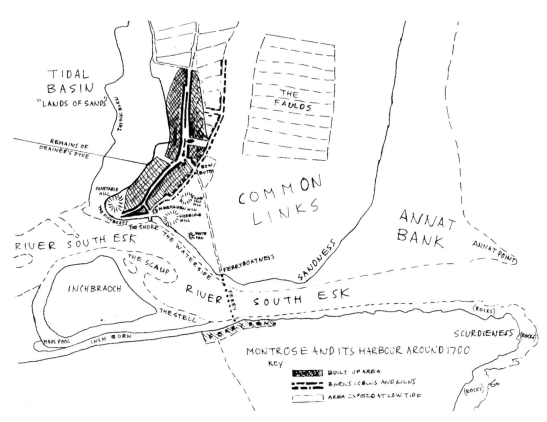

38 Davy's sketch map of Montrose and its harbour c.1700 – note 'the fishboats' opposite Inchbraoch

which had a monopoly trading precinct from the Dighty Water immediately north and east of Dundee and Broughty Ferry to the Findon Burn. Some evasion of Customs is implied when the burgh's charter was renewed in 1506, forbidding places on the Mearns coast, and specifically Gourdon and Stonehaven, from packing or exporting fish.

The fishing community before 1800

It seems likely that Montrose in the middle ages may have had one of the largest fishing communities in the district. In 1488 property in the Fishergait or Seagait was recorded in a sasine witnessed by a fisherman, Thomas Gilyeam. The same street was also referred to as the 'common vennel leading to the Fishboats'. This was where boats landed, on the site of the much later bridge; Bridge Street did not exist then. The fisher community resided mainly in the triangle formed by Seagait, Pier (or Shore) Wynd and Wharf Street amongst other seafarers and as near as possible to where their boats were beached. The names Fishergait or Seagait were used alternatively into the 19th century while Wharf Street was originally called the Laigh (Low) Fishergait. Skirling's Wynd, which once connected it to Seagait, is clearly named after a fisherman who once lived there, as the surname is recorded in the 17th century amongst the fisher community. Archaeological

116

excavation in the Castlegait, to the north-east of Seagait, has shown that in the 14th and 15th centuries cod, and molluscs such as buckies (periwinkles), cockles, mussels, limpets and dogwhelk were eaten or used as bait.

There are some indications of the importance of the fisher community to the burgh, and of its size, from the 17th century. It was said by Monipennie in 1633 that the town or its shores were 'abundant with all kynde of fishes'. Edwards in 1678 implied that large quantities of various species of white fish, mackerel and lobsters were caught 'at no great distance from the shore' while Ochterlony around 1682x85 also considered Montrose to be supplied with an abundance of all sorts of fish. The burgh authorities always regarded the prime function of the resident white-fishers as being to provide a regular, plentiful and cheap supply of fish to the inhabitants of the burgh. So they forbade them to sell fish direct from their boats, ordering them to display it for sale to all at the market cross, thereby preventing 'forestalling', or buying up for resale, by individuals to the detriment of the community as a whole. The export of surplus fish was the monopoly of merchants and any attempt by fishers to sell directly to outsiders was forbidden. Thus on 22 April 1635 the Town Council warned the 'haill fishers' against the 'shipping and making of great boats'. This could imply either that they might have landed their fish elsewhere if they had larger boats, or perhaps that they could have gone further out to sea and sold directly to foreign shipping. On 15 July 1636 the fishcurers in Montrose, in particular David Newton and the masters of eight boats he owned, agreed not to sell fish between entering the water and returning to the fish shore, not to 'pack or peill' any salt fish except for their own consumption, or to let any cadger or others come within their boats, on pain of a fine of £6 and confiscation of their fish. It is interesting that a merchant fishcurer owned several boats and presumably controlled most, or all, of the burgh's fishing effort as it is unlikely that there were many more than eight boats. There was apparently some resentment at this control as in December 1636 David Newton was murdered, allegedly at the hands of a white-fisher. If each boat had a crew of five or six, as in later times, this would imply a minimum of over 40 active fishers. By the 1670s, about the same time as specific areas were set aside for meal and flesh markets, a fish market was also set up in part of the High Street, where the fish were apparently displayed from poles. Almost eighty years later, in September 1751, the Town Council noted that 'forestallers and regraters' were buying up fish (and other commodities) before it was presented at market at the lawful time. So it was ordained that fish was only to be sold at the mercat cross and no other place and none was to be sold to cadgers until it had remained there for two hours. The fish market remained in being until 1802.

The fishing community is likely to have been fairly stable or even slightly larger by the mid-18th century, when it may have peaked although little is known of its exact size then. In the decade 1710–20 the names of 17 white-fishers happen to be recorded in a series of burgh court claims for petty debt, 30-odd in the following decade (and with a greater variety of surnames than at any other period recorded) but only about seven in the 1780s and 1790s. There was continuity of some of the surnames recorded in 1636 into the early-18th century although there were also many new ones, showing that the community was never static or inbred and it probably grew slightly until the 1760s as a response to industrial and population expansion in the burgh and district. The fishers' peculiar way of life set them apart from the rest of the burgh populace who called them 'sandsuckers' from their activity in the Back Sands collecting bait. But they could depend on the sympathy of the whole community in hard times: money was advanced to enable them to replace lines lost in storms in 1720 and in 1791; a fund was established for the widows and orphans of fishermen lost at sea in 1725; while money was also distributed among 'poor fishers' in 1761 when storms prevented them from fishing. Aged and infirm fishers might also, like others in the burgh, enjoy a small pension from the burgh's Hospital funds and the kirk session. Some may also have been members of one of the two local seamen's friendly societies which also gave pensions to sick and decrepit members.

The available evidence points to a severe decline in Montrose's fishing community in the later-18th century, undoubtedly due to the activity of press gangs soon after 1755. In 1776 five Usan fishermen, led by David Pert, petitioned the Town Council for freedom to gather bait as they intended to take up residence in the burgh and carry on fishing with a 'stout boat' manned by themselves and a boy, offering to supply the town with fish since Montrose was then 'very ill supplied with fishermen'. Two years later, having to remove from their houses due to a dispute with their landlord, they requested the Council to build houses for them to rent at the Waterside. This was agreed 'as the fishers here are mostly gone and those remaining are mostly very old and infirm'. So a site was leased cheaply to a builder to provide houses, which apparently had red pantiled roofs and are later shown on Wood's town plan of 1822 between the salt works and Ferryboatness. Curers had set up premises at the Waterside from the 1750s for salmon boiling but were also wet-pickling cod for export from early in the century and may also have traded dried fish. In 1774 there were seven fishcurers active, in 1786 six, so apparently no great decline in the fish trade itself. But in 1790 there were only 16 to 18 active fishers at Montrose, implying four or five boats or yauls, and it was said that many of them were very old, that for some years the fishing had been followed with indifferent success and that the distant banks were ignored. Pennant in 1772 and Headrick in 1813 also noted the lack of vigour in catching an apparent abundance of fish on the more distant banks. In 1783 the Customs collector reported that all the fish caught at Montrose was consumed locally, although the previous year he had reported that dried fish was frequently dispatched from the outlying creeks. So it seems that a depleted fisher community was barely supplying the burgh by then. The dearth of haddock, the mainstay of inshore fishing, around 1783–93, combined with the renewal of press gang seizures during the 1794–1815 wars, further inhibited fishing, and the community was at a pretty low ebb by the end of the century. In 1800 a despairing Town Council tried to remedy the dearth of fishers by arranging housing for some expected to come from the 'North country', but they failed to arrive.

In the late-18th century there were a couple of short-lived capitalist ventures into white-fishing. In 1771 Sir Alexander Ramsay of Balmain and several leading Montrose merchants formed a Trawl Net Company to catch flat-fish to which the Town Council subscribed five guineas as it thought that it might 'prove beneficial to the inhabitants'. The company had hired a fisherman experienced in this method but no more is recorded of this early Scottish trawling experiment. Later in the century trawl-nets were tried off Cellardyke, while at Aberdeen fishermen from north-east England were brought in to experiment with turbot nets. In March 1787 the Montrose Iceland Fishing Company fitted out the *Two Brothers* for cod fishing in Icelandic waters with 1000 bushels of Scottish salt and in December the same year exported 436 hundredweight of cod, ling and tusk-fish with a variety of local textiles to Alicante, Spain in the same vessel. This experiment was not repeated and the vessel afterwards returned to normal trading under the same skipper. In 1789 Knox states that dried cod and ling were exported to the Baltic, Hamburg, Holland and France. But if the burgh's own fishers once supplied this trade, by the end of the century cod, ling and tusk-fish were being imported from Shetland for re-export.

The fishing community and white-fishing since 1800

There were signs of revival of the community soon after the Napoleonic War. In 1798 and 1808 at least two Ferryden fishers had moved to Montrose and were granted house sites from the Council at the Waterside. In 1817 ten white-fishers 'at the Waterside' petitioned the Council for relief as they had been reduced to dire poverty by 'tempestuous seas' preventing them fishing. In 1819 there were six skippers at Montrose, and so around 30-odd fishermen. In 1841 there were no fisher families resident in the original triangle of Seagait, Shore Wynd and Wharf Street but all lived downstream of the pier at the Waterside. After the 1840s the fisher population went into a slow decline, though by 1871 some fisherfolk again resided in the Shore Wynd area. Latterly the few fishers left were all scattered around the same area and in the newer streets nearby such as Bridge Street and Hill Street. The original landing place, the Fishboats, at the end of Seagait, had been lost to the site of the bridge and a boatyard by the 1790s and it is uncertain where the boats may have landed in the early-19th century. But by the end of the century they were probably landing by the old pier, as commercial vessels by then berthed downstream. Although the great expansion of the local fisher population in the 19th century took place across the South Esk at Ferryden, the Montrose curers were to dominate the industry and much of the white-fish, as well as herring, was landed at the Montrose side of the river.

In 1802 a fish market with stone tables and running water had been created in George Street but in 1846 a new one was created off John Street. It was not successful and was bought up by Joseph Johnston, who was becoming the dominant fish buyer and curer in Montrose. By then retailers probably had their own shops dispersed through the town. Joseph Johnston's original interests were in salmon fishing but his family firm also came to control a large share of the white- and herring fishing industry in the Montrose area. The 1841 census accounts for 23 fishermen aged 30 to 60 who may have manned four boats, with another seven, including boys of 14 to 18 and old men of 70 to 80, who may have manned a couple of yauls. In 1842 it was merely noted that 'great quantities of cod and other white-fish are taken off the coast, and after being dried, sent to the English markets'. In 1849 James Thomson noted that there was no herring fishing from the port but that Montrose was famous for pickled cod, smoked haddocks and (cured) herrings with a long-established market in London. Wet-cured cod was an old-established product but the smoking of fish was recent, since there had been no commercial smoking in Angus in 1813 according to Headrick.

By 1855 the fishing community remained small and there were only two haddock boats and four yauls worked by 22 fishers at Montrose, but fish processing by contrast was very important. There were no less than 169 persons involved: five curers, 42 coopers, 51 gutters or packers and 71 others vending and making nets etc. and this was before Montrose became a herring port from 1861. But the resident fisher community declined as Ferryden's grew and in 1881 there were only seven yauls and 12 fishermen at Montrose. In 1884 Joseph Johnston & Sons invested in a steam trawler and by 1886 there were seven trawlers, all paddle steamers, belonging to the port, responsible for three-quarters of the white-fish landed at Montrose, the remainder almost entirely from Ferryden line boats. Two of the early paddle trawlers spent most of their time as tugs assisting the sailing fleet. From the 1890s there were only three trawlers, all belonging to the Johnstons, which spent most of their time fishing out of Aberdeen. Around 1890, of 14 resident fishermen, four or five, who later disappear, had English surnames. They were trawlermen and may later have moved on to Torry. A fleet of three trawlers seems to have been maintained up to about 1940, mostly working and landing at Aberdeen and elsewhere rather than Montrose. The resident fisher community continued to decline slowly; there were only six active fishers in 1915, by 1921 only two, and other than tiny yauls the various types of boats operated from Montrose were almost exclusively manned by Ferrydenners.

A Montrose Fishing Company was formed in November 1917 with an original capital of £20,000 by a number of local and outside investors, including farmers and solicitors, none of whom had any previous experience or interest in the industry. They first acquired two motor liners and three motor yachts which were converted to small trawlers. In late 1918 the company purchased three steam trawlers from the Admiralty, which were only delivered by 2 March 1919. After five months' successful fishing they took out an option on another 12 ex-Admiralty trawlers with the intention of establishing Montrose as a real trawling port. A site for a fish auction market was allocated by the Harbour Trust and it was intended to establish an ice-making plant and to acquire housing for 40 to 50 trawlermen and their families. The company made a profit up to June 1920 but then ran into trouble. In July-September large catches glutted the market and so prices were low, while a coal strike in October–November laid up half the fleet. The company had grossed over £210,300 profits but made a net loss of over £21,200, it was reported in March 1921. By then the company owned 20 steam trawlers but they were all working out of Granton and Aberdeen, where the company also owned some plant or premises, as the harbour bar at low tides at Montrose meant that large trawlers could not regularly work out of this port. The local yearbooks record that the company also operated a fleet out of Montrose around 1920–22 consisting of: one motor liner, three unspecified (probably small motor trawlers), 13 ketches and three schooners (nearly all newly built 1918–19) which seem more likely to have been great liners. Strangely none of these are mentioned in any of the newspaper reports of several crisis meetings of shareholders held in Edinburgh during March–September 1921. By 1923 the company's Montrose fleet had declined to 17 vessels. No yearbook for 1924 seems to have survived but by 1925 they only had one small motor vessel registered at Montrose and by 1926 the company was said to be in liquidation. In September 1921 it had been revealed that the company was in dire straights, not helped by a strike of Granton trawlermen. The local investors were annoyed not only in the drop in value of their £1 shares to five shillings and the request for more capital, which was refused, but also by the fact that Montrose itself had not been established as an important trawler port. The company's assets in trawlers could not be sold at anything like their original cost to realise capital as demand was low. It appears that they fished on with a declining fleet until 1926, although nothing seems to have been reported in the newspapers of their fortunes during 1922–26 or of the final liquidation.

From the mid-1920s Montrose only had three steam trawlers, two steam drifters and a couple of small motor vessels. By around 1930 however there were only three small motor boats owned by Joseph Johnston & Sons and a tiny motor yaul owned by a fisherman which were probably all converted sail boats, along with three trawlers which probably worked out of Aberdeen or Granton. The 1939–45 war seems to have seen an end to the modest fleet of three steam trawlers and small motor boats and for a time it seems Montrose had few, if any, boats at all. From the mid-1950s there was a single small motor seiner owned by Andrew Mearns of Ferryden who was also the only South Esk pilot until he retired in 1968. From the 1960s there have been several part-time creel boats as well as two small motor trawlers, the *Angus Rose II* and *Rosemary*, belonging to Ferryden men working out of Montrose. Later there was only *Angus Rose III*, a seiner/

trawler. In 1971 there were five seiners from 37 to 49 feet fishing locally inshore, by 1982 only two landing regularly. There were numbers of part-time small craft working creels, some also cod-nets, up to around 1995, thereafter the 20-odd small boats were all used only for sea-angling. One small trawler, not locally owned, worked out of Montrose. In the 1980s the Harbour Trust made a small rubble pier beside the old pier, long-abandoned by trading vessels, as an area for fishing boats to land, but Montrose's days as a real fishing port have long passed.

The mussel beds

The South Esk estuary and the shallow tidal basin behind the town, once called the Lands of Sands, more recently the Back Sands or Backies, were long a source of bait not only to the fishermen of Montrose, Ferryden and Usan but to fishers as far north as Torry. As well as extensive mussel beds, other bait such as lugworm and ragworm were found there. The burgh long assumed and maintained effective public ownership of this asset. In 1470 the Town Council charged three named skippers, from some outlying place, three shillings each for a boatload of mussels. It was long the custom to allow free access to the burgh's fishers but to charge outsiders for supplies and to deny them supplies when there was a dearth of mussels. In the period 1492–1502 John Erskine of Dun ejected the burgh's fishers from the sands west of the Tayock Burn. His son became provost in the mid-16th century and probably tolerated the local fishers gathering bait. Montrose Town Council controlled the exploitation of the mussel beds in the estuary and Back Sands. On 12 April 1704 mussels were plentiful so were to be sold to outsiders at two 'dollars' a boatful, the proceeds to go towards repairing the pier. By 19 September 1705 sale to 'foreign boats' was prohibited and townspeople were only to take bait upstream from the Fort Hill, i.e. they were to take them from the Back Sands and not from the Mussel Scaup in the estuary. Again in 1724, 1765 and 1790 the sale of mussels to outsiders was prohibited. After an initial attempt to stop Ferryden fishers taking mussels freely in 1716, by 1720 an agreement with the proprietor of Rossie seems to have allowed them the same rights as the Montrose fishers.

From 1812 however the proprietor of Dun, Miss Alice Erskine, began to claim ownership of the largest part of the Back Sands west of the Tayock Burn and north of the river. The local fishers continued to take mussels from this area but on 19 January 1819 an interdict was issued against six named skippers of Montrose, ten of Ferryden and four from Usan. On 30 March that year Miss Erskine brought a legal process against the magistrates of Montrose, two named fisherfolk and others to quit any claim over the 'Lands of Sands' and a final interdict was issued on 8 April 1820. Afterwards when the estuary outside that area could not provide enough mussels presumably the fishers had to pay for bait. In 1852 the Ferryden and Usan Mussel Society formed with 152 members, which leased and cultivated its own beds in the river and Back Sands. By 1876 the society had 350 members and by 1885 four-hundred and twenty-eight members. Presumably the handful of Montrose fishers could also be members.

Joseph Johnston & Sons also owned and maintained beds which supplied another third of the mussels needed locally. Until recently they supplied bait to the last of the Gourdon line-fishers.

Herring fishing

Montrose exported tiny amounts of cured herring in the 15th and 16th centuries and it is uncertain if it was caught locally or re-exported. A small consignment was exported in 1685 but all the circumstantial evidence points to this being a re-export from elsewhere. In June 1720 Montrose Town Council received a circular from London concerning the company of the Royal Fishery of England announcing an additional subscription of £300,000, of which £3000 had been allotted to Montrose. The Council referred this to the Convention of Royal Burghs and to any interested freemen of the burgh. In November James Scott of Logie announced he was willing to take up the burgh's share and was granted all right and interest. There is no evidence, however, that any herring fishing was organised from Montrose in connection with this. Later in the century a new company based at the port exploited fishings in the far north and west for about twenty years and exported the cured catch.

In 1750 a Montrose Chamber of the Free British Fishery was set up, partly with local and partly with London capital under an Act of Parliament in 1749. This guaranteed a three percent annual return, and a 30-shilling bounty was paid on vessels of 20 to 80 tons burden owned by companies and individuals and a two shillings and eight pence bounty on all exports. Since Montrose had a Customs office, where salt had to be cleared, it was a suitable base. The leading merchants with shares in the Chamber also dominated the Town Council so it gave every encouragement, granting £5 annually for the rent of a house for the use of the Chamber, and in November 1751 it waived all shore dues on all necessary busses (herring boats), tenders, goods and equipment. In June 1753 the Council also granted ground to erect sheds for making twine and nets, to house a boiler for tanning nets and to store casks, salt etc. at the Waterside to the east of the pier between Horloge Hill and Ferryboatness on a 14-year rent-free lease, later at a 'reasonable' rent.

By 1758 three herring busses were in use: *Charming Mally*, *Montrose* and *Dispatch*. An increase in the bounty to boats from 30 to 50 shillings per ton burden in 1757 no doubt encouraged expansion but enthusiasm soon waned and in 1760 there were only 13 busses in the whole of Scotland. Herring busses had a crew of about 11 and had two or three masts, the mainmast lowered when fishing. They were square-rigged and of a suitable size for distant water fishing. They commenced fishing off Shetland on 13 June, following the herring shoals south through the Minch to Campbeltown by early October and fished in the Clyde until 31 December, returning home by January. The crew, whether local or not, may have engaged in white-fishing the remainder of the year. The herring were salted and loosely packed at sea into casks called 'sea sticks' and were repacked on shore at the home port with extra salt into 32-gallon barrels. The industry did not rely on the home market since a bounty encouraged exports. Some was sold to foreigners at the fishing grounds, but most was brought home and exported to northern Europe, very seldom was any sold locally. But problems arose. In August 1760 *Charming Mally* was wrecked on the coast north of Aberdeen. The Montrose Chamber survived a crisis in 1768 when bounties were not paid but in January 1769 *Montrose* was wrecked at the harbour mouth returning from fishing. She was carrying 910 barrels of herring, 198 empty barrels and no less than 30,800 square yards of netting! By November 1770 she had been replaced by the *Hope* and it seems the Chamber had high hopes of continuing but the reduction of the bounty to 30 shillings per ton in 1771 made the future hopeless and by June 1772 they had dissolved and given up their premises and later assigned their assets to the Town Council.

Knox gives 1750–76 as the period Montrose was a herring port exporting 50–100 barrels annually. But there is nothing in the Customs records to support the existence of a regular herring fishing at the latter date and re-exports accounted for most herring exports after 1771. Herring from Stornoway was dispatched in April 1771, over 2000 barrels, most of which was sent to London. In August 1774 two Montrose vessels brought in 182 barrels of herring bought at the fishing, but it was specifically stated that they were not fitted out for fishing. Cured herring for local consumption was usually brought from the Forth. In October 1792 it was reported that the schooner *Fisher*, of which a local fish curer was part owner, had sailed with 82 bushels of foreign salt the previous October to the herring fishing via Orkney, had last been seen at 'Loch Herring Pool' (Loch Eriboll, Sutherland) and was presumed lost. This seems to have been the last capitalist venture. In 1795 the Customs collector reported no deep sea or herring fisheries from Montrose and in 1788 and 1801 no herring vessels over 15 tons burden. In March 1799, however, a local vessel, the *Barbara*, belonging to Daniel Watt, landed 195 barrels of herring but was not entitled to the 20 shillings per ton bounty on vessels as it was under 15 tons burden. Later there appear to have been no regular herring landings at Montrose until the 1860s, although occasional small landings, sold fresh, may have been made when shoals intermittently came inshore.

Although Montrose curers, following on the pioneering Ferrydenners, began to recruit local fishers from the district to fish out of Peterhead for herring from 1832, it was only 30 years later that Montrose itself became a herring port. In 1838 the Town Council, inspired by other burghs such as Aberdeen, proposed giving a bounty of £7 to herring boats if a minimum of 30 could be attracted to fish out of Montrose. This was also on condition that the boats were properly manned and equipped to the satisfaction of a competent inspector and would work exclusively out of Montrose during the summer season. The Council were also to grant land for curing sheds and to dry nets on, free. The fish curers also requested the Council to provide a steam tug (there was none until 1857) to tow the boats in and out of the harbour in calm weather, but this was refused. For various reasons the industry did not take off at that time. But Stonehaven had become a herring port from the 1840s and this seems to have inspired James Johnston, who joined his father Joseph's business in 1857. He induced Cellardyke fishers to fish further out than usual off Gourdon and they were often successful (the fishing in the Forth had been unsuccessful for several years). James also encouraged the Ferrydenners to go further out to sea. He even acquired a boat, which in August 1858 landed 50 barrels of herring, skippered by James Paton of Ferryden. But nothing was caught at the next attempt and it was only from 1861 that Montrose really became a herring station for the following 50-odd years up to the First World War.

In 1861, after the local boats had had two poor seasons out of Peterhead, James Johnston engaged them to fish out of Montrose in the first part of the season, then later out of Peterhead. The fishing 30 miles off-shore was successful so the local boats began to be drawn into a regular summer fishing, sailing nightly to the grounds. In 1861, 1600 crans were landed and this steadily increased up to 1893 when 26,403 crans were landed by boats with a total of 300 fishermen, not all local of course. In 1877 James Johnston claimed to have engaged 50 to 60 boats so the firm were curing much of the local catch and began to concentrate their herring curing interests in Montrose itself. There were hiccups in the growth of the industry as in 1866 the curers were reluctant to engage as many boats as usual due to the doubtful state of the continental markets. So the price per cran and the amount landed fell. But the industry soon revived and grew and in 1880 several curing premises were being extended and improved. In 1882 the curers requested the Harbour Trust to build a fish quay between the old shore and the wet dock as the larger herring boats were finding it difficult to get off at ebb tide. This was achieved by April 1885 and later that year horse-drawn tramways connected to the main rail lines were built along the quayside. The Johnstons by then had their own steamer which delivered cured herring directly to the Baltic and North German ports. The industry was at its height around 1875–84 with good prices in continental markets. Occasional ups and downs due to fluctuations in the herring shoals were still typical of the industry; in 1885 19,175 barrels of cured herring were exported from Montrose but only 8,648 the following year. In 1891 it was stated that the average value of the herring landed the previous three years was £35,019. A total of 286 men and 34 boys on 153 boats from Ferryden had been engaged and a further 309 men and 34 boys on another 156 boats also worked out of Montrose.

Towards the end of the century there were poor seasons and the local herring industry went into permanent decline. Some of the curing firms ceased to exist as the owners retired and no one else chose to take over since the situation was not promising. In 1898

Joseph Johnston & Sons, who made many of their own barrels, were able to sell excess barrels rather than buy in as formerly. By 1904 only 50 to 60 Ferryden fishers were engaged. In 1907, however, the Montrose Steam Drifter Company Ltd was formed with a share capital of £2,800 but operated a single boat. The main partners were the two remaining curers, Joseph Johnston & Sons and Alexander Mearns, with an office at 93 High Street. The Johnstons also operated another steam drifter on their own behalf. Both were built new in 1907. A third belonged to Gourdon owners and must have been a converted sailing lugger as it was originally built in 1883, but was successful enough to be used up to about 1925. The Steam Drifter Company was moderately successful up to the end of 1914 but by 1919 had sold its boat to St Monans owners although it was still registered at Montrose in that year. Joseph Johnston & Sons sold their herring curing premises in 1919 as the continental market had collapsed and local catches had declined. Although the two remaining steam drifters were active into the early 1920s they must have spent their time fishing elsewhere, from Shetland to East Anglia or the Minch.

Whaling

Various factors encouraged whaling from Montrose by the 1780s. The loss of the American colonies meant that the price of whale oil rose and former colonial ships of a suitable size came on the market cheap, along with the flight of some experienced crews from New England. There had also been a government bounty of £2 per ton burden on vessels and 30 shillings per tun (standard cask) on blubber from 1750, insufficient in itself to tempt earlier Montrose capital, although the Forth and Clyde ports, Dundee and Aberdeen had all been involved at an earlier date. It was in these circumstances that the Greenland Whale Fishery Company was formed in Montrose in 1785 and bought a 624 ton ex-American vessel which first sailed north in April that year. They leased a half-acre site at the Waterside for a boiling yard at a moderate rent and later bought the ground. Only one whale was caught the first season and not even the £528 bounty repaid the costs. But they persevered and had more success from the later 1780s. In 1786 the New Whale Fishing Company was set up with a yard at the West Pier and had two vessels by 1787. The next six years the three barques sailed out together in what was the high point of the first phase of whaling from Montrose. They favoured the Davis Straits as having larger whales, but it was more dangerous than off East Greenland. Good years such as 1791 were followed by bad when in 1792 the *George Dempster* only brought home 18 tuns of blubber, the *Eliza Swan* nil while the *Montrose* was crushed by ice and lost although the crew were saved. Despite being insured, the Greenland Company dissolved on the loss of their barque and their yard became a salt works from 1794. The *George Dempster* was lost with all hands in 1794 and the New Company withdrew their remaining vessel *Eliza Swan* after the 1795 season and also ceased fishing.

A new group, the Montrose Whale Fishing Company, emerged and from 1798 had some very successful seasons with the *Eliza Swan*, which it had bought. As the vessel was old by then a new, larger *Eliza Swan* of 302 tons was invested in, but increased running costs and poor seasons did not encourage the use of more vessels until the price of oil began to rise astronomically towards the end of the 1794–1815 French wars. So in 1813 the company acquired the *Monarch* and in 1820 the *Hero*, so had three fine ships. In 1813 a rival Union Whale Fishing Company had also started with an old ship, *London*, and from 1815 also the *Spencer*. Both companies did comparatively well into the mid-1820s after which there was a slow downward trend in sailings and catches. Catches fluctuated greatly from year to year and ships were caught and damaged in the ice. The worst year was 1830 when the *Spencer* was lost, two ships came back with no catch and one with only five whales. Although the Montrose Whale Fishing Company still had two ships the industry was becoming uneconomic as supplies of foreign oils were coming in and it wound up by November 1833. The Union Whale Fishing Company was also compelled to give up by 1834 when its remaining ship, *London*, was also lost. But the failure to sell the yard or ships meant that the Montrose Company's manager continued to send *Eliza Swan* and *Monarch* to the Davis Straits on his own account despite poor returns until they were eventually sold to a leading ship owner and timber merchant and used in ordinary commercial voyages. An attempt was made to set up a whale and seal fishery again in 1889 but not enough shareholders were prepared to take the risk, even if it was not all that evident that Dundee's whaling industry was beginning to decline.

In their heyday in the 1820s the Montrose whalers had averaged nearly 12 whales per season and over 100 tuns of oil, latterly only two whales and just over 26 tuns of oil. The local merchants and others who had invested in whaling all had many other commercial and industrial interests and the risk was spread between many owners. When occasional exceptional seasons could occur after several poor ones it was difficult to make a decision when to cut losses by giving up for good. Some of the crews were recruited from the local seafarers, although 'stout country lads' were advertised for as apprentices. Others were picked up in Orkney and Shetland, although the Ferryden fishers considered themselves better seamen than any. At a time when whaling men were exempt from naval service and seizure by the press gangs, many fishermen and mariners joined the whalers, which took them away for over six months in summer.

Salmon fishing [1]

Montrose has long been one of Scotland's premier salmon exporting ports. The river North Esk was the most productive in the area, followed by the South Esk, but salmon from Lunan Bay, Inverbervie and elsewhere within the burgh's exclusive trading precinct

---

1 Adapted from the author's *Report on the History of Salmon Fishing in the Montrose Area from c.1360 to 1835*, 1985 (typescript).

from the Dighty to the Findon Burn was also exported via Montrose. The curing and packing of all salmon (and other fish) within this precinct was also meant to be exclusively carried out in the burgh. This monopoly was effectively maintained to about 1600, but fell off thereafter. Most 17th- and 18th-century commentators remark on the export of salmon or that it was a particularly valuable item of commerce.

In the middle ages salmon exports seem mainly to have gone to England, France and the Low Countries. Customs records from the 1740s to 1830 show that Campvere, the Scottish staple port in Holland, was a major destination most years, sometimes Rotterdam and occasionally Northern France. Salmon was shipped to Bilbao in Northern Spain in 1748 and 1774, to Lisbon in 1747, and also to Italian destinations including Venice, which in some years took about a third of the total exported. The last shipment to Venice was in 1781. Most of the vessels belonged to Montrose but other Scottish vessels were used, and often large Dutch vessels carried consignments of up to 1000 barrels to Venice.

The last shipment of the traditional barrelled salmon seems to have been made to Campvere in 1793. By that time the salmon was almost all iced or kitted for the London market.

Apart from fishings in the North Esk, detailed in the previous chapter, the burgh also owned the estuary fishing on the north bank of the South Esk from Beany Sands west of the mouth of the Tayock Burn to the point of Annat Bank and also the Sands fishing from the Annat Bank to the burgh boundary with Charleton, less productive until stake-nets were introduced in 1806. The south bank of the Southesk was attached to the lands of Rossie and Usan. From 1742 both banks were fished by the proprietors of Rossie, with the Sands from 1779. By the mid-19th century most of the fishings were leased or feued to Joseph Johnston & Sons and other commercial concerns.

The Sands fishing

The first record of this fishing is from 1663 when a tack of the sands 'at the bak of the town' was granted to Alexander Duncan, a carpenter burgess of Montrose. In 1723, however, it was described as 'for many years bygone altogether neglected' and a similar complaint was made in 1759. After complaints that Archibald Scott of Rossie's fishers were encroaching north of Annat Bank, the most valuable part of the fishing, in the absence of a proper boundary, the Council decided to roup the fishing, and in 1768 the Sands fishings were rouped to the Scotts of Rossie. In 1779, when the tack was stated to be vacated and void (the result of a dispute, it seems, with George Carnegie of Pitarrow, proprietor of Charleton), the Council agreed unanimously to grant a new feu charter to Patrick Scott of Rossie, who had succeeded his father Archibald in 1773 and who had already bought Scott of Logie's part of the town's South Esk fishing to add to his own. The new charter incorporated all of Rossie's fishings, both in the South Esk and on the Sands, but no record of the entry fee or annual feu duty seems to have been kept.

The South Esk fishings: north bank

This belonged to the burgh. In 1463 the fishings were leased in return for a render of 51 salmon. In 1478 the fishing was leased in quarters, for 20 shillings each, to John Cruickshank, David Nanweik, Robert Ferrier and David Rukby, burgesses of Montrose. By 1636 by contrast the fishing was leased in tenths, Alexander Erskine of Dun paying £6 3s 4d for a lease of three tenths. Probably the fishings were feued in the 17th century to the Scotts, the wealthy merchant family who became local landowners and progenitors of the Scotts of Rossie, Logie, Usan and Commieston. There seems to be no further record until 1742, when the fishings were shared between Rossie and Logie. In 1780 Patrick Scott of Rossie, having already bought Robert Scott of Logie's share of the South Esk fishings, was granted a charter of the town's South Esk fishing along with the Sands. In 1783, however, he being declared insolvent, his creditors sold his estates, including a fishing station near the Ferry of Montrose and the whole fishings held of the town, to Hercules Ross. In 1816 it was noted that 'Rossie's' fishing held of the town was worth £50 annually.

The South Esk fishings: south bank

This had no connection with the burgh but comprised some of the most valuable fishings which formed the source of its export trade. The fishings must have always belonged to the estates of Rossie, Craig and Usan. Around 1650 most of the parish of Craig was acquired by Patrick Scott, fourth son of James Scott of Logie. He died in 1690 and was succeeded in Rossie and Craig by his son Patrick, two other sons having Usan and Dunninald. This Patrick was succeeded in 1731 by his son Archibald Scott (mentioned above in connection with the town's fishings), and he in turn by his son Patrick whose creditors sold the estate to Hercules Ross in 1783. A map of 1807 shows Rossie's fishings stretching from Rossie Mills to the Sata or Salthouse Bank, where the heritors of Rossie had their fish-house or salt-house, and the Sata Sand and Black Rig adjacent. West of Inchbraoch or Rossie Island was the Trout Shot, still known for yielding sea-trout, and on the east the Scalp and the Stell. To the east of Ferryden was the Sheriff Hole Shot and the Cuttie Rock Shot. The map also shows that the fishings on the north bank, held of the town, stretched from Beany Sands, Beany Brig and Beany Point, west of the Tayock Burn, to the point of the Annat Bank.

Fisher names

Thomas Gilyeam fisherman was recorded in 1488, one of the earliest records of any fisher surname anywhere. In 1636 the names Gowans, Skirling, Newton, Ross, Garmack, Mackie and Miln(e) were borne by eight skippers. Around 1700–20 the last three, as Cormack/Kermack, Mackie/Mackay and Mill/Milne were still common, while other names current then were Doers, Allan and Fraser. There was a larger variety of names from the 1730s–50s, indicating an expansion of the fisher community. The commonest surnames then were Pert/Peart and Morrice/Morres/Morris while others were Twedal,

Young and Orkney. Fourteen other surnames are recorded only once; the only ones familiar from other parts of the district were Mearns, Adam and Shepherd. In 1776 fishers from Usan called Pert, Peterkin, Lawson and Lindsay migrated to Montrose. Around 1780–1800 the names Pert/Peart, Peterkin, Allan, Law, Anderson and Cargill are recorded. In the period around 1815–40 the commonest names in order of frequency were: Pert, Paton, Inglis, Cowie, Hosack and Ewan. Other names occurring only once were Anderson, Cushnie and Tindal. In 1841 there were: 14 Perts, six Patons, three Andersons and two Inglis, other names being Monro, Tindal, Cowie and Hosack. By the 1880s the names Pert, Paton and Moir were the only ones borne by more than a single fisherman. Other names current then were: Milne, Craigie, Mitchell, Clark, Torry and Rattray. Around 1890 English trawlermen called Weaselham, Rewcastle, Snowling, Hayward and Burton were resident for a few years. In 1915 the six remaining resident fishers bore the surnames Pert, Coull, Rattray, Torrie, Crane and Crowe.

Some variations of the place-name and spelling

Monros	1641x50
Montross vulgo Monross	1693
Montrosse	1747x55
Montrose	1790–91, 1794 to date

Number of fishermen and boats

Year	Fishers	Boats	Type
1488	?	?	'fishboats'
1636	40–50?	8	boats under 25 feet?
c.1730	30–50+?	6–10?	boats under 25 feet?
1758	50+?	9–12?	3 herring busses, several line boats
1790–91	16–18	4–5	yauls
1819	30–36	6	boats and yauls
1841	30	6?	4 boats and 2 yauls?
1855	22	6	2 boats and 4 yauls
1881	12	7	yauls?
1886	?	7(+)	7 trawlers (plus yauls?)
1900	8*	5–6	3 trawlers, 2–3 yauls?
1915	6*	7–8	3 trawlers, 3 steam drifters, 1–2 yauls?
1921	2*	22	2 steam drifters, 1 motor liner, 13 ketches, 3 schooners, 3 unspecified (small motor trawlers?)
(1928 boat account includes Ferryden)			
1930s	1*	7	3 trawlers, 3 motor boats, 1 motor yaul
1950	–	–	–
mid-1950s	?	1	seiner
1975	?	6	2 seiner/trawlers, 4 creel boats
1995	?	20+	1 small trawler, 20+ small boats

* Many of the trawler crews may have been from Aberdeen and Granton although Ferryden men may also have crewed them. Recently most boats have been owned and manned by Ferryden men.

Ferryden [1]   Craig NO715566

Ferryden was a fisher community in Craig parish, on the south bank of the River South Esk, immediately opposite the burgh of Montrose. Ferryden was not one of the older fishertouns. Slezer's view of 1678 shows only one house. Although listed by Ochterlony in 1682x85 along with the local white-fishing communities the first real evidence of such a community is in 1716 when several Ferryden boats were stopped from collecting mussels in the tidal basin by the magistrates of Montrose. Adair's map of 1693 shows only three buildings or houses at Ferryden and it may only have been a salmon fishing settlement at that time (but see Salmon fishing, below). The name derives from the den leading to the ferry across the South Esk and was originally the name of a farm. The laird Patrick Scott of Rossie with his brother the laird of Dunninald were among the earliest enclosers and agricultural improvers in Angus and it seems that Rossie must have encouraged white-fishers to settle at Ferryden at the beginning of the 18th century. The predominant names were West or Wast, Coull, Pert, Paton, Mearns and Findlay. The Coulls have been traced to Speymouth and the Wasts to Crovie, predecessor of Gardenstown or Gamrie. Findlay is a common name at Cullen, Banffshire though they are found at an early date in Mearns coast fishertouns south of Stonehaven. By tradition, David Pert was the first to settle and build a substantial house, followed by a James Wast or West. The Perts and Patons seem to have been indigenous to Usan in the same parish and to the Montrose area, the Mearns to Johnshaven, north of Montrose.

In 1791 there were 38 families resident in Ferryden and six small four-man boats were used. There is evidence for a decline in many local fisher communities from the 1760s due to the press gangs which particularly hit the young men, preventing use of the great lines for distant fishing in larger boats. By 1835 the population was 679, of which 590 belonged to 85 fisher families. At that time the fishing boom was just beginning and there were 18 large six-man boats, four of which went to the great line fishing about 30 miles out, and seven smaller four- or five-man boats. Herring fishing off the Buchan coast had just begun and several boats went from Ferryden. Fishing was at its height in the 1880s and 90s, when the population reached nearly 2000 and around 160 boats were operated by 300 Ferryden men and boys; only a handful of fishers and boats belonged to Montrose where most of the fish was landed, packed and cured. Decline set in before 1914 when there were only 22 boats and after the war and slump of 1923 a new generation virtually abandoned fishing. Two or three boats carried on line fishing until the mid-1960s.

In the 1960s two seiner/trawlers, *Angus Rose II* and *Rosemary*, owned by Ferryden men, fished out of Montrose, and there were half-a-dozen open boats used in mussel raking or for lobsters.

---

1 From an early hand-written draft.

Salmon fishing

On 11 July 1670 Charles Maitland of Halton was confirmed in the barony of Rossie including 'that pendicle called Ferriden with harbour and fishings of the same'. These were probably salmon fishings.[1] In 1684–85 Patrick Scott of Rossie was proprietor of Ullishaven (Usan) and Ferredene 'and hath salmond fishings there'.

Fisher names

According to family tradition the Ferryden Wasts or Wests migrated south from Crovie in Banffshire before 1720–30. A gravestone in Inchbraoch Cemetery erected in the 1760s by John Wast, 'skipper Ferryden', commemorates his children born between 1731 and 1745. Craig parish registers (extant from 1657) record names in Ferryden from 1686. These include Coull, Peart, Mearns and Findlow, names common later, along with Jamieson, Smart, Greig, Scott, Twedale, Thom, Bremner/Brebner/Brymer, Watson and Allardice, and, from the 1720s, also Morice, West, Walker, Bruce, Hill and Reid. From 1753–56 Patton/Paton and Peart, common names later, appear along with Johnston, Anderson, Inglis, Ewan, Alexander, Donald, Young and Smith. The John Main recorded in 1757 (who gave his name to Johnny Main's Harbour) may have originated from Portlethen. In 1819 Miss Alice Erskine's interdict against fishers taking mussels from the Lands of Sands included ten Ferryden fishers whose names were: Watt, West, Summers, Paton (two of each), Mearns and Cob. Three Findlays and another Mearns are recorded in the same year.

In the 1841 census the predominant name is Coull with 45 occurrences (over a quarter of the village), followed by Pert/Peart (31), West, Paton and Findlay. The Valuation Roll of 1895–96, out of some 230 households, records 56 householders named Coull, followed by West (34), Paton (31) and Pert (25). Other common names are Findlay (13), Mearns (12) and Watt (11) while Stephen, Nicoll, Anderson, Young and Duncan occur five times or more.

Some variations of the place-name and spelling

Ferryden	1641x50, 1791, 1794, 1835 to date
Ferriden	1670
Ferredene	1682x85
Ferry-den	1693
Ferry Den	1747x55

---

1 This point was contested with the author by Gordon Johnson, Peterculter (pers. comm. 17 September 1996), who believed that white-fishings were meant and drew attention to the reference to Inchbrayock in the same charter, where salmon fishings were particularly specified. If correct, this gives an earlier date for the origins of Ferryden than those cited above (ed.).

Number of fishermen and boats

Year	Fishers	Boats	Type
1716	?	'several'	?
1791	24	6	small
1835	100+?	25	18 large, 2 medium, 5 small
1846	100+?	20–30	all sizes, including large
1855	186	68	all sizes
1881	350	156	all sizes
1890s	300	163	all sizes
1914	?	22	?
1960s	c.8?	2 or 3	small open boats

In the 1920s and 30s a number of Ferryden men may have crewed the Montrose fleet of trawlers and drifters.

Heicham/Higham   Craig NO728568

A salmon fishers' hamlet near Ferryden, part of the barony of Usan. No record after 1753.

Some variations of the place-name and spelling

Hechem	1587
Heichame	1602/03
Higham	1714–53

Usan   Craig NO725546

Although the lands of 'Hulysham' or Usan are recorded from 1245 the haven of Usan is only recorded from 1511 and the fishertoun or *villa piscaria* from 1548. Usan had an excellent natural haven with the houses perched less than 50 feet above it and so it may have been settled from a very early period. The traditions concerning the office of King's Cadger are clear evidence of its existence from at least the 13th century when King Alexander II (1214–49) and his son King Alexander III (1249–86) regularly stayed at Forfar castle and made it their Christmas residence, so it was an important centre of royal administration. The castle was destroyed in the Wars of Independence at the end of 1308 and ceased to be an important royal residence. So it seems the office of Cadger and the road must have been created by the 13th century at least, possibly even earlier. The King's Cadger held 30 acres of land near the fishertoun on condition of supplying the court, when at Forfar, with fresh fish daily. The King's Cadger's Road traversed the 17 miles from the shore of Usan to the market cross of Forfar until 1780, when, long disused, it was divided up between the landowners on the route.

The fishertoun took its name from the estate it belonged to, which from 1245 to recent times has had an incredible variety of spellings, sometimes with the element –haven tacked on the end. The estate belonged to the Lychton or Leighton family from the 13th century to 1618, after which it was sold to the Carnegies. The fishertoun and fishings are again mentioned in 1567, 1592 and 1632. Afterwards the estate changed hands several times, for a time to the Scott family, but in 1815 it was bought by George Keith, a wealthy Carolina planter who had started life as a house painter in Montrose; his family were to own Usan until the 1930s.

There was originally a single cluster of cottages and other buildings on the site of the village and Seaton farm until Keith took it over. Adair's map of 1703 indicates Usan towne by four buildings, while Ainslie on a larger scale map of 1794 indicates Uzon Fishtown as a scatter of about nine buildings on either side of a track on the site of the present farm and village. The Craig parish registers record fishers resident at Seaton or Fishtown of Usan and cottars at Cotton or Husbandtown of Usan. The two adjacent settlements would have been a cluster of single-storey theekit clay biggins. In 1822 Keith completely rebuilt the fishertoun in stone and lime as a row of 28 two-room cottages with the tower near the centre as a landmark. The adjacent farmstead of Seaton of Usan was probably redeveloped and renamed about the same time.

39 The derelict tower and village of Usan

The community

There may have been two boats' crews at Usan before the 18th century and there appear to have been at least three in the 1770s before a crew of five men and a boy migrated to Montrose around 1778 after some disagreement with the landlord, Archibald Scott of Usan. In 1787 there were 22 households and a total of 61 persons resident at 'Fisher Usan' and there may have been 12 to 15 fishers forming two to three crews. In 1791 there were 18 fishers manning three boats, about 20 families and a total population of about 100. Between 1794 and the 1820s the population also included a dozen or so salt workers and a full-time salt officer and officer of excise and there may have been a dram-shop or ale-house by that time. There seem to be no hints of any drastic decline due to the activities of the press gangs as is evident at Ferryden, Montrose and elsewhere, although 24 men from Usan and Ferryden had served in the Navy in the wars of the 1770s. The press gangs must have seized a few more men during the French wars of 1793–1815, but if there was a decline then the community soon recovered, since four skippers were accounted for in 1819. By 1835 there were 36 fishers working six boats, and 16 fisher households forming 85 souls out of a total population of 142, the remainder of which must have been the five coastguards, farm workers and their families since the salt works had closed. The 1841 census records 34 households at Usan Village, including a 'vintner' (innkeeper) and 21 fisher families. The 1855 boat account records a peak of fishing activity with 39 fishermen and boys operating 12 boats and 41 others involved in gutting, curing, vending and otherwise assisting. There were four boats over 30 feet, six standard boats and two yauls. The population dropped slowly but steadily afterwards. In 1881 there were 30 fishers manning 15 boats of various sizes and by 1891, 22 fishers from 16 families out of only 22 households were resident. Usan, like other small havens, declined before the 1880s and rapidly after 1900. By 1910 there were 12 houses let to townspeople as weekend retreats, and only 10 working fishers. By 1928 there were only five old fishermen each working a tiny yaul. One had a paraffin motor by the 1930s but by 1938 fishing had ceased as the men became too old. Only part-time creel fishing has been carried out since then.

From about 1900 the vacant houses were let to professional folk as weekend and holiday homes. The village was sold by the last of the Keith-MacIntoshes to the farmer in the 1930s. Unlike Ethie Haven or Stranathro the houses were never sold off or properly maintained so the village gradually became depopulated by the 1950s and so the long row of cottages and the tower have become derelict despite several suggested schemes to improve them.

Village institutions, social and cultural life

For such a small village Usan enjoyed many conveniences and varied activities, particularly in the 19th century. The Usan fishers shared with those of Ferryden a Mussel Society which leased its own beds in Montrose Basin, at one time managed by 'Mussel Jamie' West from Ferryden, who also preached on occasion at the Usan mission on Sunday evenings. Usan also shared a fishermen's friendly society with Ferryden from 1814. A savings bank set up in the parish was mainly used by the fishers, coastguards and domestic servants. A parochial library set up in 1809 had 96 volumes kept for the Usan villagers, mainly of religion, history, biography etc. There was however some rivalry between Usan and Ferryden, which had ten times the population. The Usan folk thought Ferryden folk assertive and grasping while they in turn looked on the Usan folk as 'canny' or slow-witted, if not simple, an attitude found elsewhere between large and small fishing communities.

The village had an inn before 1860, much frequented by visitors to nearby Boddin, St Skae's and Elephant Rock. It was once tenanted by a John Thomson, reputedly the originator of the saying, "We're a' Jock Tamson's bairns". Around the 1880s Usan had a flute band patronised by the Keith lairds, which played as far away as Brechin Castle. They had a uniform of short trousers with a white stripe, short reefer jackets (probably navy blue) with brass buttons and presumably peaked caps. The Usan women were great singers and D H Edwards, proprietor and editor of the *Brechin Advertiser* made recordings of them in the 1920s, but these have apparently not survived.

A school was set up at Usan in the early-19th century to serve the southern part of the parish of Craig, half the 'missie's' annual salary was paid by the Keith laird of Usan and half by the Arkleys of Dunninald. Small fees were also payable to the teacher. The building consisted of one long room with a tiny two-roomed flat at one end for the teacher. The children were encouraged to adapt to trades other than fishing and the odd 'lad o' pairts' went on to become a minister, the zenith of educated man's ambition then. The school seems to have closed by 1900 and the children had to walk nearly three miles to Ferryden. The school was also used as a mission on Sunday evenings by lay preachers from Ferryden, superintended by the parish and Free Church ministers. All used fishing metaphors in their sermons. The singing was unaccompanied, led by a precentor using a tuning fork. Services held prior to the departure of the herring fleet were particularly solemn. The schoolroom was also used for many a jolly wedding and social into the 1930s with a fiddle or two and a melodeon providing dance music. The school was latterly converted into a house and was the only inhabited one in recent times until the old salmon bothy was also converted.

The coastguard station

The coastguard came to Usan and were leased the watchtower and houses from 1835. The ground floor of the tower later housed the rocket cart used to fire rescue lines to ships. The first floor housed telegraphic instruments, rifles, flags and other signalling equipment. The second floor was the officer's office while the battlemented top gave an outlook equipped with telescope and semaphore. A rocket lifesaving brigade was eventually established with volunteers from the fishing community and men from adjacent Seaton farm. The cart was drawn by the best pair from the farm. It held black coffin-like boxes which contained the ropes. Rescues were made as far south as Red Head from grounded vessels and quarterly drills were held into the 1930s. The coastguards originally lived in the cottages at the seaward end of the row, which were larger, having lofts. They may originally have been built for the salt officer and excise officer and saltwork manager or foreman. In the 1890s a new purpose-built coastguard station was built next the farm, with a watchtower and accommodation block. Since about 1980 it has been sold off as private houses and auxiliaries cover the coast from Land Rovers.

The saltworks

Close by the shore is a large square windowless building, the sole survivor of three salt pans. In 1793 the tax on coal carried north of Red Head, levied since the Union of 1707, was repealed. By June 1794 two pans had been built at Usan by David Scott of Dunninald, MP for Forfarshire 1790–96, who had agitated for the repeal. He was the brother of Archibald Scott, proprietor of Usan. It was hoped to make 9,000 bushels of salt annually, supplying a third of local consumption. But even after a third pan was built only 3,700 bushels was produced annually. Seventy percent was sold locally, at Montrose and Ferryden for fish curing. A channel was cut through the flat bed of rocks north of the haven to let sea water into the pans and also for coal sloops to deliver coal close to the pans. It took up to six tons of coal to produce one ton of salt from sea water. The water partially evaporated in a rock basin in summer, the pans being filled three to five times. The industry brought good wages into the village and increased the value of the estate, but the duties on salt entering Scotland were repealed in 1823, cheap rock salt from Cheshire flooded in and all the Scottish saltworks soon closed down. The channel cut in the rocks, known as 'the Cut', has since been used as a harbour for small fishing vessels.

Salmon fishing

Salmon fishing by sweep-net seems to have been carried on, perhaps intermittently, from the 17th century if not earlier. It received no mention in 1791 or 1835, possibly overlooked since the most valuable fishings in the parish were in the estuary of the South Esk. The salmon bothy, between the school and the saltworks, was probably built in the early-19th century, the space beneath it was used for curing white fish. Bag-nets were presumably introduced by about 1840. The remaining salthouse, abandoned after the 1820s, was converted to an ice-house, later used as a net store. In the 1920s and 30s the salmon gaffer lived in No.8 and the men came from Gourdon and Johnshaven and lived in the bothy during the season (February to late September). The salmon fishings were leased out by the estate and in recent times they were worked by Tay Fisheries with hired men until the mid-1980s when they were leased by a salmon fisher who lived on site. The salmon bothy was then converted to a family house.[1]

---

1 Usan Salmon Fishing Company is currently (2010) the only company practising coastal salmon fishing between the Dee and the Tay. Besides their own fishings, which extend from Scurdiness to Auchmithie, the company leases part of the Lunan sands fishings from Redcastle Salmon Fishing Company. Bag and jumper nets are used. The latter has superseded the stake net and comprises a fixed net whose upper edge hangs from cork floats while the weighted lower edge lies on the bottom; its advantage is that it is more easily removed (ed.).

Fisher names

The name Scott was common in the parish in the 17th century from 1612 to the 1670s, but by 1700 had disappeared. Other names common in the parish were Clerk, Trumbull (Turnbull) and Patterson but it is not certain if any were Usan fishers, only from the 1690s are residents of Usan specified. But Patton and Peart (after 1800 spelt Paton and Pert) were common names from the 1660s and 1680s and throughout most of Usan's later history, the latter being the commonest by far before 1800. There was a far greater variety of surnames in the village in the 18th century, including: Lawson, Inglis, Sim, Patterson, Lindsay and Pitterecken (Peterkin). In 1787 there were no less than 23 surnames in the village including those of married women. Of 61 residents there were 24 Perts and nine Patons, other names occurring more than once were: Watt, Fitchet, Anderson, Lawson, Gadie and Cargill. Others were Mearns, Peterkin, Lawrence and Lyall. By 1841 of 21 fisher families there were 14 Patons, two Perts, one Cargill and one Coull, in 1861 much the same except for an Anderson. By the 1890s there were 15 families of Patons, only one called Pert and no others. By the 20th century Paton became the sole surname among active fishers.

Some variations of the place-name and spelling

Hulysham	1245
Howsane	1467
Houshevin/Houshawin	1481
Owsane	1484, 1487
Ousane, Owsawyn	1485
Osan	1486
Willishavin	1488
Houshavin/Houshavyn	1493
Wilishavin	1495
Howlshavin	1496
Wllishavin, Ulishawyn	1497
Ulyshaven	1502
Ullishaven	1511, 1548, 1641, 1675, c.1685
Wolfishavyn	1512
Ullishevin	1592
Wllishevin	1603
Ulilschavin	1621
Ullisheavin	1632
Vlisheaven	1650
Uzin	1676
Uzan	1693
Uzon	1697
Usan Towne	1703
Usan	1703, 1714–98, 1835, 1841 to date
Ullysseshaven	1743, 1795

Aousan, Ousane	1750
Ullisseshaven	1776
Fisher Usan	1787
Uzon Fishtown	1794
Usan Village	1841–91

The usual full name would have been Seaton or Fishtoun of … (i.e. of Usan in any of its spellings). Note that u, v and w were once interchangeable.

Number of fishermen and boats

Year	Fishers	Boats	Type
1776	18–24?	3–4?	under 25ft?
1791	18	3	under 25ft?
1819	24	4	under 25ft?
1835	36	6	4 c.30ft, 2 under 25ft
1855	39	12	4 large, 6 standard, 2 yauls
1881	30	15	all sizes
1891	22	10?	all sizes?
1910	10	?	yauls?
1928	5	5	yauls
1938	–	–	

Boddin   Craig NO712536

© The Estate of Colin Gibson

40 *Salmon fishers' and lime workers' cottages*

Salmon fishing

In 1604 the haven and fishings attached to the lands of Dunninald are mentioned; in 1611 the haven and landing place, with salmon and other fishings; and in 1624 the Fischerlands are mentioned. The full name of the station was Boddin of Dunninald. There may have been a sweep-net salmon fishing here since medieval times. Any 'other fishings' apart from sea trout are doubtful or incidental, and this was probably legal waffle. The mention of the Fischerlands implies that the salmon fishers had arable land for subsistence in the winter. Salmon fishing had ceased around 1791 but a sweep-net fishing recommenced in 1822, while bag-nets were probably introduced by 1840. This fishing seems to have continued, perhaps with breaks, until the present day. There was also once a single stake-net set at an angle from the gravel beach south of the lime-kiln, usually they were only used from sandy beaches.[1]

---

1 Usan Salmon Fishing Company still (2010) employs a fly net at Boddin, the stakes being set into holes bored in the rock (ed.).

On the north side of the peninsula is a row of derelict buildings which once housed salmon fishers and lime workers. At the southern end is a salmon bothy, once the gaffer's house. At the north end are two two-storey blocks, the upper floors of which were separate flats reached by outside stairs. They were built of a mixture of limestone and sandstone and had slate and red pantile roofs. Built into the brae is an ice-house and above it is the more recent salmon gaffer's house.

The lime-kiln

© The Estate of Colin Gibson

41 *Boddin Point*

Boddin Point projects into the sea, dominated by what looks like a castle but was in fact a gigantic lime-kiln built by David Scott, laird of Dunninald. The outcrop of limestone at Boddin Point had apparently been worked since 1696, one of the earliest recorded limeworkings in Angus. The huge kiln, the largest in Angus, was built in 1771. Coal sloops landed by a 30-foot channel and any swell or brisk gale prevented landing. The Customs were asked to send a tide-waiter to collect dues on coal landed to save a three hour round trip to Montrose. Lime from Boddin was being landed at Montrose from 1779. In 1783 Scott informed Montrose Town Council that he intended to build a pier and hoped that the shipmasters of Montrose and Aberdeen would petition in favour of the public aid required. Whether with such help or at his own expense it seems that the 'pier' or wharf was built about then. The present slipway used to launch and land the salmon coble has masonry resembling the old shore of Montrose carried out in 1779 and 1795. In 1791 it was said that the limework was carried on to a great extent, and to it all the improvements in husbandry in the neighbouring country were in great measure owing. Exploitation was at first inhibited by a tax on coal carried north of the Red Head, levied since the Union of 1707. This was removed in 1793, partly by the efforts of the above David Scott who was MP for Forfarshire at the time. It was also he who built the saltworks on his brother's property of

© The Estate of Colin Gibson

42 *Boddin lime-kiln*

Usan in 1794. Production from the kiln soared to 40,000 bolls of lime annually. Due to the near exhaustion of the seam, expenses increased and the working was finally abandoned in 1831. The kiln has since been badly eroded by waves and the whole south wall fell into the sea in 1988.

Lunan Bay [1]

Lunan/Inverkeilor NO6952 to NO6949

It is likely that salmon fishing has been carried out around the mouth of the Lunan since early times. A charter of Robert II of 1377, confirming the lands of Inverlounane (north of the river-mouth) in favour of Alexander Stewart, mentions fishings, though not specifically salmon. The licence granted to Thomas Stewart, Lord Innermeith and Baron of Inverkeilor, by Arbroath Abbey in 1506 for a fish-boat at Ethie Haven (q.v.) almost certainly implies salmon fishing as no reference is made to the fisherlands required by a

© The Estate of Colin Gibson

43 *Stake-nets in Lunan Bay*

white-fishing community. The earliest actual reference to salmon fishing is in a charter of 1624 which permits the taking of salmon and other fish 'in salt water and fresh'.

Neither Edwards (1678) nor Ochterlony (1682x85) mention salmon fishing at Lunan and it seems that the fishing may have died out for some time, as the author of the Old Statistical Account for Inverkeilor, writing in 1790–91, states that salmon fishing had 'begun' on Redcastle and Lunan sands in 1760. After a profitable start it soon became unproductive, probably owing to the practice of steeping flax in the river. The minister of Lunan likewise confirms that salmon have deserted the bay 'where they were sometimes caught in great plenty'; in 1790 the fishings were annexed to the farm at Lunan and no particular rent was specified for them, suggesting they were of little value.

© The Estate of Colin Gibson

44 *Red Castle with nets and a neat stack of stakes on the beach in the foreground*

By 1835 this situation had greatly improved. Salmon fishing was stated to be carried out 'very successfully' on the sands with stake-nets, while a bag-net had lately been installed at the south end of the bay.

---

1 Contributed by editor.

141

© The Estate of Colin Gibson

45 *The mouth of the Lunan*

The Ethie fisheries were valued at £140, those at Lunan at £420, a considerable sum. The census returns from 1841 onwards record salmon fishers resident at Lunan, Redcastle and Ethie Haven. The ice-house at Lunan, with its castellated entry tower, has been dated to c.1850.

From the early-20th century the north end of the bay was fished by Joseph Johnston of Montrose and the south end intermittently by the Tay Salmon Fisheries Co of Perth. In recent years the latter have sold out to Usan Salmon Fisheries, who today also lease the north end from Redcastle Salmon Fisheries Ltd. Fishing today (2010) is by means of 'jumper nets' where the leader floats free on corks rather than being fixed to stakes, making it easier to install and remove.

Ethie Haven   Inverkeilor NO699487

This erstwhile fishing hamlet is comparatively remote, well away from the A92 coast road between Arbroath and Montrose, about three twisting miles east of Inverkeilor along farm roads and situated on the rocky coast on the south side of Lunan Bay. It is known to few folk outside the immediate area. The houses can be glimpsed from the A92 north of Inverkeilor, particularly if their whitewash catches the sun. The lands of Ethie were originally part of the regality of Arbroath Abbey, apparently from its foundation in 1178, and formed a parish which was merged with Inverkeilor from 1611. The earliest record of the use of the haven is from 1506 when Arbroath Abbey granted licence to Thomas Stewart, Lord Innermeith and Baron of Inverkeilor to:

> bryng a fysche boit in our hawyne of Aithy for al the dais of his lywe [life] and his fyschairis to pas and repas thairto with thair stuf and geir syk as gannys thaim, and to la thair ankiris upon land, to wis [use], hing and dry nettis, to tak fysche and al other necessair thyngis to do, vse, exers and hant neidful to fyschyng craft and sawing of boit and geir.

But he was to have no ground rights and the right to use the haven was to revert to the abbey on his death. However, in 1528 the same privilege was granted to Richard Stewart, Lord Innermeith, his wife and their son and heir John Stewart. The mention of nets and the lack of ground rent or permanent habitation clearly imply that in early times only salmon fishing was carried out from the haven. From 1545 the lands of Ethie including the haven (but with no mention of fishings) were feued to Robert Carnegie of Kinnaird and remained in the hands of his descendants, the Earls of Ethie and Northesk, until sold in 1919. Charters of the regality of Arbroath in 1608, 1641 and 1662 include the lands of 'Athy' with its haven with fishings. Its vernacular name at the time was probably

Haven of Athy. John Carnegie of Ethie, who also owned Auchmithie and lands inland on the river North Esk, was created Earl of Ethie in 1647 by King Charles I, but the title was later changed to Earl of Northesk at his own request since his brother David Carnegie of Kinnaird had become Earl of Southesk, and he also had lands near the Northwater Bridge; Ethie Castle, however, was the main residence of the earls. Ethie Haven was not mentioned by Ochterlony around 1682x85

© The Estate of Colin Gibson

46 *Ethie Haven*

and it is specifically stated that the earl was supplied with fish from Auchmithie, so if there was any fishing from Ethie Haven before 1700 it was only for salmon and there was no permanent habitation there. The haven itself is merely an L-shaped creek barely 20 feet wide in places, apparently a natural break in the rocky foreshore (although it may have been improved by man), leading to a pebble beach on which small boats could be drawn up.

The community

The inception of a white-fishertoun at Ethie Haven appears to date only from 1701 when two men called Torn (or Thorn) were leased house sites by the Earl of Northesk. Both men were named Francis Torn, one living 1669–1737, the other 1666–1742 so both were in their prime when they arrived at Ethie Haven. They may have been brothers, despite having the same name. They, like other settlers, may have come from Auchmithie, or possibly Usan. On their tombstone in Inverkeilor kirkyard both are described as 'shipmaster' but they could have been joint skippers of a single boat manned by them, their sons and others. If there were two boats in the early-18th century there must have been several other families to provide the minimum of ten men and boys required. If so, they might have been sub-tenants to the Torns, and so would not be mentioned in their lease. Although maps, printed and manuscript sources from the 1700s invariably refer to Ethie Haven or Ethiehaven the local fishers usually called it 'Torrenshaven' or 'Torn's Haven' and so the Fishery Board recorded it as 'Thornshaven'. It has even been mis-transcribed as 'Thorshaven', giving it a spurious Scandinavian origin.

One of the Torns had a son called John whose wife was called Katherine. In 1740 the *Katherine* of Ethie Haven, master John Thorn, was hired by a Montrose merchant to carry 30 matts (4500 lbs) of Virginia leaf tobacco to Leith but this was refused by the Customs authorities. The *Katherine* may have been a fishing boat rather than a trading bark or sloop. Some of the fishers in the locality commonly carried dried fish to the Forth at the end of the summer great line fishing and returned with coal for their own use, so their small boats were quite capable of such a voyage. John Torn died in 1767 and left £36 13s 4d Scots (£3 1s 1d Stg.) for the poor of the parish to the kirk session of Inverkeilor on condition that his name and a picture of a 'ship' were painted on the west loft of the kirk, where he had usually sat. So it may be that John Torn had a small bark or sloop as well as a fishing boat. He had certainly acquired a fair bit of money for a fishing skipper, but there could have been another route to comparative wealth. The smuggling of tobacco and other goods was rife in the mid-18th century in the area, and the landing of goods from ships hovering off Lunan Bay and Usan was notorious; although Ethie Haven is not specifically mentioned, its very remoteness must have made it an ideal spot for smuggling.

Ethie Haven seems to have flourished in a small way throughout the 18th century and being so small may not have suffered from the press gangs like larger communities. In the 1760s and 1770s two skippers in Newhaven of Ethie had children baptised, so there were apparently two or three boats then. In 1790 there were ten 'industrious fishers' manning two boats, catching haddock, skate, cod, ling, halibut and occasionally turbot, so great line as well as sma' line fishing was carried out. In 1755 lobster fishing for the London market had commenced. This must have affected the summer great line fishing (which was abandoned in favour of creel fishing when the returns were good) as the demand for salt dried cod traditionally sent to London fell off at this time. Ainslie's map of 1794 and Blackadder's of 1822 seem to indicate four cottages on the site of the present houses and another three nearer the shore. So it seems there were seven families, which would be expected from the number of active fishers. In 1835, however, white-fishing was moribund and the boats seldom went out since it was said 'the old men are afraid to venture, and the young men seek employment where there is greater encouragement'. The 1841 census reveals a total of 19 persons in three inhabited houses and the salmon bothy. The men and boys over 14 were all salmon fishers or farm workers while three seasonal young salmon fishers lived in the bothy. The only white-fisher was aged 90. However, the resident salmon fishers all had white-fisher surnames and may have fished with sma' lines in winter, rather than working on the land, and some creels were probably fished in summertime as a part-time activity. In 1852 however the Earl of Northesk replaced the old houses with a two-storey block providing 12 two-room apartments, the upper flats reached by bridges from the steep bank behind. A row of coal cellars and privies and the fish house were presumably built around the same time.

The new houses had the desired effect since by 1855 there were 13 fishermen and boys operating six boats: two over 30 feet, two standard boats and two yauls. In 1856 the place was described as 'a small desolate fishing village on the south side of Lunan Bay'. 'Desolate' in this instance meant isolated and it surely was the most remote fishing hamlet on the east coast. Herring fishing in the usual six-week summer season away from home must have started from the 1850s since larger boats were being used. In January

1858 a winter herring fishing was tried offshore in the bay with a few nets. They had some success, initially catching five crans; these were sold to a Montrose curer who made them into bloaters for the London market within 24 hours. But stormy weather brought the experiment to an end when the nets were lost in the first week of February. For some reason the community did not continue to flourish. The incomers stayed only a few seasons before moving elsewhere and new transients only settled for a season or two. In 1881 there were only two boats and seven fishermen, so only inshore white-fishing and creel fishing was maintained by then. The 12 flats in fact were seldom all occupied. Eight were occupied in 1861 and all 12 in 1881 and seven in 1891. By 1895 there were only three fishermen and only five permanent households while at least three were let as holiday homes. After 1900 there was only a single white-fisher until 1908 but one or two resident salmon fishers, and in summer three in the bothy, who came from Auchmithie and Johnshaven. Since then only occasional part-time creel and handline fishing has been carried out by resident salmon fishers and others. In 1919 the earl sold the estate and Ethie Haven was bought by the farmer of Ethie Mains who continued to lease the vacant flats as holiday homes. There was apparently a grandiose scheme to develop the place as a holiday resort but nothing came of it. In 1938 the whole hamlet and its land was bought by an Edinburgh businessman who sold off the untenanted houses to the same class of business and professional folk who had rented them before. Only a single salmon fisher (who worked at Lunan) and his family, a widow and a single woman resided latterly, and the last permanent resident died in the mid-50s. The various proprietors who now own the flats maintain the road and other common amenities and have drawn up an agreement to restrain development in the village.

Salmon fishing

As mentioned above salmon fishing has been carried out intermittently since at least 1506 and probably much earlier. Fishings mentioned later in the 16th and 17th century undoubtedly refer to salmon. Although there is no hint of salmon fishing in the 18th century it is unlikely that it was abandoned. Stake-nets could not be set up at Ethie Haven but a 'suspension net' had been set up by 1835. This was probably a bag-net as they were certainly in use in the area by the 1840s. In 1841 there were four resident salmon fishers and three seasonal men from Auchmithie in the bothy and salmon fishing seems to have continued at least intermittently throughout the 19th century. From 1909 until 1925, when it was abandoned, the salmon fishing was tenanted by Joseph Johnston & Sons of Montrose. In 1926 however the Tay Salmon Fisheries Company of Perth bought the rights; they tried fishing in 1937 but it was unsuccessful and they abandoned it until 1985 when it was started again successfully for a time.[1]

---

1 This part of the coast is currently (2010) fished by Usan Salmon Fishing Co (ed.).

Fisher names

The origin of the first settlers, called Torn or Thorn, is unknown but the name is of Angus origin. Never a common surname, it did occur in the parishes of Arbroath and St Vigeans and Craig, so the Torns may have come from either Auchmithie or Usan. However the parish registers do not give the place of residence within the parish or occupation so early and the surname does not occur at either fishertoun later in the 18th century. William Gady, a skipper, is recorded around 1770–78, his surname only otherwise known from Usan in 1787. The name Lawson is recorded between the 1760s and 1840s and occurred at both Usan and Auchmithie in the later 18th century. The name Cargill, of Auchmithie origin, is recorded from the 1770s and throughout the 19th century. The name Coull, of Ferryden origin, occurred from the 1840s to the 1880s (as that of a salmon fisher) along with more transient residents called Stephen, Smith and Pert. By the 1890s the single white-fisher was a Swankie (from Auchmithie) along with salmon fishers called Waiter (a very rare name whose only other occurrences are at Johnshaven and Gourdon) and a Duncan, a fisher name occurring occasionally in the district.

Some variations of the place-name and spelling

Hawyn of Athy	1508, 1528
Ethie Haven	1737, 1742, 1790, 1794, 1835, 1841 to date
Newhaven of Ethie	1763–78
Thornshaven	1855, 1881
Ethiehaven	1856, 1882
Thornhaven	1858

Locally Torrenshaven, Torn's Ha'en or simply the Ha'en

Number of fishermen and boats

Year	Fishers	Boats	Type
1701	5–10?	1 or 2	under 25ft?
1760s–70s	15?	3?	under 25ft?
1790	10	2	under 25ft?
1835	?	?	?
1841	1	1	yaul
1855	13	6	2 large, 2 standard, 2 yauls
1881	7	2	yauls?
1908	1	1	yaul
1928	–	–	

Auchmithie Arbroath & St Vigeans NO681444

The lands of Auchmithie were part of the 'shire' of Aberbrothock given to Arbroath Abbey on its foundation in 1178. The name is Gaelic *achadh muthaich*, 'field of the cowherd', which must have been coined between 850 and 1150 when Gaelic was the predominant language in Angus. This pastureland may have begun to be cultivated by 1200 or earlier but the earliest record of the name is from 1434, when, in a lease of lands to the north, passage was reserved for animals belonging to the 'husbandmen of Achmuthy'. A series of leases of Auchmithie by the abbey from 1468–1535 reveal something of how this farming and fishing community was organised and what obligations the occupants had towards their monastic landlords. The *ville* of Auchmithie, as it was referred to in Latin, can be translated into Scots as fermtoun. It was leased in quarters and eighths, jointly to tenants and their wives and sometimes their heirs for 19 years or life, while sons could inherit the lease. The lands of Auchmithie then included not only Mains of Auchmithie but Seafield, West Mains and Seaton of Auchmithie (which were only created as separate farms in the late-18th century) and also Windyhills to the south, which was feued separately after 1560. Usually land at that time was held on short leases of one to five years, but such long leases were common on ecclesiastical estates. Other tenants may have held shorter unwritten leases as not all the fractions were accounted for. The farmers had cottar sub-tenants who actually worked the land, and also fisher sub-tenants. The rent was paid partly in cash and partly in animals or services, such as the carriage of peat or building stone etc. when required. Each lessee of a quarter also had to provide a fishing boat or crew, fully equipped for fishing. Lessees of an eighth paid half the rent and were responsible for half of a boat and crew. The earliest recorded lease, of 1468, refers to this requirement 'as is the custom of the husbandmen of Achmuthy', while a lease of 1482 stipulated that the boat and its crew were to catch fish for the monastic community, after which surplus fish could be sold 'at the usual price'. The same lease also stipulated the right of the abbey to introduce another boat and crew. There was also a *brasina* or brewhouse of Auchmithie associated with the fishertoun. By the 17th century it was referred to as the ailhouse. Its primary function would have been to brew the tenants' and sub-tenants' ale for their own use, but it appears that it also sold ale and was probably the predecessor of the later inn and hotel and on the same site, perched above the path to the shore. Its tenant of around 1500 paid a money rent of one merk (13 shillings and four pence Scots) annually, together with the obligation to keep it in good repair. Leases, as of the land, were to man and wife jointly for 19 years or life, but were often given up after two years. Three of the five leases recorded, from 1468, 1496 and 1535, also stated the obligation to provide a boat and its crew equipped for fishing. But a lease of 1488 makes no mention of this, while a lease of the brewhouse together with an eighth of the land in 1533 to Marjory Ogilvie (mistress of Abbot David

© The Estate of Colin Gibson

47 *The village of Auchmithie on the cliff top*

Beaton) specifically exempted her from the obligation to maintain a boat and crew. She had several other properties and the lease implies that it was let to sub-tenants. The Reformation of 1560 abolished the abbey's religious function and its assets became the property of the Hamilton family. In 1564 the fishertoun with its lands, houses and crofts was sold to John Carnegie of Seaton who died in 1604. The fishertoun and the largest part of the lands of Auchmithie were inherited by his brother and by 1626 by his nephew John Carnegie of Ethie, who was created Earl of Ethie in 1647. In 1666 the title was changed to Earl of Northesk since his brother had become Earl of Southesk. The title derived from lands around Edzell and Pert on the river North Esk but his main lands were Ethie and adjacent Auchmithie. The successive Earls of Northesk continued to be feudal lords of Auchmithie and its fishers until 1919 when the estate was sold. Their relationship with the fishers varied from the tyrannical and unjust around 1700 to more paternalistic by the 1790s.

The community before 1800

Auchmithie had a fine natural haven with a shingle beach ideal for landing and launching boats and a fisher community undoubtedly existed long before 1468. Since the fishers were originally sub-tenants of the husbandmen it would seem likely that they emerged from a semi-agricultural past, with obligations on the land. The fishers may originally have paid their rent to the husbandmen with work at harvest and other times, later perhaps in money. Since the normal complement of boats in the late middle ages was five this would probably imply 25 to 30 active fishers and a fisher population of around 125 to 150 persons. The abbey regarded their main function as being to supply fish but this was paid for, after which any surplus could be sold to others. A document of 1488 records the amount and price of various foodstuffs to be bought annually by the abbey cellarer.

This included 1500 dried keiling (large cod) for £45 in Lent and in winter, along with 12,000 dried haddock and speldings at £8; £60 annually was also to be spent on the day-to-day buying of fresh fish. The dried fish may have been acquired from Broughty Ferry, Catterline and Torry, which the abbey also owned, but the fresh fish presumably came mainly from Auchmithie. From 1564 the fishers became the direct tenants of the Carnegie lairds and paid a money rent to them for the lands, houses (or house sites) and the right to use the haven and to fish in the sea. By then, although they had some land to cultivate and probably pasture to graze a cow, they were almost fully occupied with fishing.

Around 1682x85 Ochterlony stated that the Earl of Northesk 'hath a fishertoun belonging thereto [Ethie] called Auchmuthie, whereby they are abundantly served of all kind of fishes all seasons of the yeir'. From 11 November 1686 the earl leased to David Cargill and his sons Robert and John, for a period of 19 years and in return for an annual money rent, houses, arable land and the right to fish with great and small boats. They also had 'servants', meaning employees, who crewed their boats. So the fishers still then cultivated some land and were not totally dependent on fishing as they were later. As when the abbey was landlord the rent was not paid in fish but there was an obligation to provide constant supplies of fish to the landlord's household, after which the surplus could be sold. The earls also collected the teinds, a tenth of all produce, including fish, payable to the kirk. By 1793 the only payments mentioned as due to the earl were from one shilling and sixpence to three shillings and sixpence annually for house sites, plus the teinds of fish. Having become full-time fishers by then the former fisherlands had been incorporated into the adjacent farms and even small gardens were lacking. From the mid-18th century the expansion of industry and population in Arbroath must have created a greater market for fish and it had few fishers of its own. There is no record of Auchmithie being affected by press gang seizures from the 1760s but it seems that this factor must have inhibited any growth of the community in the later-18th century since in 1793 there were only six boats manned by 30 to 35 men and a total fisher population of 180 persons, little more than there had been 300 years earlier. It was also said in 1793 that Arbroath could have consumed ten times as much fish as it did. Shortly before this the earl had built a cart road to the beach, prior to which the winding path was the only access. It may be that the road was intended primarily to enable coal and lime to be carried from small sloops landing at the haven, although there is no actual record of this. Some years earlier a small earthenware jar had been found beneath a cottage floor containing 33 coins, some of Charles II (1660–89) and William II (1689–1702) and also some earlier coins of German states and Henry IV of France (1589–1610). Later, in 1876, a storm disturbed the shingle bank beside the haven and revealed thousands of trade tokens and buttons, also copper coins from the time of James V (1514–42) to Queen Victoria and a silver franc of Henry III of France (1574–89). It was very common for foreign coinage to circulate in Scotland before the union of 1707 and it would seem that cadgers must have paid for fish at the haven at one time and were the source of these. Smuggling had been rife in the 18th century with fishing boats used to carry goods ashore. The many caves and landing places below the cliffs between Auchmithie and Arbroath were ideal for such activity; goods were landed at Brandy Cove, Cove Haven, Dickmont's Den and Auchmithie itself, where the innkeeper was also suspected of being a ringleader. But smuggling fell off from the 1760s with patrols by revenue cutters and by the 1790s was virtually at an end.

Fisher serfdom: the Auchmithie case of 1705

In May 1705 the Earl of Northesk brought a case against two fishermen, the brothers John and Robert Cargill, before the Privy Council, which notoriously upheld his claim that they were legally serfs and should return from Arbroath to his service. Nothing in Scots law stated that fishers were unfree and if brought before the Court of Session the case would have failed. In February that year the Session had already decided against extending the law maintaining colliers and salt workers as serfs to fishers. The former were not finally free until 1799 but there is not a shred of evidence that fishers were ever serfs in post-medieval times. But the earl had powerful cronies in the Privy Council and the fishermen were forced to return. In fact, in 1686, with their father David Cargill, skipper, the Cargill brothers had contracted a written lease from the earl for 19 years' rental of houses, arable land and fishing rights at Auchmithie. This had run out at Martinmas 1704. It seems they did not quit then, and were ordered to do so by Whit Sunday 1705. So with their families, boats, gear and servants they duly moved to Arbroath where they were welcomed and made burgesses, a status few fishers ever achieved. But the earl was apparently displeased at their quitting Auchmithie entirely. The fact that unfree men could not have made a lease did not prevent the Privy Council forcing their return although this was patently unjust and unlawful.

The community since 1800

After the end of the French wars by 1815, the Auchmithie fishers were able to exploit the growing markets not only of Arbroath but also of Forfar, Dundee and villages in the area. So the population grew from 180 in 1793 to 280 by 1842 with a doubling of the number of active fishers from 30 to 60, manning twice as many boats. The total population continued to grow with just over 400 persons between 1861 and 1871, dropping in later decades to around 350. The number of active fishermen peaked at 78 in 1855, dropping slightly to 70 in 1881, 54 in 1894 and about 30 by 1910. The community, like many others, grew from around 1815 to the 1870s, but most rapidly from 1832 when herring fishing commenced. The growth was native, the census shows that out of 44 heads of fisher households in 1841 only three were incomers and there seem to have been no later incoming men. The 1861 census records the curious fact that many households included 'servants', fisher lassies from Ferryden called Coull, Inglis and Pert. They were not domestic servants but were there to collect bait, sheil mussels and bait lines for unmarried sons, some of them eventually marrying into Auchmithie. No incomers were recorded in the 1891 census, by which time the community was in slow decline. Despite the drop in population some cottages still housed two families. Some only paid ground rent to the earl as they, or their forebears, had built their own houses. There were no formal leases of houses then and the fishers were all 'kindly tenants'. The earl built Fountain Square in 1880, providing some new houses while also improving the water supply and drainage. Water had been pumped up to the village from 1863 by hydraulic ram, prior to which it all had to be carried from a spring at the foot of the brae.

Migration out of the village to Arbroath began in 1829. But despite the fact that Arbroath had rail links to Dundee and Forfar from 1838, a good harbour (enlarged in the 1840s), no cliff to toil up and down, and a ready market in the burgh itself, a great many fishers still preferred to live in Auchmithie. In fact the Auchmithie women used to walk to Dundee and back to save the rail fare, a round trip of 40 miles! It seems, however, that there was a constant trickle, particularly of young men, to Arbroath. The movement grew by the 1890s so that the number of fishermen at Auchmithie halved in about 20 years. Certainly by 1900 many old folk in Auchmithie had sons and daughters in Arbroath. Herring and great line fishing seems to have ceased before 1914 and an ageing group of fishermen carried on sma' line and creel fishing up to around 1930. Many of the younger men went to the salmon fishing in summer on the Angus coast and further afield. Latterly a few old men operated small sailing yauls at creel and handline fishing in the bay. Others worked on farms or cycled to work in Arbroath and continued to live in the village, a few keeping a boat for creel fishing in summer. Some white-fish was dried and smokies continued to be made. In fact one family made smokies as late as the 1980s, the fish brought in and then distributed by van. In 1928 there were ten small yauls, mostly with a crew of one man. This dropped to six in 1938 and to three by 1940 while a single yaul carried on until 1944 if not later. In the post-war period a few part-timers, often non-residents, have occasionally carried out creel fishing with small motor boats.

Village services and institutions

The earliest evidence for the existence of an inn is from September 1787 when Robert Burns breakfasted there having ridden from Montrose. He then took a boat to Arbroath in order to see the cliffs but made no comment on Auchmithie. Sir Walter Scott spent some time at the inn in 1814 and *The Antiquary* (1816) is based on his experiences of Auchmithie. At that time the inn was called the Northesk Arms and was tenanted by Mrs 'Lucky' Walker, who later re-named it the Waverley Inn. By 1870 it was the Northesk Arms Hotel and it continued to belong to the earl until 1919. It was naturally famous for fish dinners and was a social centre for the fishers as well as catering for increasing numbers of tourists; not only the spectacular cliffs and caves but also the picturesque village and its 'quaint' folk were the attraction, several visitors recording their impressions of the fisherfolk and their hard-working but cheerful lifestyle. From being a 'dry' or temperance hotel from 1912 and a tearoom in the 1930s, from 1943–63 it became a youth hostel which attracted crowds of young cyclists and hikers. Today Auchmithie has a choice of licensed restaurants, which naturally feature seafood, including smokie dishes.

There were several tradesmen and services in the 19th century. The 1841 census reveals that apart from 44 fisher households there were two shoemakers, a tailor, a grocer, a fish curer, plus a couple of wrights and a smith to service the estate farms. There was a post office in the Pound by 1861, later in the Square. The fisherfolk in the 1890s were not impressed by the encroachments of the 'Coonty Cooncil' on the village, nor by the rates they had to pay for improved drainage and water supply, their own scaffie and bobby and stricter school attendance and inspection. There was a small schoolroom in 1841 served by a schoolmaster and a 'missie' but in 1859 the earl built a new school with a schoolmaster's house attached to the west of the village. Although claims were made in the 1880s, when it had 72 pupils, that the fisher bairns were barely literate, it seems they did learn the 'three Rs' if little else. But they often missed school for seasonal work such as tattie lifting, for bait gathering or to mind infants, and when Mrs Annie Gilruth, wife of the farmer at adjacent Seaton of Auchmithie, campaigned for the improvement of the school in 1887 the cry was, "Fishers need nae leer!" It was claimed that Arbroath bairns were 'just fair trachled with getting their faces washed and police runnin eftir them to tak them to schuil'! In 1919 the school was taken over by the Forfarshire Education Authority and upgraded. In the 1920s it had 65 pupils taught by a qualified schoolmaster and female assistant. The school roll dropped slowly through the 1940s, then more rapidly and it closed in 1971 with only four pupils, just a few years before new housing was built in 1976, bringing many more families into the village.

The Countess of Northesk built a chapel to the west of the village which opened in 1834, although baptisms, weddings and funerals still had to be held at Kirkton of St Vigeans, where several distinctive fisher headstones can be seen. By the 1880s, burials were at the Western Cemetery, Arbroath. A series of resident missionaries served the chapel, with mixed success. Due to the agitation of the redoubtable Mrs Annie Gilruth, a new kirk and manse with its own minister opened in 1885 but attendance was never very high. A few fishers were Episcopalians or Free Kirkers but many never went to any church. The charge was united with St Vigeans and the kirk closed by the Church of Scotland in 1980, though the episcopal minister in Arbroath, who had already started a mission in the village, began to hold services in it.

Since Mrs Gilruth had been denied the use of the church for concerts and the school for meetings she campaigned for a village hall, soliciting subscriptions from the local aristocracy and gentry. The hall opened in December 1888. All manner of talks, exhibitions, weddings and socials were held in the hall, and concerts were given by the fisherfolk as well as visitors. There was a lending library and a reading room. The hall continued to flourish with whist drives, dances and annual Burns suppers until the 1960s and has since been used more occasionally for badminton, bingo, children's activities and Community Council meetings. The village also had a football team from the 1920s, which was revived after the war and active until the 1950s.

The harbour

In 1852 the earl had consulted an engineer about the viability of a pier or harbour. Nothing was done but his intention caused the fishers to invest in larger boats. By the 1880s a steam winch had been installed for hauling up the herring boats but the women of Auchmithie still had the onerous task of wading into the freezing water to launch them. In 1883 the succeeding earl revived the subject. The ubiquitous Mrs Gilruth took an interest and engaged the support of the Member of Parliament, as a result of which the Fishery Board for Scotland, without a survey, estimated a cost of £2500. A Board of Trustees was appointed and in 1889 it was resolved to proceed with a design submitted by a Mr Barron, engineer of Wick harbour. The Fishery Board agreed

48 *Auchmithie harbour*

© The Estate of Colin Gibson

to pay three-quarters of the estimated cost of £4500; £1100 had already been raised by Annie Gilruth's campaign (in which she used photographs of the Auchmithie women launching the boats), and small amounts were also raised by the Auchmithie and Ferryden fishers. The foundation stone was laid in July 1890 with great ceremony and celebration and by 1891 the north and east walls of the harbour had been completed. But an outer bulwark, which would have protected it from the sea surging in from the south-east, was never built as the money ran out and the harbour remained incomplete. In 1895 several fishers were called before the Arbroath Small Debt Court for non-payment of harbour dues; they protested that the harbour was useless and that the dues of two shillings monthly per crewman were in excess of those at Arbroath, a much superior harbour. Eventually the Fishery Board offered to pay half the estimated cost of the outer breakwater. But by October 1898 a new Fishery Board under a Tory government reneged on the promise. The trustees spent some remaining money improving the road to the shore and many tons of rock was blasted and used to batten the outer side of the harbour walls. Annie Gilruth died in 1903. Two of the most active trustees were also dead by then and no more work was done on the harbour. Soon the last of the big herring boats had been drawn up for the last time and Auchmithie as a thriving fishing village had entered terminal decline. Even if the breakwater had been built the harbour would have been a white elephant by 1914. Auchmithie by then had few more inshore fishermen than places with no harbour and there were no finances to maintain or repair it.

The coastguard station

This was probably founded around 1830 as it is recorded in the 1841 census. It is a purpose-built two-storey block similar to that at Muchalls with accommodation for five families. In 1869 it was described as being whitewashed and having a flagstaff. Possibly the earl would not lease a site on his property near the village since it was built on a site belonging to Windyhills south of the burn. Although around 200 yards from the village as the crow flies it is much further from the beach by road. A boat was kept at Auchmithie beach but at high tide the shore was only accessible via the village. Almost nothing is recorded of the coastguard station and there is no record of a rocket life-saving team as found elsewhere. Relations with the fishers could not have been bad as there was at least one marriage of an Auchmithie lass to a Welsh coastguard named Cadogan. Two Norwegian vessels were wrecked nearby in 1880 and 1897 but there is no record of who rescued or assisted them except that in the first incident the Auchmithie folk tended a survivor with a broken leg. The station seems to have been one of those closed down around 1904–05. It was bought by the proprietor of Windyhills and used to house his chauffeur, farm workers and Irish tattie squads. By the 1970s it was sold off as private houses.

Salmon fishing

There is no early evidence for this. In 1842 it was stated that stake-nets and bag-nets had been tried in the area but had not repaid the cost. A single salmon fisher was resident in the village in 1861. In 1890 it was recorded that salmon fishers occasionally dried their nets at the shore.

The smokie [1]

Although other smoked haddock cures such as the peat-smoked finnan haddies and bervies were well-known, at least locally, by the 17th and 18th century, there is no early record of the smokie. James Headrick, writing in 1813, noted that some individuals smoked haddock and codling for their private use but that there was no commercial establishment for smoking haddocks. He suggested that this method of curing should be introduced to Angus, noting that finnans sent by mail coach to Edinburgh and London were fetching high prices. The sending of smoked haddocks to Dundee is mentioned in 1842, the earliest actual record that smoked haddocks were prepared at Auchmithie.

---

1 Adapted from the author's *Auchmithie: home of the smokie* (1995).

The method was first described in detail in 1882 and also around 1893 by J B Salmond in a vivid portrait of Auchmithie. The haddocks were first gutted and decapitated then tied by the tail in pairs and hung to dry in the sun for two or three hours. When properly dried the pairs of haddocks were suspended from wooden bars over a half-barrel sunk into the earth, in which a fire of green beech wood had been kindled and then dampened with sawdust. Damp sacks were thrown over the haddocks. After an hour the haddocks were ready to dispatch in boxes and rips to Arbroath, Dundee, Edinburgh, Glasgow and elsewhere.

Since the bulk of the Arbroath fishers came from, or had their antecedents in, Auchmithie, they too made smokies by a similar method. With the demise of Auchmithie haddock fishing by the 1920s the Arbroath smokie's fame spread abroad. The original Auchmithie smokies were brownish-black on the outside but the flesh inside was white and sweet. They were dry, fully cooked and smoked principally as a basic means of preservation, unlike the modern Arbroath smokie which is moister and smoked for flavour.

Fisher names

The surnames Cargill, Shepherd, Spink, Smith and Bedie/Beddy/Beddie/Beatty or Beattie, which continued to be common in the village, are recorded from 1669 when the parish registers begin. The name Swankie is not recorded until 1730 but has been very common since and is virtually unknown outside Auchmithie and Arbroath. The names Ayton or Eaton and Watt only appeared from 1766 and remained fairly common later. Lawson occurs only in the 18th century, as it did at Ethie Haven and Usan. In the 19th century the number of families bearing the name Cargill increased from about one third of the population in 1841 to half by 1900. The next most common names in the 19th century, borne by four or five families each, were: Swankie, Shepherd, Spink, Smith and Watt. The names Eaton and Beattie were only borne by a couple of families while other names borne by only a single family were: Swan, Murray, Harper, Paton and Gall, the latter two immigrants from Ferryden and Broughty Ferry. The Beatties and Watts disappeared from the village by the 1880s or 90s, probably through migration to Arbroath. After 1900 Cargill remained the commonest fisher name by far. There were also several families of Spinks, Smiths and Swankies resident around 1930 but only one or two Shepherds and Eatons.

Some variations of the place-name and spelling

Achmuthy	1434–1535, 1641x50
Aichmuthy	1496–1512
Aychmuthe	1530
Achynmuthe	1533
Echmuthe	1564
Achmethie	1591, 1662

Echmutie	1597
Aichinmouthie	c.1600
Achymwthy	1608
Auchmouttie	1634
Auchmutie, Achiemoutie	1641
Auchmuthie	1682x85, 1740
Auchmithie	1705, 1741, 1794, 1841 to date
Auchtermutty	1747x55
'Muthie (Robert Burns)	1787
Auchmithy	1793
Achmithy	1807

The earliest spelling is the nearest to local pronunciation. The prefixes Auchter- and Auchen- are erroneous. A village in Fife with the same name became standardised as Auchmuty. The fishertoun itself was sometimes prefixed Fishertoun of … or in Latin *villa piscaria de* … in the 16th and 17th centuries. It was prefaced Seatoun of … in the 1740s; the Village of … in 1793; but Fishtown of … in 1794; and simply Auchmithie Village by the 19th century.

Number of fishermen and boats

Year	Fishers	Boats	Type
c.1500	25–30?	5	small?
c.1700	?	?	large and small
1793	30–35	6	under 25ft
1842	60	12	under 30 feet
1855	78	33	14 large, 15 standard, 4 yauls
1881	70	40	all sizes
1890	c.65	38	6 large, 12 standard, 20 yauls
1894	54	29	2 large, plus standard boats and yauls
1896	40+	21	boats and yauls?
1910	c.30	?	mostly yauls
1928	11	10	yauls (sailing)
1938	12	6	yauls (sailing)
1948	2	1	small motor

Cove Haven   Arbroath & St Vigeans NO669420

This little bay is on the Seaton estate a mile north-east of Arbroath and has a broad shingle beach below a low cliff, fairly easy of access. In 1581 Peter Young, preceptor of the Chapel Royal at Stirling and almoner to King James VI, was granted the 'sunny half' of Seaton of Arbroath, with its haven called Coif-haven or Cove-hewin with its teind fish and the right to gather wrack and ware (flotsam and seaweed) within the tidemark. This was confirmed in 1586 and 1587 along with half of Dickmontlaw, which is one and a half miles to the west but presumably had some connection with nearby Dickmont's Den which may have been a detached part of the lands of Dickmontlaw. These lands were all part of the Regality of Arbroath, once the property of Arbroath Abbey, but the tiny haven is not recorded earlier, nor is anything of substance later. On Ainslie's map of Angus of 1794 and Blackadder's of 1822 two cottages marked 'Covehaven' are indicated, but by the head of Dickmont's Den over 200 yards to the south of the haven. They had gone by the time of the Ordnance Survey of 1858. J Brodie in his guide to the cliffs of Arbroath of 1904 only recorded a vague tradition of smuggling. The cave which gives Cove Haven its name is known as the Masons' Cave, where the Arbroath Freemasons met on special occasions. It was used as a boathouse by

© The Estate of Colin Gibson

49 *The Masons' Cave*

the proprietor of Seaton in the late-19th century and once had wooden doors. It seems likely that this was the site of a net and coble salmon fishing but there appears to be no evidence that it was ever worked in recent times. Until the late-17th century seals used to breed and give birth in the caves and shingle beaches in the area but later had been hunted to extermination.

Arbroath [1]   Arbroath & St Vigeans NO6440

The burgh originally belonged to the Abbey of St Thomas founded in 1178. It developed along the road leading from the abbey to the shore called the Copgait, later the High Street. A harbour for small merchant vessels was created at the mouth of the Brothock Burn in 1344. This was only replaced by a new harbour to the west, dug out of part of the shore, in 1725. There seem to be no hints in the abbey register that there was a medieval fishing community here. Although it is likely that there may have been a few fishermen supplying the monks and inhabitants with fish, Auchmithie seems to have been their main source. Apart from nearby Auchmithie, which could supply fresh fish daily, the abbey also owned Broughty Ferry, Ferryden, Catterline, Cove and Torry, from where it got barrels of cured salmon and supplies of dried white fish. Nonetheless it is somewhat surprising that there is no clear evidence for the existence of a resident fishing community in Arbroath until the late-18th century, since other coastal burghs all had their own fishing fleets from early times. A royal charter granted to the burgh in 1599 allowed the creation of trade incorporations including fishmongers but such a body never formed. There was a fish market around 1682x85, which from Ochterlony's description seems to have been in the vaulted undercroft of the Abbot's House, at the other end of the burgh from the harbour. A list of shore dues fixed by the Town Council in 1691 included two shillings Scots payable on every 'creill' of fish or 'lapsters' brought by cadgers, which

---

1 Compiled by editor from author's roughs.

implies that they were brought in and does not prove the existence of any actual fishing from Arbroath. An area of ground called the Fisheracre was strangely at the northern extremity of the medieval burgh rather than near the shore. Despite this, it can only have been a croft allocated to the fishers.

The fishing community before 1830

Despite the total lack of evidence for any fishing community in medieval times it is hard to believe there were not at least a couple of boats which would have found a ready market for fresh fish in the town as well as the abbey. From 1654, when the parish registers begin, we find a few persons bearing the familiar fisher surnames found in neighbouring communities and in later times in Arbroath. In 1705 a family of Cargills migrated from Auchmithie but were forced to return there. There may have been four boats in the mid-18th century. In 1764 the Kirk Session noted that some fishermen had been lost at sea and that a collection was to be made for their dependents. In 1772 there were three small boats and the Town Council was arranging to pay for the removal of a boat's crew of five men and a boy, with their families, from 'Hacterland, near Bervie' (Catterline) on their producing references of good character, since there were so few fishermen to supply the burgh. But there is no further reference to these fishers and their distinctive surnames, Alexander and Bridgefoord, are not recorded in Arbroath. In 1792 there were 14 active fishers so perhaps two boats under 25 feet with crews of five or six and a smaller yaul. It was said that they made more of a living as pilots than from fishing but this was during the haddock dearth of around 1783–93.

It is more than likely that the few fisher families lived among other seafarers at Old Shorehead and adjacent parts at the foot of Marketgate and the High Street. Wood's town plan of 1822 shows most of Seagate (marked as East Wynd) as being built up on both sides with a slaughter-house at the eastern end. Arbroath then had around 60 trading vessels so merchant mariners must have greatly outnumbered fishers at the 'Fit o' the Toun'. It was estimated by McBain (writing in 1887) that around 1830 there were six boats with their gear, not exceeding £100 in value. The fisherfolk are said to have numbered 80 persons. So there were around 30 active fishers from about 20 families.

The fishing community from around 1830

In 1829 some Auchmithie fishers announced to the Town Council that they were to remove to Arbroath with their families. The Council decided to grant them sites for houses at the Low Common. The fishers, however, ignored this and instead settled at the Fit o' the Toun where the existing fishing community lived. The 1841 census records 49 fishermen and boys (and around ten pilots), some under 18 with seven over the age of 65. This implies around eight or nine boats and yauls. They all lived at Old Shorehead, Seagate (still known as East Wynd) and adjacent parts of the High Street and Marketgate, and in the newly developed South Street and adjacent parts of (West) Newgate. Only a

© The Estate of Colin Gibson

50 Gulls (Swankie's doos) at Arbroath

few merchant mariners lived amongst them. Conversely not a single fisher family lived west of the Brothock: Ladyloan, Grimsby, West Port and (New) Shorehead were the abode of seamen, shipmasters, ship-carpenters, ship-owners, sailmakers, coastguards and Customs men. By 1859 the area east of West Newgate and South Street had been developed and the census figures for 1851 and 1861 show that fisher families by then had also colonised Ladybridge Street and the parts of Marketgate, the High Street and West Newgate about half-way northwards to the line of Horner's Wynd (Commerce Street) and Hill Street. In 1855 there were 69 fishermen and 29 boats and yauls, including eight over 30 feet. There was a fish curer, a cooper and six gutters and packers (presumably packing salt cod), and a total of 148 persons, including those in ancillary industries, involved in fishing. By 1871 there were nearly 90 fishermen and boys and in 1881 no less than 150 fishers operating 92 boats of all sizes. The number of fishermen may have peaked in 1891 with 175 men and 53 boats. Numbers stabilised with 50-odd boats up to 1905.

Around 1916 one-hundred and thirty fishermen had 51 boats, of which over half had auxiliary motors. In 1920 there were 160 fishermen and 60 boats 'almost all motor', only the small inshore yauls would have been sail only, used by older men. In 1928 there were 162 fishermen and 44 boats; 25 were over 30 feet, 11 under 30 feet, all motor, plus eight sailing yauls. In 1930 the Arbroath Yearbook listed 35 boats by name and stated that all were motor, but the Fishery Board accounted for 158 fishers and only 33 boats. The 1931 accounts give 158 fishermen and 37 boats, of which 23 were over 30 feet, ten under 30 feet, all motor, plus four sailing yauls. The yearbook for 1935 listed 24 boats by name but the Fishery Board accounted for 182 fishermen and 32 boats. The reason for these discrepancies is a mystery.

The fishing community from 1939

Due to men being called up during the war, by late 1939 the number of boats had dropped to 26 and in 1940 ninety-seven fishermen operated 27 boats. By late 1945 the fleet had recovered to 126 fishermen and 30 boats and in the early 1950s one-hundred and seventy fishermen and 40-odd boats: seiners, trawlers and liners. Sma' line fishing continued into the 1960s. By the late 1960s there were around 150 fishermen and 45 boats from 30 to 70 feet but no line-fishing by then. A new fish market opened in December 1969. By 1971 there was a fleet of 27 seine-netters and trawlers from 30 to 70 feet, mostly working within 40 miles of home. The oldest was a converted sail-boat, the *Isabella*

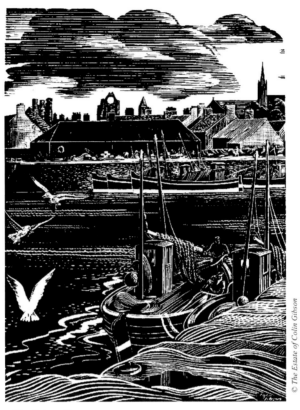

51 *Arbroath*

Fortuna, built in 1890. Smaller boats were used for creel fishing in summer, the full-timers also setting cod nets from them in winter. By 1982 the larger vessels also carried out pair-trawling up to 50 miles from home. This was very successful: landings increased around 1984–87 and several new boats were commissioned. But this method was too successful and catches began to decline although prices were high for a time. When prices fell some turned to trawling for 'praans' (Dublin Bay prawns or Norwegian lobster, *Nephrops sp.*) with two or even three prawn trawls operated from each boat. This also turned out to be too efficient and enormous catches resulted in falling prices. In fact it was so destructive of stocks that it was banned in all coastal waters. So the fleet remained in a state of over-capacity and prices never recovered. Both prawn and white-fishing boats had to operate over a wider area, from Peterhead to North Shields in the 'famine years' of 1989–91. A desperate drop in white-fish catches saw only a dozen auctions in the first six months of 1991 when formerly there could be nearly as many in a single week! The North Sea haddock quota was more than quartered but the fishers believed that it was again 'thick' with haddock.[1]

---

1 Written in 1992. No white fish are currently (2010) landed at Arbroath (though some fishing for shellfish is still practised) and the harbour has been developed as a marina (ed.).

Herring fishing

The New Statistical Account of 1833 makes no mention of the fishing community at all although many other occupations are listed. But under the heading of zoology it was stated that the neighbouring ocean had a plentiful supply of fish, mainly haddock, cod and flounder, with herring and mackerel in their season, while crabs and lobsters were also procured in plenty. So herring fishing had begun, probably from the previous year when Montrose curers first hired fishers in the district to fish off Buchan unless the reference is to occasional local shoals. Arbroath became a herring station in 1858 and in August of that year 20 boats were active, increasing to 39 by 1862. By the 1870s over 50 women were employed as gutters and packers. By 1889 all 19 local herring boats were engaged by Joseph Johnston & Sons of Montrose.

By 1909 herring fishing began to decline and 1912 was the poorest year ever. By 1920 the big 72-foot herring boats were becoming uneconomic and 1925 was the last season they sailed to Yarmouth. A 'drifter', the *Good Friend*, was recorded around 1913–16 but by 1920 had gone. This was presumably a steam drifter since the larger sail boats, with or without engines, would have been drifter/great-liners. No firms invested in steam drifters and families could not afford the larger type which were unsuited in any case to the harbour. The future lay in family-owned motor seine-netters and later also small motor trawlers.

Salmon fishing

The burgh owned the adjacent salmon fishings but little is recorded of them. They were let for a 15-year lease from 1606 for an annual rent of 24 shillings. In 1625, 'together with all other fishing within the haill bounds of the said burgh's liberties of the watter of Brothock', the fishing was leased to Andrew Wood for 13 years for an annual rent of 40 shillings. The lessees were probably burgesses who would have hired salmon fishers to work the net and coble. At that time it seems the fishing was mainly at the mouth of the Brothock. Nothing further seems to be recorded until much later but the fishing may have continued with few breaks into the 19th century. In 1833 it was said that stake-nets had been introduced a few years before with the hope of establishing a salmon station but had not even repaid the cost. There appears to be no evidence as to whether bag-nets were ever tried later. Two or three salmon fishers were resident in the late-19th century but it is uncertain where they worked.

Fisher names

The parish registers, extant from 1654, unfortunately do not give occupations until the 1780s and even then it is uncertain whether 'skipper' implies a fishing skipper or a mariner or seaman; only occasionally from 1787 is anyone specified as a fisherman. The baptism register is most useful as it gives not only the couple's names but also two witnesses, not always relations. So if the couple both have surnames found later, or at roughly the same time in nearby fishertouns, it is fairly safe to assume that they are likely to be fisherfolk. From the 1650s to 1700 we find men called Spink (the predominant name), Caithness and Cargill married to women called Lyell, Allan, Chrystie, Bedy and Mill. From 1700 to the 1780s Spink continues to be common. Other names are Watt, Clark and Kyd, and their wives' names include Inglis, Petrikins (i.e. Peterkin, a surname occurring at Usan in the same period), Torn, Coull and Fairweather. Most of these names are found in fishertouns elsewhere in Angus in the 18th century. Kenny was the name of a family of merchant skippers and shipbuilders but some were married to Allans and Spinks and may have been fishermen. From the 1780s occupation is sometimes given and we have shipowners called Spink, Cargill, Kyd and Smith (married to a Swankie). In 1787 the fisherman Robert Spink is recorded, in 1792 George Duncan and James Spink (the latter married to Helen Smith). In 1813 James Dryden, fisherman had a wife Elizabeth Anderson. In 1815–90 Caithness, Beattie, Marshall, Knight, Skirling, Tait and Moir were pilots or mariners. John Smith, fisher is recorded in 1834 and in 1837 Patrick Swankie and his wife Margaret Spink had a child baptised.

The 1841 census records 49 fishermen and boys. They include 15 Smiths, 12 Cargills, seven Swankies, four Spinks, four Taits, two Bremners, two Swans and, singly, Beattie, Watt and Marshall. In 1871, of nearly 90 active fishermen, almost two-thirds were Smiths; there were 16 Cargills, 15 Swankies, fewer Beatties, Shepherds, Watts, Spinks, Swans and Carries and single instances of Bremner, Tait, Garland, Young and Alexander. In 1891, out of over 170 fishers, Cargills (nearly 50), Smiths and Swankies made up two-thirds, along with Shepherds (12), Beatties (10) and fewer numbers of Watts, Swans, Perts, Bruces, Lindsays and Spinks. The names Eaton, Teviotdale, Annat, Young, Kidd, Ritchie, Tarvet, Robb and Nairn occurred once.

Some variations of the place-name and spelling

Aberbrothoc	1641x50
Aberbrothik	1678
Arbroth	1682x85
Arbroath	1682x85, 1792 to date
Aberbrothock	1682x85, 1794, 1822, 1825
Aberbrothwick	1747x55, 1813

Number of fishermen and boats

Year	Fishers	Boats	Type
1772	15–18?	3	under 25ft
1792	14	3?	2 boats and 1 yaul?
1830s	c.30	6	under 30ft
1841	49	8–9	boats and yauls
1855	69	29	8 large, 14 standard, 7 yauls
1881	150	92	all sizes

Year	Fishers	Boats	Type
1887	160	65–75?	16 large, 39 standard, 10–20 yauls?
1891	175	53	all sizes
1905	?	50+	all sizes
1916	130	51	3 herring/gretlin boats, 29 motor, 1 steam drifter and yauls
1920	160	60	'almost all motor'
1928	162	44	25 motor seiners over 30 feet, 11 liners under 30 feet, 8 sailing yauls
1931	158	37	23 over 30ft, 10 under 30ft, 4 sailing yauls
1940	97	27	motor seiners and liners
1965	177	45	seiners and trawlers
1971	?	30+	27 seiners and trawlers 30–70 feet and smaller creel boats/cod netters
1982	?	35+	35 full-time (over 30 feet) and part-time small creel boats and cod-netters
1980s	?	24–26+	4 large, 12 seiner-trawlers 50–60 feet, 8–10 40–50 feet, and creel boats

East Haven   Panbride NO590362

East Haven was part of the barony of Panmure which constituted the largest part of the parish of Panbride. It was particularly associated with the lands of Scryne which formed the southern half of the barony. The earliest known proprietors of Panmure were the de Valognes, an Anglo-Norman family favoured by King William I (1165–1214). Sir Peter Maule, also of Norman ancestry, married the de Valognes heiress in 1224 and their descendants, Earls of Panmure from 1646 and of Dalhousie from 1860, were to hold the lands, with a short break, to the present day. Around 1214 Philip de Valognes granted the monks of Coupar-Angus an acre of land in his port of Stinchendehavene for a toft to build on, with a toll on fishings and the right to use the haven. The monks' rights in 'Stinkende-havine' were confirmed by the Maules in 1456 and 1490. The 'Monks aker' was recorded in 1611 and the 'Munkis-aiker' in 1622 but its whereabouts are long forgotten. In 1510 half of the lands of Scryne including Roys Heawin were feud off by Maule of Panmure and in 1514 Easterhawyn with its haven was referred to. In 1533 only the fishings and haven were mentioned. In 1541 Thomas Maule was confirmed by the Crown in all his property including Scryne with *orientalem portum de Panmure* (east haven of Panmure) which was created a burgh of barony. In 1600 and 1622 a quarter of the toun

52 Channel through the rocks at East Haven

© The Estate of Colin Gibson

163

and lands of Eisterheven with its fishings was occupied by Andrew Maule of Gauldie, Henry Spink, Henry Clark and Thomas Gray. In 1622 Patrick Maule was confirmed by the Crown in possession of his lands including: *orientalis portus de Panmure* with the seaware, tolls and anchorage dues. The privileges of a burgh of barony and free port of *orientalis portus* or Eister-heaven were also confirmed. In 1622 a quarter part of the lands including the Munkis-aiker was occupied by an Arthur Boyes. In 1632 Eistertoun of Panmure with the free port and haven belonging was confirmed in possession of Patrick Maule. The barony and haven remained in the hands of the Maules until James Maule the 4th Earl was dispossessed for being a leader of the 1715–16 Jacobite Rebellion but his son managed to buy back the lands in 1764.

The community before 1800

It seems that Stinking-haven was a part-farming, part-fishing community around 1214. This would appear to make it perhaps the oldest recorded fishing community in Scotland. In early times the fishers probably had some duties on the land, becoming more or less full-time fishers in later times. In 1541 East Haven was erected into a burgh of barony with rights granted to the inhabitants to buy and sell goods, to be burgesses and to elect bailies annually, to have a market cross and a weekly market on Tuesdays. It was also permitted an annual fair to last eight days from St Luke's Day (18 October), with rights to charge tolls and fees. The Maules were also empowered to make hereditary leases of burgage plots. It is doubtful if much resulted from this, as in the case of many other such burghs of barony. The coastal plain of Angus did, however, produce surplus grain in good years and grain was certainly exported from Montrose in the 1540s, so it is possible that Panmure estate could also have produced a grain surplus then. Dried fish is another likely surplus, but there is simply no evidence as to whether these commodities were exported, or whether coal was brought in at that time. In 1622 the right to have a burgh of barony at East Haven was renewed in favour of Patrick Maule of Panmure but the weekly market day was changed to Friday and an additional eight-day annual fair was to be held from 1 August. Maule was also granted the right to charge tolls and anchorage dues on vessels using the haven. This was renewed in 1632 so a modicum of trade may be implied by then. The inhabitants of East Haven around 1600–22 may largely have been peasants and fishermen. Two of those named, Spink and Clark, had surnames found among fishers in the parish somewhat later. Andrew Maule of Gauldie and Arthur Boyes may have been farmers descended from the petty gentry of the parish to judge from their surnames. Such people could have combined agriculture with commerce or inn-keeping as was quite usual in rural areas at the time but there is simply no evidence.

The renewal of the status of burgh of barony in 1622 and 1632 is significant. At that time Patrick Maule was engaged in improving his estate by various means. In 1622 a great many trees were planted, possibly for sheltering crops as well as for appearance, since the landscape at that time was predominantly treeless. There were limited and spasmodic exports of grain from 1600 to 1630 after which they became larger and more regular until disrupted by the Civil Wars of 1639–51. Grain shipments through East Haven revived by the 1660s, the largest proportion going to Leith. There was a notable increase in the amount of arable land on the estate in the 1670s and 1680s, Panmure Mains alone had 100 acres of arable by then. From the 1640s onwards cattle were also being bred for sale in Perth, Dundee, Arbroath and St Andrews. The latter destination must have involved shipping. There were several upstream ferries across the Tay at Broughty and Dundee which may have been used, although a direct route across the Tay is as likely. The income generated enabled George Maule, 3rd Earl of Panmure to build a new house of Panmure in 1678 and a new parish church incorporating a laird's loft above a family burial vault.

In his description of Angus of 1678, Robert Edwards, minister of Murroes, stated that having completed his new house of Panmure, the earl 'for the good of his country, and the convenience of sailors … has begun to build a harbour in his estate, to the east of the mouth of the Tay, where vessels are invited to take shelter, when by contrary winds they are prevented from getting up the river'. Edwards published a map of the county at the same time inscribed in honour of his patron, the Earl of Panmure. The map shows the intended harbour as consisting of a short pier on the west and another longer one to the east, returning at right angles to the shore, leaving an entrance on the south-west. It seems Panmure may have been seeking contributions towards the cost of his harbour in having its public value proclaimed by Edwards. As early as 1611 however Robert Maule, the family historian, had commented, 'This hewine is very commodious for small fische botes and might easlie be maid fit for gryter vessels be cutting away twa small crags in the entrie thearof, as I heawe hard men of experience say'. It is doubtful if the harbour got much beyond the stage of planning. Even if destroyed by storms, some signs would surely have remained. In 1793 James Trail, translator of Edwards' Latin and a son of Panbride manse whose father and grandfather had served the parish, suggested that the harbour only got as far as some stones being collected. He also expressed regret that it had not been built and said that a small quay at either East or West Haven would have been beneficial by then since the whole neighbourhood was supplied with coals and lime via these havens. Vessels could not land in the winter and even found difficulty at times in summer with south-east winds. Unfortunately neither Edwards or Trail clearly indicate whether trading vessels carried any goods out of East Haven. The earl had granaries at East Haven in the 1670s, but since he dealt directly with merchants from Edinburgh and elsewhere there was little need or opportunity for resident merchants. It is also somewhat doubtful if the burgh ever functioned as intended with elected bailies, markets and fairs although it was referred to as Maulesburgh or Mauleshaven into the mid-18th century. Around 1682x85 however it was referred to as Fishertoun of Panmure, which probably more accurately described its nature. The export of grain to Leith continued however, and from 1689 to Glasgow, shipped to Bo'ness or Grangemouth and then carted overland before the Forth and Clyde Canal opened in 1790. In 1715, at the beginning of the Jacobite Rebellion, James, the 4th Earl, had sailed from Leith to East Haven in a small vessel.

The parish registers, extant from 1693, are no help regarding the variety of occupations practised in East Haven although the surnames later common among fishers and mariners occur. By the late-18th century East Haven certainly seems to have been mainly a fishing community, although apparently having an inn and a few essential resident tradesmen and retailers. In 1790 the fishers paid 5 merks Scots annually, the equivalent of the five shillings and eight pence Stg. specified in 1833, for the privilege of fishing. The number of boats is not recorded but two seems likely, then and in earlier times. Shortly before 1800 there was a trading sloop operated by William Spink. Coal and lime were imported but no mention of grain exports was made then. By around 1800 the former lands of East Haven had been incorporated into East Scryne farm, the fishers having long been full time with little time to cultivate more than a kailyard. The scant evidence suggests that East Haven was of a similar size and social composition to West Haven in the late-18th century.

The community from 1800

The fisher community grew gradually after 1800. In 1833 there were three boats, each with a crew of five or six and so around 16 to 17 active fishers. There were probably around a dozen or more fisher families forming about 50 to 60 persons out of a population of 118. By 1841 there were 22 active fishers and possibly four boats by then with 15 fisher households out of 34 households in the village. There was an inn and brewery and, apart from the innkeeper and the brewer, grocers, a baker, a cooper, weavers, railwaymen and farm workers. A sloop or two operated out of the haven in 1833 and probably later in the century. The growth of the community exactly matched that of West Haven into the 1840s. Unlike it, where most of the fishers were native with only three surnames borne by 13 out of 16 fisher families, at East Haven, out of 15 fisher families, only three bore surnames found in the parish in the 18th century while 11 surnames were current. So it seems there must have been an influx of newcomers after about 1815 but none of the new surnames were the better-known ones from other Angus and Mearns fishertouns.

The parallel growth with West Haven was not to continue. In 1848 scarlet fever killed a sixth of the population, probably children mainly, and in the following year cholera was as fatal. This permanently inhibited the potential growth of the community. By 1851 the population was 145 in 38 households but in 1855 there were only 12 fishermen and five boats as compared to twice as many in West Haven. At its peak around 1881 East Haven still had only half as much fishing effort as its neighbour (eight boats and 15 fishermen) despite the advantage of a railway station. Why the epidemics hit East Haven so much harder than West Haven is a mystery. Poor quality housing and the overshadowing of many houses by the railway embankment have been suggested. Photographs taken in 1870 show that most of the houses had thatched roofs and some had the gable built of turf and wooden lums for peat rather than coal fires, but this was not unusual at the time. Photographs of West Haven taken in 1880 show slated and tile roofs with thatch only on a derelict abandoned house. In 1881 there were 38 inhabited houses at East Haven, no more than 30 years earlier.

Before the railway came in 1838 the road continued past Long Row to Elliot. The layout of the village was very different to that of around 1900. In addition to Long Row, Station Row and Shore Row which exist today there were two short rows on either side of the road next to Station Row and the centre was occupied by a large rambling inn and brewery. There were no station buildings until 1859. Just before 1880 the Earl of Dalhousie had six new cottages built to the north of the village, called Tankerville Row in honour of the countess, a daughter of Lord Tankerville of County Durham. Despite the toll of disease the village was still a bustling place in the mid-19th century; the inn, brewery and a bakery functioned around 1860 and there was a resident fish curer. Apart from fisherfolk there were weavers, bleachers, farmworkers and railwaymen, some of them members of fisher families. Busy scenes occurred, the fishers sat sheiling mussels, baiting or redding lines by their doors. Carts travelled back and forth to the railway station or from coal sloops beached at the shore. After the mid-1880s the fishing community began to decline gradually with the abandonment of herring fishing. An ageing workforce with few, if any, new recruits continued sma' line and creel fishing. By 1895 there were only nine or ten active fishers and perhaps four boats or yauls up to about 1914. In 1892 East Haven was described as giving 'a most unfavourable impression from the sight of so many dilapidated houses'. There was also 'the tottering fabric of what was formerly an inn, which enjoyed a certain amount of favour in olden times, and the mouldering walls of a brewery'. By 1895 there were only 28 inhabited houses so by then the inn, brewery and two short rows north of Station Row had been demolished. A new feature was the building of villas between the railway and the shore to the south and east of East Haven by middle class Dundonians who travelled to work by train. There were three in 1895, about a dozen by 1920, socially and geographically separated from the original population of fishers and ordinary working folk. Between the wars, after 1927 when one fisherman aged 67 had tragically been killed by a train, there were only three old fishermen, the brothers Sandy, Jeemie and William Herd, using two yauls, *Rachel* and *Sisters*, alternately, mainly at creel fishing. Two of the brothers seem to have carried on until about the end of the 1939–45 war. Since then there have only been a few part-time creel fishers, not all resident. But the village was still a fairly lively place between the wars with numerous children and there were three small shops, one also serving teas to visitors while an Easthaven & District Social Club was started up by the station-master in the late 1920s. In the early 1930s Princesses Elizabeth and Margaret used to be brought from Glamis Castle to the beach to play mid-week when there were seldom any other visitors to witness them, Lunan Bay was another coastal spot they were taken to. The village became much quieter after the war, only the post office remained for a time while the railway station closed in 1967.

Salmon fishing

There are no early references to this. It only seems to have been started shortly before 1841 with the introduction of bag-nets and appears to have ceased by the 1930s. It was re-introduced in the early 1980s but had little success and was given up.

Fisher names

The surnames Spink and Clark were recorded in 1600. The former also occurred at Arbroath in 1600 and was later common at Auchmithie. The latter name is recorded in the parish in the 18th century but from 1800 only in West Haven. From 1690 the parish registers record the fisher names Watt, Paton and Teviotdale, known later at Ferryden and Arbroath. In the 18th century names known later to be fisher surnames, Lyall and Caithness, are found intermarried with Spinks, Clarks and Watts. By 1841 there was little continuity and many more surnames, suggesting that there had been some migration into East Haven. There were four Scotts, two Herds, a Lyall and a Crawford and seven other surnames each borne by a single family. By 1891 Herd, Ramsay and Lyall were names borne by more than one family while Scott, Crawford, Esplin and three or four other names occurred. By the 1920s and 30s the last fishers bore the names of Herd and Ramsay.

Some variations of the place-name and spelling

Stinchendehavene	1214
Ross Heawine	1380
Stinkende-havine	1456, 1490
Roys Heawin	1510
Easterhawyn	1514
Orientalis portus de Panmure (East Haven of Panmure)	1541, 1622, 1682x85
Fishertowne of Skryne	1599
Eisterheven/Easter-heavin/Eister-heaven	1600, 1622
East Hewine/Ross Heawen	1611
Eistertoun of Panmure	1632
Fishertoun of Panmure	1682x85
Mauleshaven	17th–18th century
Maulsburgh	1747x55
East Haven of Panbride	1800
East Haven	1833 to date
Locally the Ha'en	

Number of fishermen and boats

Year	Fishermen	Boats	Type
1790	10–12?	2?	under 25ft
1833	16–17?	3	under 25ft
1841	22	4?	23 to 30ft?
1855	12	5	1 large, 2 standard, 2 yauls
1881	15	8	all sizes
1895	9–10	4–5?	yauls
1910	8	4–5?	yauls
1928	3	2	yauls
1938	2	2	yauls
1944	2	1	yaul

West Haven   Panbride NO572346

This was part of the barony of Panbride which belonged to the Norman Malherbe family in the 13th century but changed hands and reverted to the Crown several times. In 1341 King David II granted it to the Boys or Boece family who were later to hold parts of the barony lands as petty gentry farmers into the 17th century. The barony as a whole changed nominal superiors many times but parts were feued and sub-feued to resident landholders. In 1492 John Forbes of Brux, who held part of the lands, granted a quarter part of Seaton of Panbride to an Alexander Boys. This is the earliest reference to what must have been West Haven. In 1507 the Crown granted the nominal superiority of Panbride to Lord Crichton of Sanquhar. The Scrymgeours held it from them but from 1513 into the 17th century members of two families called Boys and Ramsay were actual possessors of parts of the barony. In 1522 Robert Carnegie of Kinnaird owned specific parts of the barony, including parts of Kirkton with the haven belonging. In 1568 John Carnegie owned Kirkton of Panbride and the Ratoun Row Hevin with the acres and fishings belonging. The Carnegies of Kinnaird, Earls of Southesk from 1640, continued to own the superiority of the barony for about 200 years. The heirs came to be granted the barony and styled 'of Panbride'. In 1653 the barony lands included Rotten Row with the port and haven. In 1682x85 Panbride was listed as a fishertoun by Ochterlony. In 1716 the earl was forfeited for his part in the Jacobite rebellion but in 1764 the lands were bought back by the heir and sold to the adjoining proprietor, William Maule, Earl of Panmure, in exchange for lands nearer his own estate of Kinnaird near Brechin.

The community before 1800

The natural haven may well have been settled as early as its near neighbour East Haven. The Seaton of Panbride of 1492 would seem to have been a fermtoun as well as a fishertoun with its own 'acres' or arable land attached, later West Haven farm. The fishers probably had some ties to the land in the middle ages and later may have had crofts to

169

© The Estate of Colin Gibson

53 West Haven

work up to the 18th century. Fishings, mentioned first in 1507, are also mentioned in 1551, 1552, 1568 and 1767. The settlement was regarded as a part of the Kirkton of Panbride, or more particularly in 1568 and 1653 as being attached to Rottenrow. This was a farm constituting part of the Kirkton lying half a mile north of West Haven, the site now built over. In 1682x85 simply referred to as 'Panbryd', the full name at that time may have been Haven of, or Fishertoun of, Panbride. It was only after 1764 when acquired by the Earl of Panmure that it was recorded as 'West Haven of Panbride' or simply 'West Haven', although its neighbour had been known as the Easter Haven as early as 1514.

Nothing before the early-19th century indicates the number of boats and fishers but it is likely that there was only a single boat and crew of five or six in early times, possibly two boats and crews by the mid-18th century, implying a possible ten to 12 active fishers and a maximum total fisher population of 40 to 50. There were also farm workers and possibly a few tradesmen by about 1800 such as weavers, a tailor and a shoemaker, while there was also an inn. A gravestone in Panbride kirkyard commemorates George Caithness R.N., innkeeper at West Haven, who died in 1812 aged only 35. Another stone from the same decade records John Caithness, shipmaster in Haven of Panbride and has a carving of a coasting sloop such as carried coal into the haven in summer. A third, dated 1800 and also carved with a sloop, was in memory of Thomas Clark, shipmaster in West Haven. There were three sloops of just under 40 tons burden in the parish around 1790 so it appears two of them belonged to West Haven. The settlement is indicated on Ainslie's map of 1794 as two short rows of buildings flanking the main road adjacent to the farm, with another cluster near the haven but no long rows as found later. The whole population was probably then little more than 75 persons, certainly no more than 100.

The community since 1800

The community, like many others, began to grow after 1815. By 1833 there were three boats with a crew of five or six each, so there were 16 or 17 active fishers; but the total population of West Haven combined with the hamlet of Gallowlaw to the west was 305, of which less than a third could have belonged to fisher families. The population was quite varied in the 19th century although railway and bleachfield workers, resident from 1838 or soon after, were often members of fisher families, as were farm workers. Panbride Bleachfield, on the coast between East and West Havens, employed many men and women in the surrounding villages from its inception soon after the coming of the railway in 1838 until shortly after 1918. There were other works in Carnoustie employing residents of the village. There were also by the 1830s: five coastguards, masons, weavers, yarnwinders, seamstresses, a fish curer and merchant, a cooper, a grocer, salmon fishers and others. Before 1840 there had been a baker, and in 1841 there were also a sewing-school mistress and watchmaker. The West Haven Inn, which stood on the main road, had its own brewery and was redeveloped to become the Dalhousie Hotel, but closed by the 1890s. From 1838 the railway line separated the farm, inn and houses along the main road (merging into Gallowlaw on the west) from the fisher houses facing the shore. By 1860 these were mainly in three rows, East Row, Long Row and Mariner Row, and with few exceptions were single storey but and ben cottages.

In 1833 there were four trading vessels of 45 to 65 tons burden in the parish, two or more of which must have belonged to West Haven. A hundred years later old folk could still remember the smart little sloops which had brought coal into the haven, although by then they had long been put out of commission by steamers and the railway. The sloops were only unloaded as farmers and others came with carts to buy a cartload at a time, so for a week or so carts crowded Carlogie Road. Once a year the schooner *Agnes* came with a cargo of lime. All these vessels would simply have landed on the beach and been re-launched at high tide. Before the building of the railway in 1838, when it had to close, many of the boats and small sloops sailing out of both West and East Haven had probably been built at a boatyard belonging to Thomas Ferrier, 'carpenter', half a mile to the west of West Haven, the site of a later railway goods yard opposite the Station Hotel, Carnoustie. Sloops landed with timber at the mouth of the Lochty Burn, where rocks give way to sand, and the boats were launched by way of a 'rude canal' cut to the shore.

In 1841 there were 23 fishermen and boys so a minimum of four boats. By 1855 there was only one more fisher but no less than 14 boats: four over 30 feet, four standard boats and six yauls, showing that specialisation in different fishings had begun with involvement in herring fishing by the 1840s. Fishing effort peaked around 1881 with 31 fishers and 15 boats. It seems that herring fishing had been abandoned by the 1890s since there were only 13 or 14 active fishers and 24 families of fisher origin resident out of a total of 45 households. By 1900 there were only seven small yauls worked by one or two men apiece at inshore creel fishing in summer and white-fishing in winter with hand lines or sma' lines. In 1910 there were only nine fishermen operating four or five yauls and only 14 householders with the typical local fisher surnames. The fishermen were all middle-aged or elderly so the First World War did not speed the decline. By 1928 two boats were worked by six men and in the late 1930s there was still one boat crewed by two old men but none by 1944, although some part-time fishing seems to have been carried out then, and since the war. With the decline of fishing and the closure of the Panbride Bleachfield after 1918, which had employed many folk in the village, there were very few manual workers left in the village and more owner-occupier professional folk settled. Socially, West Haven became a residential suburb of Carnoustie, into which burgh it had formally been incorporated since 1889. Carnoustie has grown eastwards south of the railway in recent times to meet the old fisher cottages but these still retain their distinctive character around the haven. A more modern feature is the large number of weekend beach huts.

The coastguard station and life-saving

The West Haven station was probably founded by around 1830. The officer and four boatmen and their families originally lived in the village. A look-out tower was built to the west of the village and is still in use. Initially they would have had a small boat for general service, life-saving not being a prime function. Fewer ships were wrecked on the rocky coast or on the Tay sandbanks after the Abertay lightship was established in 1877. However by the latter part of the century life-saving facilities had been established at West Haven. Not only was there a rocket-cart, kept in a shed, but a life-boat kept in a purpose-built boat-house, which came into existence shortly before 1892 and belonged to the coastguard service. A new purpose-built block had also been built to house the coastguards and their families behind the look-out tower: it and the boat-house behind East Row are built of the same materials and in the same style. The RNLI have no record of a lifeboat at West Haven so this boat may have been of the 'surfboat' type as kept at Gourdon for inshore rescue, supplementing the Buddon Ness lifeboat before 1893. The look-out was connected by electric telegraph by this time, prior to that semaphore or other visual signals must have been used. The station was only connected by telephone with the lifeboats at Broughty Ferry and Arbroath from 1925. The lifeboat may have been scrapped during the 1914–18 war when the coastguard were called up for active service and the West Haven station apparently became a radio station manned by naval personnel. The rocket cart continued in use right up to about 1939–40. It was originally drawn by the best pair of horses from West Haven farm, latterly by a motor lorry. Since the war, coordination of rescue services became the station's main function. From the 1950s more powerful lifeboats and a helicopter at Leuchars were available. Until around 1980 there were three full-time coastguards at West Haven, since reduced to one full-time sector officer assisted by auxiliaries using Land Rovers to cover the coast between stations.

Salmon fishing

There seem to be no early references to salmon fishing, although a net and coble fishing would seem feasible from the haven. Salmon fishers were resident in West Haven and adjacent Gallowlaw by 1841 and a bag-net fishing seems to have been carried out until the 1930s. There was another fishing with a bothy close by Carnoustie station to the west of the village.

Fisher names

The parish registers of Panbride, extant from 1690, do not give occupations or places of residence until about 1800 and there was probably always some movement, especially by intermarriage, between the two fishertouns of the parish. The name Clark, found at East Haven as early as 1600, is found in the parish throughout the 18th century. By 1800, and right up to the final demise of its fisher community in the 1930s, Clarks are only found in West Haven. Other fisher names occurring at an early date, such as Lyall, Caithness and Spink, were probably from East Haven, as is the case after 1800. The name Watt, better known up the coast, occurs in the 18th century but is not located specifically. The name Paris only appears from the 1790s. By 1841 Caithness was the commonest fisher name in West Haven, followed by Bisset and Clark, with other individuals called Ramsay, Paris and Peters. By the 1890s there were three Bissets, two Ramsays, two Simpsons, a Caithness, a Peters and several new names of single individuals. By the 1920s–30s the only active fishers bore the names Bisset, Clark and Ramsay.

Some variations of the place-name and spelling

Seaton of Panbride	1492
Ratoun Row Hevin	1568
(Haven of/Fishertoun of) Panbryde	1682x85
West Haven of Panbride	after 1764
West Haven	1794, 1800, 1812, 1833 to date
Haven of Panbride	1800

Number of fishermen and boats

Year	Fishers	Boats	Type
1790	10–12?	2?	under 23 ft
1833	16–17	3	under 23 ft
1841	23	4?	23–30 ft?
1855	24	14	4 large, 4 standard, 6 yauls
1881	31	15	all sizes
1895	13	7–10?	boats and yauls?
1900	10–12?	7	yauls
1910	9	4–5	yauls
1928	6	2	yauls
1938	2	1	yaul

Buddon Ness salmon fishings [1]   Barry/Monifieth NO5633 to NO5032

The valuable sands fishings at the mouth of the Tay have been exploited since the middle ages. By the beginning of the 19th century the fishings were pursued largely by Maule of Panmure. The introduction of stake-nets in 1802 and the use of ice for packing brought about a huge increase in their value. (See under Broughty Ferry for more details.)

Maule owned land on both the east and west sides of the Barry Buddon peninsula while the central section, a broad strip tapering towards the coast, was the property of David Hunter of Pitskelly. A plan of 1826 shows nine salmon stations around Buddon Ness, some fished by net and coble, others by stake-net. By 1843 this had been reduced to five.

A number of salmon bothies once stood along the coastline; most of them were probably simple huts but a stone house built by Hunter of Pitskelly in the 1820s later also became a bothy. Near to this was an ice-house, built probably in the 1830s and serving the single fishing station on Hunter's relatively short coastal frontage.

In 1817 the Hon. William Maule of Panmure was involved in a dispute with the Duke of Atholl over his rights to use stake-nets (which he, Maule, had introduced to the area). The duke and other proprietors of riparian fishings on the Tay claimed that such netting was illegal within the firth. The complaint was upheld and the outcome was the drawing of a line to mark the end of the estuary and therefore the limits of stake-net fishing. Two blocks of sandstone were placed to mark the line; one, known as the Sea Stane, is in a field near St Andrews, the other, the Chancellor's Stone, was erected at Buddon Ness, though it was later buried under windblown sand. In 1842 the fishing was said to be much decreased because of this.

In 1853 Fox Maule Ramsay, Baron Panmure and later 11th Earl of Dalhousie, was able to purchase the Pitskelly estate and bring the whole of Barry Buddon into single ownership. In 1891–93, however, the War Department compulsorily purchased the estate, along with the salmon-fishing rights, to secure its future as a military training ground. The fishing rights continued to be let by the War Department. From 1927 they were let to the Tay Salmon Fisheries Company, who also rented, and then purchased, the Panmure fishings at Carnoustie. By 1939 the fishings were abandoned as uneconomic although the TSFC continued to hold them unfished, for the benefit of the river's salmon stocks, until the late 1970s.

Buddon lifeboat

In 1830 the first Tay lifeboat was established by public subscription at Buddon Ness; it had 12 rowing and two steering oars and could hold 25 to 30 besides the crew. A regular crew was not enrolled until the 1860s but in emergencies West Haven and Broughty Ferry

---

1 Largely contributed by the editor, with grateful thanks to Colin R McLeod. The paragraph on the lifeboat is by the author.

fishers and coastguards turned out. The first regularly constituted rescue society, the River Tay Lifeboat and Humane Society, was formed on 5 June 1837 and ran for 13 years despite lack of funds to reward crews. In 1848 a larger lifeboat was stationed on the south side of the river at Green Scalp, two miles downstream from Tayport, but this was of little use and it was transferred to Buddon Ness according to Malcolm. A regular pilot service

54 *Buddon lighthouses*

from about 1850 reduced risks to shipping and in this year the Lifeboat Society handed over their assets to the Joint Committee of the Harbour Trustees and Fraternity of Masters

55 *Ruined WWII defences on Monifieth beach*

and Seamen in Dundee on Pilotage. Soon afterwards problems arose when the railway company who ran the ferry from Broughty refused free use of the ruined castle for the storage of signals, rocket equipment etc. The Joint Committee carried on until 1861 but money was still inadequate and they applied to the RNLI. The Dundee branch was formed on 19 December 1861, a boathouse was erected at Broughty and two coxwains, John Knight and George Anderson, Broughty fishers, were ap-

pointed to enrol crews and month about to look after the Buddon boat. The first Broughty lifeboat, Mary Hartley, arrived at the new station in March 1862. The railway ferries

assisted at launches by towing the lifeboat downriver before a motor lifeboat was installed in 1909. In 1865 electric telegraph was established between Buddon lighthouses and Broughty Lifeboat Station. An average of one rescue a year was achieved by the boats but the Buddon Ness boat was now deemed to be of little use and was removed on 17 February 1894.

56 *View up the Tay estuary from Buddon Ness*

North Ferry of Portincrag / East Ferry / Broughty Ferry [*]

The sheltered bay formerly known as North Ferry of Portincrag, with a shingle beach protected by the projecting rock to the east, forms a natural haven, while Monifieth Sands farther east forms one of the largest mussel beds in Angus; so it is likely that white-fishing has been practised here from a very early period. There were also rich salmon fishings. The haven was also the site of the easternmost ferry on the Tay from medieval times, hence the name East Ferry recorded in 1587, 1611, 1793 and in more recent times.

Around 1188 Gillebrigte, Earl of Angus, granted land at Portincrag to Arbroath Abbey to build a hospice or inn. This was confirmed by his son Earl Gilchrist around 1201x07 with his fishings from the Craig westwards and by the Crown in 1213. These would be salmon fishings. Malcolm Earl of Angus also confirmed the grant around 1218 and the original grant was again confirmed by the Crown in 1243. The hospice, like those on the Forth at Queensferry (established c.1090) and Earlsferry (1150–77), was probably intended for poor pilgrims, but in this case not to St Andrews but to St Thomas's Abbey, Arbroath. There is however not a shred of evidence that the hospice was ever established. The abbey did however continue to own land and fishings at North Ferry of Portincrag, to give it its full name, although it was referred to mostly as Portincrag or North Ferry (Tayport, at the south side where the ferryman and boat were based, was originally South Ferry of Portincrag). The name has often been misinterpreted as partan craig, meaning 'crab rock', but the early spellings are always Portincrag or Portyncrag from Gaelic *port na creige*, meaning 'port of the rock' or 'rock haven'; so the name refers not to the projecting rock but to the natural haven to the west, protected by it from the open sea and tides. The rock itself continued to belong to the earls of Angus until 1490 when it was given to the first Lord Gray; the castle was rebuilt by 1496. It was known as the rock of Bruchtie or Brughty, later Broughty, its only asset a valuable salmon fishing attached although the lands of Balgillo served as an estate between 1491 and 1650, both then owned by the Lords Gray who occasionally lived in the castle. The rock was sold by the 8th Lord Gray to the Fotheringhams of Powrie in 1666.

Leases by Arbroath Abbey of Portincrag or North Ferry are recorded between 1433 and 1531. They reveal that it was a farm or arable land with salmon fishings. The fishings and parts of the farm were leased separately at times, the rents usually being paid in barrels of salmon or grain according to what was leased. The earliest evidence for the existence of a white-fisher community is from 27 April 1477 when an indenture was drawn up between Alexander Luvel of Ballumbie and the abbot and convent of Arbroath, following on an agreement reached in 1476. Luvel conceded to the abbot's white-fishers of North Ferry of Portincrag (*passagio boriali de Portyncrag*) the right to dig, collect

---

[*] Compiled by editor from author's notes.

© The Estate of Colin Gibson

and take bait on the sands and seashore within his lands in the parish of Monifieth on condition that for every small line (*linia gracili*) used they would pay Luvel and his successors six white fish. In return the abbey granted Luvel a lease of the teinds of Murroes. In addition it was agreed that neither would allow each other's fishers to settle on their land without licence, undertaking to return them, if they should attempt the move, within fifteen days on pain of five merks damages. Luvel's

57 A bait-digger on Monifieth sands

fishers are likely to have been salmon fishers as there is no suitable place for, nor any record of, a white-fisher settlement on Monifieth Bay. They may have dredged mussels to supply visiting white-fishers, a resource exploited by the Broughty fishers until fairly recent times.

North Ferry, or parts of it, came into the hands of the Fotheringhams of Powrie, held in feu of the Regality of Arbroath in the 16th and 17th centuries. On 10 November 1579 Thomas Fotheringham sold his eighth part of 'Bruchtie', occupied by George Keill, to his brother-in-law Patrick Lindsay of the Byres. A John Michaelson in 'Breuchtie' was a witness. Although 'Bruchtie' strictly denoted the castle, it must here refer to the *ville* or fermtoun of North Ferry since the castle had no arable land attached and in any case belonged to Lord Gray. In 1603 'North Ferrie near the castle of Bruchtie' was feued by the Commendator of the Regality of Arbroath to John Hamilton of Blair and his wife Jean Fairny with its teinds, rabbit warrens (*terris cunicularis*) and fishings in the Tay. In 1608 a charter of the Regality of Arbroath included North Ferry with salmon and white-fishings, the first evidence of the latter since 1477. The same was recorded again in 1641, 1642 and 1662. These charters were only of the feudal superiority, the place still seems to have belonged to the Fotheringhams, who would have leased the lands and fishings. The lands seem to have been a fairly small area, from the parish boundary around the foot of modern Church Street to Castle Green and as far back as about Brook Street. In 1666 the Fotheringhams bought the rock and castle, with its salmon fishings, from the 8th Lord Gray but the land was uncultivable and the castle abandoned and ruinous by the 18th century, a mere landmark. In 1682x85 Northferrie was listed as a fishertoun by Ochterlony.

By the mid-18th century North Ferry was held by the Hunters of Burnside from the Fotheringhams, but by 1767 it was sub-infeued to Maule of Panmure and actually held in liferent by an Edinburgh solicitor. In 1742 the farmer of Balgillo held a joint lease of North Ferry with half of the teind fish of the three fish boats there. Since the salmon fishings were leased separately the three boats must have been white-fish boats. North Ferry was then said to have consisted of 'a few steadings of houses known by the name of the Ferry', with the derelict castle and sandy ground, 'the dwelling place of rabbits' (the *terris cunicularis* of 1603), on the site of Castle Green and Beach Crescent. About 1790 Maule of Panmure began to feu off plots to weavers and other 'mechanics'. The settlement at that time was later described as half a dozen fishers' huts but it was a little more than that: already by 1793 the population numbered 230, perhaps a third to a quarter of which was formed by fisher families. Ainslie's map of 1794 shows 'E. Ferry' (in distinction from 'W. Ferry' in Dundee parish) as four blocks of buildings near the shore on the site of modern Fisher Street from Church Street only about as far along as David Street or Fort Street, with another two blocks behind them at the eastern end.

Already 'multitudes' resorted every summer to West Ferry and East Ferry for the newly fashionable health fad of sea bathing and residents profited by letting houses and otherwise catering for the moneyed class. General Hunter, who inherited Balgillo and the feu of North Ferry around then, by 1801 had a map engraved of the proposed 'New Town at the North Ferry' on a grid plan devised by John Ley, schoolmaster of Monifieth. From around this time the name 'Broughty' became the official or usual name; Broughty Ferry was used in the parish registers in 1807. From 1839 the railway allowed the Dundee middle classes to develop the place into a fashionable suburb; by 1842 the population had grown to nearly 2,200 inhabitants including West Ferry and it had its own church, a secession chapel, eight schools and a great variety of trades and shops. By 1891 the population had risen to 9,256 and there were seven churches and nine schools, several public buildings including a library, several hotels and all the usual conveniences and institutions of a late Victorian burgh which may or may not have been considered an advantage by the fisher community.

Up to the middle of the 19th century small barks or sloops were accustomed to land near the Ferry and on Monifieth Sands to take on grain and to land lime and coal. The ferry itself was operated from the South Ferry (Tayport) end, and carried only passengers. From 1872 the North British Railway Company built a harbour and railway ferry, the latter operated to 1887. By 1900 about 40 trading vessels entered the harbour annually.

The fishing community

The fishing community must always have been sub-tenants, renting houses and small plots of land from the farmer tenants of North Ferry, and even in the 20th century very few owned their own houses. The houses have always been in the area of Fisher Street, with the boats, until the demise of the community, conveniently drawn up no distance from their doors, more fortunate than many white-fishers. The indenture of 1477 would seem to imply restrictions on their movements within the parish but not necessarily outwith it; rather than being serfs it is likely that they sub-let from farmer tenants who themselves only held 19-year leases. Although the abbey valued their continued presence for a supply of fish, only teind fish were payable to the abbey, which may have purchased any surplus they required. From thc latc-12th century they may have supplied Dundee, always their most important market, as well as Perth and smaller inland towns like Forfar.

The later growth of the fishing community had little to do with the development of Broughty as a burgh, the main stimulus must have been the demand from Dundee itself, too far from the best fishing grounds. From an estimated 12 to 15 fisher families in the second half of the 18th century and 50-odd in 1842, the fisher community increased to 71 families by 1895. By that time the fishers inhabited not only Fisher Street and the beach area to the east but the streets and lanes off there back to King Street, where the odd mariner and sailmaker lived but no fishers. They lived in a compact block around Fisher Street, Dundas Street, Fort Street, Chapel Lane, Bell's Lane, David Street and Ambrose Street, their boats and paraphernalia littering the beach in that area, and lived their own way of life oblivious to the genteel streets and inquisitive tourists around them.

Salmon fishing

Leases by Arbroath Abbey of North Ferry of Portincrag include salmon fishings from an early period. The rock itself, the property of the Earls of Angus until 1490, later Lord Gray, had the valuable salmon fishing as its only asset. A lease of the salmon fishing of Bruchtie to Robert Fleschaer in 1594 included a vaulted fish house. In 1682x85 the salmon fishings in Monifieth parish were listed as Kirkton (belonging to the Laird of Ballumbie, Panmure's brother), Grange (Durham), Balgillo (Hunter), Broughty Castle (Fotheringham) along with several other ancient fishings east of Broughty.

In 1793 the salmon rent of Monifieth parish was £150, the fish being sent to the London market. When stake-nets were first set up by Maule of Panmure, on the shore east of Broughty in 1802, catches increased dramatically: in 1825 a total of 729 fish was taken at one tide. Two ice-houses were installed at Broughty, including one in the castle ditch. During the 19th century, however, salmon fishing in the area declined to such an

© The Estate of Colin Gibson

58 Broughty Castle and Fisher Street in the 19th century

extent that the rent fell from £1500 in 1825 to £345 in 1845, and by 1850 only one salmon fisher resided in Broughty Ferry. The decline was attributed to new laws concerning stake-nets, which forbade their use in estuary fishing, and to the concentration of salmon fishing in the upper reaches of the Tay. The Broughty salmon fishings, however, despite the concerns of riparian proprietors and conflicting interests along the sea front, continued to be leased and worked, mainly by Joseph Johnston & Sons, up to around 1900, after which they were leased by the Tay Salmon Fisheries Company in order not to be worked.

Fisher names

The parish registers of Monifieth record the names Carmichael (1654), Lawson, Wilson and Anderson 'in the Ferry' in the second half of the 17th century. From 1710, along with Anderson and Lawson, the names Knight (also common in the landward area), Ross, Webster, Simpson, Young, Norrie, Clark, Kidd, Ferrier, Whyte, Graham, Sturrock, Caithness, Finlay and (from 1776) Gall are recorded; Webster is by far the predominant name. Lorimer (a common white-fisher name later) is located only in Monifieth itself and they must have been salmon fishers at this time. In the 1841 census the predominant names are Knight, Gall, Lorimer and Kidd, followed by Anderson and Webster. Gall predominates by 1895, followed by Anderson, Webster, Knight and Lorimer; other names occurring more than once are Sturrock, Lawrence, Norrie, Smith, Dorward, Craig and Ferrier.

Some variations of the place-name and spelling

Portincrag/Portyncrag	c.1188, 1201x7, 1213, 1218, 1243, 1433, 1453, 1502, 1531
North Ferry of Portyncrag (*passagio boriali*)	1477
North Ferrie/Ferry	1477, 1485, 1489, 1512, 1521, 1527, 1535, 1603, 1608, 1641, 1642, 1662, 1682x85, 1742, 1767, 1784, 1785, 1801, 1810
Eist/ East Ferry	1587, 1611, 1617, 1793, 1794
Broughty Ferry	1807, 1841 to date

(Castle: Bruchtie/Brughtie/Broughty: 1454, 1579, 1603, 1634, 1767, 1787)

Number of fishermen and boats

Year	Fishers	Boats	Type
1742	18	3	'boats'
1793	18	3	large
1842	78	13	line boats
1855	76	30	10 large, 14 standard, 6 yauls
1871	110	?	?
1877	?	40–50	all sizes, all open-decked
1881	172	96	all sizes
1882	'almost 200'	?	23 large decked, 7 standard, plus yauls
1896	164	79	all sizes
1928	30	12	3 over 30ft, 9 under 30ft; all sail
1938	25	13	3 motor (under 30ft), 10 sailing yauls
1948	6	4	1 motor over 30ft, 3 small motor
1950	4	2	motor
1953	6	5	motor

Dundee existed as a settlement by around 1175 and if not a burgh then it was by the 1190s. As a burgh it flourished and began to eclipse the earlier established burghs of Perth and Montrose by the 13th century. The earliest settlement is believed to be on the site of Seagate and it has been suggested that the mouth of the Scouring Burn, which was where Seagate meets Gellatly Street, may have been where the earliest fishermen worked. Whether this was so or not, by the later middle ages the fishermen probably landed at Yeaman Shore to the west of St Nicholas' Craig. This projected to where Riverside Drive now begins and would have given shelter from the tides as the castle crag does at Broughty Ferry. Later they landed at Craig Harbour to the east of St Nicholas' Craig. By the 13th century Dundee had expanded westwards and the small bay between the Castle Hill (site of St Paul's Cathedral) and St Nicholas' Craig was the harbour of Dundee. There were some man-made improvements requiring repair in the mid-15th century and the shore was built up with stone by 1567. A pier and two protecting outer breakwaters existed by the mid-17th century, and were improved by an outer wall or pier on the east in the mid-18th century. A series of wet docks was created from 1825 and by the 1880s the harbour was said to stretch from Craig Pier to Carolina Port.

Fishing and fish curing to 1855

If there was any fishing in Dundee in very early times the development of a flourishing burgh by the 13th century probably stimulated fishing activity to the extent of several boats. From the later middle ages a few stray inferences suggest the continuous existence of a fishing community. There is also evidence that deep water fishing for 'great fish' – large cod and ling – was carried out in the 15th and 16th centuries (when small amounts of dried cod were exported), but this had ceased by the late-18th century. Other species were fished for in the Tay itself and molluscs were collected along its shores. In 1447 a letter patent from King James II allowed the collection of dues from all ships using Dundee harbour, the money to be spent on repairing it. Cargo vessels were to be charged ten shillings, five shillings and one shilling according to types specified, while sixpence was to be charged from a 'greite bate' and twopence from a 'small bate'. The small boats are likely to have been used in the Tay while the large boats would have gone as far as the Inchcape or Bell Rock in summer, 22 miles east of St Nicholas' Craig, where cod could be caught in more recent times. On 11 March 1522/23 it was ordained, in reference to 'gret line boats', that no-one was to buy more fish than for their own sustenance. 'Hucksters' were to be fined for holding more than four pence worth of fish in their booths, and were only allowed to buy fish 24 hours after the boats had landed, so some of the fish sold in Dundee was not exactly fresh. In 1550 the Head Court of Dundee ordained that na fescher within this brugh nor ther servands attempt to buy fish to brake and top upon neghboures under the pain of deling of thair fish fund wtin ther buithouse gidder with the unlaw of 5 merkes to our common wark unforgevin alsweill in Lentren as out of the samyn.

This appears to mean that the fishers were not to buy fish to resell to inhabitants at a profit at Lent or at any other time, implying they were only to sell fish they had landed themselves, otherwise they were to be fined.

On 11 December 1557 it was ordained that any 'flukars' who molested or injured another, on land or at sea, were to be fined: masters 20 shillings and servants five shillings payable to the Almshouse. So it seems that flukers were a rowdy lot. On a later occasion it was noted that cadgers habitually swore when the authorities sought to control their activities. Maxwell suggests that Flukergait, as the Nethergate was known until the mid-16th century, must have got its name from the flukers' houses being on the south side, near to the Yeaman Shore where their boats lay. He suggested that the flukes they fished for were the 'species of turbot' mentioned by Edwards in 1678 as being caught in the Tay near Dundee. Maxwell also stated in 1884 that small flat-fish were plentiful on the sandbanks opposite the Esplanade, but were too small to be worth catching. Halibut in Scots were usually called 'turbot' while turbot were called 'bannock fluke'. This tended to assimilate to English usage by the early-19th century but sometimes it is uncertain which are meant. It seems in fact that the above-mentioned flukes are most likely to have been immature turbot under five years old which feed in shallow water and are a maximum of one foot (30cms) long.

In October 1559 the Head Court of Dundee noted that by Act of Parliament salmon barrels were to be standardised and that the coopers were to brand them with their own marks. A year later they noted that both salmon and herring barrels were to be made to the standard measure of Leith and to be branded by the coopers' own irons so that any fish improperly packed could be traced to the cooper responsible. In April 1562 it was further 'statute and ordained' that the masters of the coopers' craft were to make salmon barrels to contain eleven-and-a-half gallons minimum, while barrels for herring and keiling (large cod) were to contain 9 gallons. These orders were to be followed on pain of escheat. In 1568 there was a complaint that cadgers and others were bringing in dried fish tied in dozens, single great fish and rotten small codlings. It was ordained that they were not to be tied but to be exposed for sale loose and only those who bought fish 'at the fisch boates' of Dundee or at other havens where fish were 'slain' were allowed to take them straight to market. As in 1550 the authorities were making sure that everyone had the same chance of buying fish openly at one place, avoiding forestalling, the cornering of the market. The above also makes it clear that Dundee, unsurprisingly, did not depend solely on its own fisher community for supplies, but fish of various kinds from outwith Dundee was brought in by cadgers. Broughty Ferry, West Haven and East Haven are the most likely outside sources of fresh fish, while dried and pickled fish may have come from much further afield. In 1580 the manor house of Auchterhouse was supplied from Dundee with white fish including 'turbot' (i.e. halibut). In 1596 the Town Council noted that the petty customs dues of the fish stock (market), 'observit inviolable in times past', were as follows:

For ilk hundred dry gret ling	four pennies
Item, ilk hundred fresh fish to be inbrocht within the burgh be the cadgers	twa pennies
Item, ilk Ferrie wyiff ilk tyde	twa pennies
Item, of the flukers for ilk tyde of outsea fishes	twa pennies

Edwards in 1678 stated that 'charies of Tay and a species of turbot' were caught in great quantities in the Tay near Dundee and a little upstream. Garvies, the local term for sprats, seems to have been meant by the former, while the latter, as detailed above, were probably immature turbot. By the later 17th century, and probably much earlier, the Town Council leased the 'fish and flesh stocks' annually by public roup and the sums paid fluctuated markedly from year to year. Originally the fish market was near the market cross, later removed to the 'Highway to the Shore', known as Fish Street, near the present Whitehall Crescent, by the 17th century. In 1731 a new table of dues for the fish and flesh stocks was drawn up. The first three items were:

Ilk fish boat or yoale containing six men and a boy, 2s 6d [Scots];

Ilk drain [train?] of line, 4d;

Ilk foreman's creel, 4d;

and the commodities listed included: Bervy fish (smoked haddock), hard fish (dried cod), herring, spirlings (sperlings or smelt), salmon, grilse, torbet, partons (crabs), lopsters, ryds (roe), buckies (winkles/whelks), cockles & mussles and oysters. Fresh haddock, cod, garvies (sprats) and flukes (immature turbot), mostly caught in the Tay, were not mentioned, so the dues were apparently only charged on items brought in from elsewhere and not landed by the burgh's own fishers, who paid instead for the right to use boats and lines. In October 1767 charges to 'unfreemen' included: sixpence each salmon; threepence each dozen lobsters or partans; two shillings each 1000 oysters; and sixpence each load of herring 'coming or going'. As in 1731 no mention of fresh white fish or garvies was made, presumably since they were landed by the burgh's own fishers.

It is only from the later-18th century that the number of boats and fishermen at Dundee is recorded. In earlier times, when deep water great line fishing was carried out as well as other fishing in the Tay, there may have been more and larger boats and many more fishers. In 1770 Pennant commented that there were then three small boats at Dundee which were unable to supply the town or area with enough fish. They used no great lines to catch cod or ling either at the Cape (Inchape Rock) or farther out at Mar's Bank as their boats were too small. In 1792 there were still three boats which were manned by

18 fishers, so they were of the usual six-man type under 25 feet long found on the Angus coast at that time and presumably similar to those used in 1731 which were expected to have a crew of six men and a boy. An engraving of the harbour of 1790 shows just such a fishing lugger with two sails. The fisher community latterly lived in and around Fish Street and the fish market to the east (later the Greenmarket), not far from where their boats were landed.

The New Statistical Account of 1832 accounts for whaling in some detail but states that other fishings were of no value, which probably refers wholly or mainly to salmon fishing as white-fishing seems to have ceased altogether by then. Engravings of the new docks and harbour of 1825, 1835 and 1843 all depict at least one fishing lugger besides cargo vessels but they may well have been Broughty boats (the 1835 view shows a single-masted yaul with a crew of four, the others the standard two-masted boat). Charles Mackie in 1836 stated that 'charies of Tay and a species of turbot' were caught near Dundee; but in this he was merely repeating Edwards' account of 1678 and not making a contemporary observation and it is likely that neither fishing existed by then. For whatever reason Dundee's fishing community had died out by the 1840s, since the 1841 census reveals that not a single fisherman lived in the area where the seafaring community, including a couple of pilots and a few fish-sellers, dwelt, namely in and around Fish Street, Butcher Row, Crichton Street, Ogilvie's Close, Scott's Close and also Wet Dock Street to the west of Earl Grey Dock. The reasons for the decline and disappearance of the Dundee fishers are not clear. As in the case of Montrose the decline of fishing took place at a period when demand was increasing and an adjacent fishing community was rapidly expanding to meet the demand.

The Fishery Board's boat account of 1855 lists no boats at Dundee but does account for 64 persons involved with fish, including vendors, coopers, gutters and packers, some employed by three curers. Some of the curing and coopering may have been of cod from Broughty and the Ha'ens but the curers were also employed in producing red herring by processing the salt-pickled item brought in from elsewhere. So it appears that there was no further fishing (apart from salmon fishing) out of Dundee until around 1880 when spratting commenced. Steam trawlers also began to make landings from the mid-1880s but Dundee had none of its own until after 1900.

Herring landings

Dundee exported significant amounts of herring in the 16th century, about 100 lasts[1] annually in the years 1535–39 and 1595–99. This made it next only to the Forth and Clyde ports as an exporter, so it would appear that there may have been regular herring shoals in the Tay estuary at the time and a catching and curing industry which was exploiting them. As noted above, in 1562 standard nine-gallon herring barrels, as at Leith,

---

1 A standard measure for herring, equivalent to 12 barrels (ed.).

were ordained to be used, the coopers to be responsible for any faulty packing. In the 1680s small amounts of cured herring were exported from Dundee, as they were from Montrose at that time, but these were very probably re-exports from elsewhere and it is noteworthy that herring are not among the locally-caught species listed by Edwards in his description of Angus in 1678. There appears to be no evidence that Dundee had a herring fleet fishing in the Minch (as Montrose had) around 1750–72. Herring were listed among the species sold at Dundee's fishmarket in the 18th century, the market dues being one shilling per load in 1731, but only sixpence per load in 1767 'coming or going'. This suggests that it was already cured and in barrels and was not caught locally. Charles Mackie in 1836 stated that herring fishing at Dundee was 'but a memory' although he is not an entirely reliable source since he merely quotes Edward's account of 1678 in relation to other fishings. But there is a possibility that this may have referred to occasional mid-summer catches after herring were discovered (or re-discovered) in the Tay with the introduction of salmon stake-nets just after 1800. Mature herring were occasionally caught in later times off Stannergate by the spratters, but such shoals were a rare and erratic occurrence.

In 1849 James Thomson remarked that Dundee had several first-rate establishments for the manufacture of red herrings, supplying the city and surrounding area. But red herring were made by re-processing pickled herring, which again, by that date, must have been brought in from elsewhere. It used to be a regular New Year custom in Dundee until fairly recent times to take a red herring dressed in coloured paper as a first foot gift on Hogmanay. Occasional landings of fresh herring may have been made by Broughty and Fife boats from the later-19th century. The 1928 boat account states that 164 hundredweight of herring were landed at Dundee that year, but who caught them, or where, is not recorded. Erratic shoals of mature herring did occur in the Tay in more recent times. In January 1938 Arbroath drifters, along with ring-netters from Girvan and Campbeltown, had a short-lived bonanza catching small herring and sprats. In winter 1951 mature herring were caught by the spratters in the Tayport to Stannergate area of the Tay but were not bought by any of the Dundee curers or fish merchants. A few years earlier Forth ring-netters had tried fishing for herring in the Tay one season but they were not used to the tidal conditions and having little success they didn't return. In January 1964 fourteen Arbroath and St Monans boats fished a similar shoal to that of 1951, landing their catches at Queen Elizabeth Wharf. During the herring boom in the mid-19th century Dundee had lacked a fishing community which might have pursued herring seasonally. But even with the advent of the steam drifter by 1900 local capital did not see fit to invest in such an industry. In 1912 the lack of curers, despite the existence of the empty eastern wharf, a mile long with deep water at low tide and eight acres of shed space, was noted.

Trawling and white-fish landings

Steam trawlers working west of the Bell Rock seem to have started making landings at Dundee from before 1890 when a register of fish brought into Dundee fishmarket began to be kept. At that time 100 to 200 hundredweight of haddock was landed daily with some ling, cod, halibut and occasionally turbot. Finnan haddies, smokies and kippers were also on sale, but not apparently processed in Dundee. In 1892 an Act was passed to enable the building of new facilities to encourage landings by trawlers but it was ten years before it was put into operation. In 1895 an anonymous article in the Dundee Year Book entitled 'Dundee as a fishery port' noted the creation of a great white-fish port and market at Aberdeen by means of steam trawlers and bemoaned the fact that Dundee only had a local market for fish, despite the fact that it was 70 miles nearer the southern markets and coal supplies. Trawlers from other ports were by then landing fish at Dundee fairly regularly, despite the lack of facilities, to the disadvantage of the Broughty line-fishers. It was suggested that similar facilities to Aberdeen could be created on vacant ground between the Cattle Market and Stannergate and rail lines extended. By an agreement in 1900 Dundee Harbour Trust agreed to pay the Town Council £100 for lost fish market dues and took over the creation and running of a new fish dock and market at Carolina Port which opened in 1902. There were great wrangles at first with the fish traders, who did not want to remove from the old fish market beside Craig Harbour, where landings had been made up to then. The Fishery records for 1896 state that 'local' trawlers were working in the area and two others off Aberdeen. In fact the only trawlers recorded in the fishery district at that time were three belonging to Montrose, two of which did regularly work out of Aberdeen. It is likely that some of the landings were by Leith and Granton trawlers.

In 1912 ex-bailie William High wrote in a report 'Fishing, Trawling and Whaling' for the British Association for the Advancement of Science, which met in Dundee that year, that the new Fish Dock was incomplete. It had been intended to have 2700 feet of quay space, 6700 square yards of depot and eight acres of water. A large area of vacant ground suitable for building stores and curing yards was also intended but none had been built, though rail sidings by then connected the dock with the Caledonian and North British Railways. A hydraulic coal hoist existed, which could service vessels of all sizes, and in close proximity the Ice & Storage Co had premises producing 25 tons of ice daily. In the previous year trawlers and liners had landed 84,947 boxes of fish and 2780 score of cod, while 200 tons of fresh and 320 tons of cured fish came by rail. But this was still only a local market supplying Dundee and to some extent also Perth, Blairgowrie and Forfar. Ex-bailie High stated that despite the facilities created, trawling had not become a large-scale industry at Dundee. Outside buyers, he wrote, would not be attracted unless a fleet of 40 to 50 trawlers were introduced, but so far Dundee capital had not seen fit to embark on this trade on a large scale.

Dundee apparently had a couple of trawlers of its own by 1904, when among 16 named trawlers recorded landing are found *Taymouth* and *Tayside*, and there were certainly three by 1910. A dozen trawlers were making landings at Dundee by this date, nine in 1915, but later during the 1914–18 war they were commandeered for minesweeping and other naval auxiliary duties and small motor liners from Angus and Fife supplied white fish to Dundee. Wartime price controls were lifted in March 1919 and the haddock price soared 85 to 90 percent above the wartime price while codling and plaice prices rose 50 percent and 30 percent respectively. In 1919 fifteen named trawlers were regularly landing at Dundee, dropping to 12 by 1924. After the war Dundee's own trawler fleet rose to five most years around 1920–26, and during 1927–38 to nine or ten, each with a crew of nine men. Landings by Aberdeen and Granton trawlers and motor liners from Arbroath and East Fife continued to supplement what remained a localised market for fish. In 1928 49,975 hundredweight, mainly of white fish, was landed at Dundee. By then Aberdeen had 228 trawlers, Granton 60 and Leith 16 while Dundee had only nine.

During the 1939–45 war the Dundee trawler fleet was reduced to five, some being commandeered again as naval auxiliaries. After the war two companies operated a handful of trawlers. Cameron, MacFarlane Ltd owned the *Bush*, bought the *Ben Loyal* from Fleetwood in 1948 and by 1949 also had the *Cave* and *Lord Darling*, while Fraser, Fenton & Co operated the *Fraser Fenton*, but all five were landing their catches at Leith and Granton. In January 1949 the Dundee Fishmongers and Poulterers Association contacted the Fishery officer at Aberdeen and the Ministry of Food was to be approached to see if Aberdeen trawlers working off the Bell Rock could divert landings to Dundee. In June 1949 a Danish trawler, the first foreigner to land since before the war, had been granted a licence to land its catch by the Ministry of Food, but the fish trade doubted if its cargo of plaice could be sold locally as the demand was for haddock, codling, sole and halibut, so it was mostly sent south. This coincided with a heavy landing by the *Ben Loyal* of 300 boxes of white fish, the surplus of which were sent to Aberdeen. By the period 1950–53 there were only three Dundee trawlers, two of which belonged to the Fentons. In January 1951 the *Lynn Fenton* landed a record catch of 640 boxes of prime haddock and cod which were mainly disposed of in the city with some surplus sent to Aberdeen and Fife. In April 1952 the *Benjamin Fenton*, after a rough trip off Shetland, landed 520 boxes, mainly of haddock. But local trawling seems to have ceased by the mid-1950s. By November 1956 the fish market was operating at a loss despite increased charges, since by then much of the trade was arranged by telephone calls on the night preceding landings or deliveries. Dundee Corporation and the Harbour Trust found that they had no legal obligation to maintain the fish market and by December their joint committee recommended that it be given up by 15 May following. Dundee & District Wholesale Fish Salesmen's Association requested a delay but the Council pointed out that they had lost £100 annually since 1951 and that trawlers had ceased to operate from Dundee. As a footnote, in January 1958 the Dundee fishmongers wanted a levy put on Arbroath vans and fishwives vending fish on the streets in Dundee. This and other road deliveries had by then superseded direct landings from boats.

Fisher names

Between 1841, when the census records begin, and 1881, when sprat-fishing commenced, no white-fishers seem to have been resident in Dundee. The author notes that in the 18th century names of sailors are often similar to those found at Broughty Ferry or West Haven, and that a number of Broughty fishers went to crew the Dundee trawler fleet (ed).

Number of fishermen and boats

Year	Fishers	Boats	Type
15th–16th c	?	?	large and small boats
1731	?	?	boats and 'yoales'
1770–92	18	3	boats under 25ft
1841	–	–	
1855	–	–	
1881	3	1	sprat smack
1896	6	2	sprat smacks
1897	18	6	sprat smacks
1904	c.40	8–9	2 or 3 trawlers, 5 or 6 spratters
1910	c.50	12	3 trawlers, 9 spratters
1920–26	c.70	15	4–6 trawlers, 9–11 spratters
1927–39	c.105	20	9–10 trawlers, 10–11 spratters (1 motor)
1940	c.70	15	5–6 trawlers, 9–10 spratters (1 motor)
1950	39	9	3 trawlers, 6 motor spratters

Steam trawlers originally had crews of nine or ten, latterly only nine.

Salmon fishing

The burgh may well have owned the salmon fishings along its shores from its foundation in the late-12th century, but nothing is recorded until much later. Apart from the large gaps in the records the stations had a bewildering number of alternative names in both Scots and Gaelic, all apparently referring to the same locality. A number of leases of the fishings survive from the 16th century and reveal that they were apparently three in number and were let together, usually to burgesses of Dundee, for periods of three years. In a lease of 1525 they were listed as 'the sklate hewch clochry and myle merk' but in documents of 1565 and 1568 as 'the Ruid fisching corsnes fisching starneris clochry/ stanneris clochere and others'. There were no clear capital letters or punctuation but both lists seem to refer to the same three stations that the burgh traditionally owned, while 'others' is probably legal waffle. The documents of 1565 name the fishings as being occupied by Robert Anderson in North Ferry (Broughty), George Wishart and Robert

Selkirk. All three were apparently salmon gaffers actually working the three fishings. In the late-15th and 16th centuries Dundee exported more salmon than Montrose despite the latter's two salmon rivers and extensive trading precinct which included Inverbervie and Lunan Bay. Apart from the burgh's own fishings, salmon from downstream stations and on the Fife bank of the Tay may all have contributed. Unlike cured herring, salmon was not usually bought in but was purely local produce. The fishings upstream from the Invergowrie Burn would have contributed to Perth's exports which were about as great.

Corsness was the small promontory midway between Dundee harbour and Broughty Castle, so marked on Adair's map of 1703. It took its name from the Rood or Cross Chapel associated with the medieval Hospital of St John the Baptist recorded in 1443. Later references are only to St John's Chapel, the Rood Chapel or 'St John of the Sklaitt Heugh' and in 1552 'St John's kirkyard beside the Ruid Chapel'. By the 17th century the site was used as a burial place for plague victims, mariners and other strangers and the site was still known as the Rood Yards in the early-19th century. Sklait Heugh referred to the grey-slate quarry below the chapel site, long worked to roof Dundee's buildings. By 1794 this same promontory was called Stannergate, apparently meaning a stone- or gravel-working. The earlier forms Starneris (*sic*) Clochry/Stanneris Clochere seem to be tautological names for the same location since stanners is old Scots for shingle or gravel or stony place while Clochry is from Gaelic *clach*, 'a stone' and means stony place or possibly a place of stony or shingly ground. If Sklaitt Heugh was an alternative name for the Rud fishing then Myle Merk by elimination seems to be an alternative name for Corsness since the promontory was just over a Scots mile (1980 yards) from the East Port of Dundee. So, after an analysis of the confusing multiplicity of names it appears that all three salmon stations were closely located around the same promontory. A charter of 1642 defined the town's fishings as being 'between the burn of Invergowrie and the rock of Kilcraig'. Maxwell interpreted this as implying that the fishings extended the length of the whole shore between the parish boundaries. He argued against identifying Kilcraig as Stannergate and claimed it was a small rock at the eastern extremity of the parish at West Ferry called the Provost's Chair. But Kilcraig means rock-chapel and seems to be yet another alternative name for the chapel which once stood above Stannergate Point. The fishings at West Ferry, although in the parish of Dundee, did not belong to the burgh but to the Douglas Earls of Angus.

In the 18th century the burgh minutes refer to leases of the 'rood yeards fishing' (in 1764), the 'Corseness fishing' in the 1770s, and simply the 'East fishing' in the 1730s. A sketch plan in the burgh records dated 1801 shows the exact position of a coble fishing immediately to the east of the promontory. It would have been threatened by a proposed harbour at one of the quarries, turned down by the Council. The plan only shows a single fishing along with three quarries and above them the old burial ground called Rood Yards. A wearisome trawl through the burgh minutes shows that the leases were seldom, if ever, mentioned after the 18th century while few documents have survived. Several leases survive from the 16th century but only two from the early-20th century.

Published annual burgh accounts from 1870 list the salmon rental under the common good. The fishing was leased annually up to 1894 and fluctuated considerably: £73 for 1871, £128 for 1875 and 1877, as low as £30 for 1882 but £111 for 1893, so there was no falling trend and the rents averaged around £78. However in 1895 the Town Council decided to roup the fishings for ten years for an upset annual rent of £50, though after consulting the Town Chamberlain this was lowered to £45. It was then leased, presumably after the usual exposure to roup, to Joseph Johnston & Sons of Montrose for ten years at the minimum £45 per annum. In 1905 Johnstons offered the same annual rent for an 11-year lease but the fishing was eventually let to an agent of the Tay Salmon Fisheries Company Ltd of Perth for the same rent. Leases happen to have survived for the seasons 1916–22 and 1923–27. For the first period the lease for the Dundee fishing, as from 1905, was to the Tay Salmon Fisheries Company Ltd at £45 per annum. But the lease for 1923–27 also included the Broughty Ferry fishings for a total of £57 per annum. Broughty Ferry had been incorporated into Dundee and the annual lease of its salmon fishings, renewed in 1915, was only £12, so the Dundee fishing fetched £45 per annum as earlier. It seems that the Broughty fishings were already being leased in order not to be fished, but this was not yet the case with the Stannergate fishing. The leases stipulated that no abatement of rent was to be made on account of any sewers existing or yet to be built, or operations of the railway, Harbour Trust or of any beach facilities introduced. Nor was there to be any restriction of public access to the shore, and any encroachment on the fishings was to be dealt with by the lessees. The annual rent of £57 remained the same until 1931 from when it was raised to £62 and it remained the same in the annual published burgh accounts until the late 1970s, after which it ceased to be separately accounted for, as did the rates on the fishings in 1984. So latterly the fishings were obviously being leased, but not worked, in order to make upriver fishings, mostly worked by the Tay Salmon Fisheries Company, more worthwhile.

Sprat fishing [1]

The generic term 'sprats' included two related species found together in shoals in salt-water estuaries such as the Tay, while a third species was occasionally found in small numbers amongst sprat shoals and was fished for upstream in brackish water using the same type of net. The true sprat or bristling (*Clupea sprattus*) grows to six inches and in the Tay was found upstream as far as Balmerino. But it was also found in mixed shoals just off Dundee between Broughty Ferry and the railway bridge in winter from October to March or April with a related species, immature herring (*Clupea harengus*). Sprats

---

1 The author gratefully acknowledged the help of the late Charlie Johnston of Newburgh in compiling this section (ed.).

and herring fry can be told apart by sight but if uncertain the serrated back of the true sprat can be detected by hand, while the herring's is smooth. The latter often comprised up to 75 to 90 percent of the shoals in January and February. They were called garvies locally, which, like the term sprats, could be generic or specific. The smaller fry of both, about two to three inches long, are whitebait (a culinary rather than a zoological term).

Garvies were apparently caught in the 17th century although they are not recorded in any of the 18th century lists of market dues. This was presumably because they were fished for by the burgh's own fishers. With the demise of the Dundee fishing community before 1840 this fishing must have ceased for a time and was only re-introduced to the Tay by Newburgh fishermen from the 1870s. The first mention of spratting in the fishery records is of landings at Dundee by Newburgh boats in 1879. There was a single fishing boat with a crew of three registered at Dundee in 1881, obviously the first spratter to belong to the port. In the 1880s around twenty Newburgh smacks were landing sprats at Dundee; but in 1895 it was stated that about half the landings of sprats were by Newburgh boats, implying that several Dundee boats were active by then. Photographs of the harbour from around 1900 show several single-masted gaff-rigged sprat smacks. They landed their catches at the Craig Harbour and were laid up there in the off-season. The Dundee crews may have owned their own boats as the Newburgh men did. The boats represented a very low capital investment compared with a drifter or even a new haddock boat as the spratters adapted old boats, too battered to work in the open sea, and possibly old nets, to catch this low-value group of species for only a few months of the year. Some of the early Dundee spratters may have been off-season merchant seamen and whalers finding the low returns better than earning nothing in winter. The Newburgh men, who had started the fishery in the 1870s, had traditionally been salmon fishers in summer and weavers in winter, so spratting was an alternative to, or replaced, handloom weaving, which began to die out after the 1860s. An account of 'Dundee as a fishery port' in the Dundee Year Book of 1895 lamented the lack of trawling or lining out of the port and did not even mention spratting, so it was clearly of little economic importance except to the few men involved. Another reason for ignoring this fishing was probably because sprats were not eaten locally and at that time were mainly or wholly used as manure or poultry food.

Spratting may have continued at about the same fluctuating level until the 1914–18 war. Towards the end of the war the country was desperately short of food, so the price of sprats rose greatly as a higher proportion began to be salt-pickled and barrelled for human consumption. By February 1918 the catches in the Tay were so good and the price offered so high that a boat could earn from £60 to £100 in a week (in some cases apparently in a night), and catches were often so heavy that a crew of two could hardly haul a net aboard. The Tay Salmon Board waived its power to control spratting during the salmon season. Boats could be cheaply fitted out and operated but there was a shortage of fishermen as so many men were away at the war, and despite the very high prices only 18 to 20 boats, including Newburgh boats and Broughty drift-netters, were landing sprats at Dundee; nonetheless they were landing enough sprats to fill 1000 to 1500 barrels daily. The 'sprats' that season were actually 90 percent immature herring though it was said the true sprat kept better and was more adapted to curing. Despite the dire food shortage Scots could not be persuaded to consume fresh or salt-pickled sprats, although herring in either form were always popular, so the entire catch was dispatched to London and other English cities.

After the war the industry returned to its old levels. In 1924 a small steamer made several trips with sprats to Stavanger where there were no less than 61 canneries crying out for them. In 1928 there were 11 sprat smacks registered at Dundee. After a few English buyers had bought some fresh, the surplus catch (in one week 80 tons) was railed to Glasgow for conversion to fish-meal. In January 1933, however, S W Smedley opened a fish cannery, Kingsway Works, in Dundee, in the hope of breaking the Norwegian monopoly of supplying canned sprats to the English. Either this didn't take off or for some reason Smedley abandoned canning the local catch, and in 1944 it was still being sold off for manure. By the late 1940s canning of the local sprat landings had been taken over by British Food Canners Ltd of Leeds at their Ancrum Road Works in Lochee.

Spratting picked up after the war when men gradually returned from the forces and motor boats began to be used. Some of the Newburgh boats were kept at Dundee in the Tidal Basin during the season along with the Dundee boats, the Newburgh men going home by bus when not fishing. By 1948 there were up to 20 Newburgh boats and seven Dundee boats landing catches for Ancrum Works. On 25 January seven Dundee boats and three Newburgh boats landed 250 crans, caught mainly off Woodhaven Pier, the best catch for five years. Ancrum Works, however, did not have adequate storage space to cope with large catches. On one occasion the excess catch was 'dumped' with an Aberdeen margarine firm for 35 shillings per cran; normally the cannery paid £2 2s per cran and a 23 shillings and fourpence subsidy was paid by the government. When the glut in supply caused the cannery to cut its price there was much bad feeling between the fishers and the cannery manager. Some boats fished on when prices were low with the attitude that half a loaf was better than none, others went on strike.

In 1950 the Ministry of Food offered space to store 100 tons in a government cold store in Perthshire, and, along with the Herring Industry Board, was to look into the possibility of converting the sprats into meal and oil. When, the following season, the boats caught large herring in the Tayport to Stannergate section of the river, an Eyemouth fish merchant offered 70 shillings per cran for as much herring as they could catch. But the fishers were in a hopeless situation: when the boats landed sprats that season the canners refused to buy any herring fry, but when the boats tried again for herring they couldn't find any big enough to sell to herring curers.

In 1953 there was unemployment in the fish cannery. When the Ancrum Works finally closed on 30 June 1961, having amalgamated the year before with the Whiteside Group of Fraserburgh, it was stated that the cannery had originally canned sprats from the Tay and the Forth but when the sprats disappeared they had relied on imported fish; sardines had become their main product and the Fraserburgh plant could handle all the work. It seems therefore that sprat fishing had failed after several poor seasons in the early- to mid-1950s, having at other times produced a glut which resulted in wasteful dumping when the cannery could not cope. The problem was the inconsistency in the size of the shoals and the mixture of species and sizes of fish. The true sprat was preferred but seldom comprised a high enough proportion of the catch and the mixture of species was too troublesome to sort. A newspaper report on the local fishing industry of 25 January 1964 suggests that a few spratters from further afield still fished occasionally but that the remnants of the Dundee spratting fleet seldom put to sea.

One of the oldest Dundee spratting families were the Livies, who owned several boats. The sprat fishers lived mainly in Union Street, Dock Street and Gellatly Street but few of those who took part are now alive. In the post-war period some were merchant seamen, others had been trawlermen. They often met in Stewart's Bar in Castle Street; the manager would advance credit and when the pay-off from the cannery came all the hangers-on would gather to scrounge drink and a lot of drinking went on. Some were even drunk on board their boats and it is surprising that there were few fatalities in the Tay.

Sperling fishing

A third species was occasionally found in small numbers amongst sprat shoals and was fished for upstream using the same type of net. This is the sperlin(g), sparlin(g) or spirlin(g) (*Osmerus eperlanus*), called smelt in England, a little-known member of the trout or salmon family which grows up to 12 inches and has a curious cucumber-like smell. They prefer brackish water and breed in spring, in the Tay just off Newburgh although they can normally be found between the mouth of the Earn and Birkhill, near Balmerino, and sometimes as far downstream as the Dundee railway bridge. Occasionally they are washed down even further and are found in small numbers mixed with the sprat shoals. Although mentioned in the table of dues for fish in 1731, the earliest evidence for sperlings being caught commercially in the Tay in relatively modern times is from Newburgh in the 1830s, using nets fixed in the tidal channel between there and Mugdrum Island. They were originally sold locally, later iced and sent to England. Many of the Newburgh salmon fishers were also involved in this lucrative fishing since the catch was highly prized and valuable, in the 1890s selling at £3 7s 9d per hundredweight (as compared with four shillings and sixpence per hundredweight for herring). In the Tay 90 men were occupied in this fishing in winter in the 1890s, but most would have been from Newburgh rather than Dundee. After the decline of the sprat fishing industry a few Newburgh boats continued to fish for sperlings with the same nets. The Newburgh fishers had difficulty in marketing sperlings. For a time there was a freezer factory at Balmerino, but latterly they took them to Glasgow fish market. Although Charles Alexander's fish lorries stopped at Perth on the way from Aberdeen to Glasgow to give the drivers a break the firm refused to pick up the catch there. From Glasgow they went to Liverpool and Cornwall but the ultimate market may have been London or abroad. Sperlings were deep-fried by English consumers and just after 1945, when there was a shortage of oils and fats, there was a slump in demand. Locally they were floured and shallow-fried. They were still occasionally fished for in the Tay out of Newburgh into the 1990s. Although few folk have even heard of them locally, in recent times a Dundee restaurant served them as a starter.

Sprat and sperling fishing methods

In early times sprats were probably caught by funnel-shaped wicker cruives as were used in the Forth between Kincardine and Alloa. These had the opening upstream to catch the sprats at ebb-tide. Another method in use in the middle Forth from the 1820s were beach-seines, worked like salmon nets. It seems that fishing for sprats and sperlings in the Tay by bag-net only began in the 1870s. The bag-nets used on the Tay (not to be confused with anchored salmon bag-nets) are identical to the stow-nets used by English spratters, although the terminology used for the net and its parts is different (on the Forth they were known as boom-nets after the two booms which held the net open). According to Charlie Johnston, member of a Newburgh fisher family, it was his grandfather John Aitken, 'the General', who first copied the design of the English nets. The story handed down is that some English spratters visited the Tay and landed at Newburgh. While they were in a pub, Aitken, who was a weaver, went down to their boats and cut a web of cloth to the pattern of the nets. Aitken presumably got his bye-name through being an acknowledged leader. He was a young man in the 1870s so this event, whether literally true or not, probably dates the introduction of bag-netting to shortly before the first sprat landings were recorded at Dundee in 1879. By the early 1880s, if not earlier, sprats were being fished for using similar nets in the Beauly Firth and the upper Forth estuary between Kincardine and Alloa, and it seems likely that it was Englishmen who introduced this method of fishing which made large catches possible. In 1883 the gross Scottish sprat catch was 43,428 crans.

The bag-nets were made of tarred hemp or flax. They formed a large bag 42 yards long with a rectangular mouth 28 feet wide tapering to a rounded tail. The net was held open at the top by a wooden floating boom and at the foot by being weighted down by an iron boom. At the bottom leading edge was a spew hole to release excess catches, more than could be hauled aboard. They were lowered a few fathoms below the boat, anchored down with a 30-hundredweight patent anchor. When fishing the boats did not move but allowed the tide to draw the fish into the net. Fishing was carried out an hour before ebb-tide and an hour after the tide turned, so depending on the tides the boat could often be out in the middle of the night. The sailing boats used for spratting were always referred to as smacks, and photographs taken at Dundee harbour around 1900 show that they had a single forward mast fitted with a gaff-sail. They were adapted from cheap second-hand sea-fishing luggers 30 to 50 feet long, too battered to work in the open sea. Before 1900 they were usually crewed by three men but by the 1920s sometimes only two. Only from 1945 were old motor yauls of 40 to 50 feet, crewed by two men, used for sprat fishing.

In the 1880s, soon after bag-netting began, the Tay Salmon Board got a Court of Session interdict forbidding the use of bag-nets in the Tay during the salmon season, which then lasted from 25 February to 25 September. The sprat season was mainly from October to the beginning of March, so there was only a short period of potential overlap and in fact many of the Newburgh men were salmon fishers in summer. There were only a handful of Dundee boats operating then and they fished mainly in mid-stream, so could pose little threat to sweep-netting for salmon from the shore, the only commercial method legal in the Tay, while the bag-netters were *supposed* to return any salmon inadvertently caught. The salmon interests were later able to make the bag-netters sign an agreement not to operate between 5 February and 20 August. But after 1945 young men returning from the forces defied the salmon interests by invoking a law allowing sea-fishing along any shore where the tide flows. Having defeated the Board in court, the fishers were able to fish on into March or April as long as the sprat shoals were worth fishing.

Names of sprat-boats and owners landing at Dundee around 1945–53

Newburgh boats and owners

Annie	Charlie Johnston
Columbine	Lewis Aitken
Constance	Lewis Aitken
Express	David Aitken
Faith	Charlie Johnston
Glide	Tom Johnston
Greta Ranee	Jim MacKenzie
Rob Roy	James Robbie
Snowdrop	David Aitken

Dundee boats and owners

Better Hope	James Livie
Comfort	James Forbes (later C Johnston, Newburgh)
Dayspring	D Wilson
Fidelity	Willie Findlay
Gowan	Peter Lorimer
Lea Rig	Hans Ormergard
Margie	James Livie
North Star	Willie Findlay
Pasadena	Jacky Dixon
Providence	James Livie
Star of the East	Stuart Livie
Trust On	Freddy Cook

Whaling and sealing

This is the only fishing industry of Dundee which has been accounted for before, and in some detail, so only a brief summary is necessary here. The raising of the government bounty to 40 shillings per tun (216 imperial gallons) for whale blubber in 1749 and from £1 to £2 per ton burden on vessels in 1750 induced the setting up of the Dundee Whale Fishing Company by 1754. There were only a couple of ships in the early days, the *Dundee* and the *Grantully*. But a rise in price led to expansion from the 1780s and by the 1790s Dundee had four ships involved, though due to the French wars 1794–1815 there was only one in 1801. After the war the fleet rapidly grew to ten ships by 1820. All were fairly successful. Several companies were involved and the locations of their boil yards are commemorated in the names Whale Lane, Baffin Street and Arctic Tannery. Great losses were sustained in the 1830s and several ports, like Montrose, dropped out of whaling. The Dundee companies replaced some of their lost vessels although the fleet was reduced to six, later to four by the 1850s. But in 1857 the *Tay* was converted to steam and Stephens launched the first purpose-built screw steam whaler *Narwhal* in 1859. It had a wooden hull and was 530 tons burden, with a 75hp engine in addition to sails. In the 1860s seven more steam whalers were built and Dundee's whaling fleet grew to 12 by 1868, dropping to nine in 1871 but rising to 11 later in the 1870s. Peterhead, which had once surpassed Dundee, failed to switch to steam and eventually dropped out by 1894. The need for whale oil to make jute supple enough to spin kept up local demand and so Dundee became Scotland's (and Britain's) last whaling port. The whaling ships had from 70 to 90 of a crew. Some were recruited in Dundee but many of the Broughty white-fishers spent a few summers whaling and latterly also fishers from other places up the coast as far north as Johnshaven. The crews were also supplemented by Orcadians and Shetlanders picked up on the way north.

An average of about ten whales and 50,000 seals were taken annually around 1865–74. Although the slaughter of seals seems phenomenal it was a fraction of the three million taken by all ships working the grounds in the same period. The use of auxiliary steam engines meant less chance of being caught becalmed with the ice closing in. The last whaler to be launched by Stephens was *Terra Nova* in 1884. The industry was in decline by then and only an early start to the season for seals made up for poor whaling catches. The Scots did not adopt the new Norwegian techniques for catching whales such as the use of explosive harpoons to make the kill. In 1892 four ships were sent to the Antarctic but this was a total failure. In 1896 only two whalers covered their costs. In 1911 only seven whales, 576 narwhals and 399 walruses were caught. The industry persisted until 1914 with few vessels recovering their costs. The *Balaena* commemorated in song was one of the last Dundee whalers. It had been built in Norway in 1872 and sailed from Dundee in the period 1891–1914.

Number of whaling ships

1754	2
1792	4
1801	1
1813	8
1820	10
1850s	4
1861	8
1868	12 steamers
1890s	c.10 steamers
1911	8 steamers
1914	3 steamers

Appendix I: Bye-names

There's Samson and Bishop and Shavie,
The Pope and Lang-nebbit John,
There's Cocker and Tam o' the Navy
And also King David and Bone.

These were essential in most fishing villages where so many people shared the same name. The fishers had few distinctive forenames, using the same common limited repertoire as their fellow Scots in the same foreshortened forms: Davie, Davit or Dite, Willie, Geordie, Jeemie, Jock, Tam, Alec or Sy and Andra for the men, and Meg, Nelly, Bet or Lizzie and May for women being the commonest. Bye-names, or tee-names, may have been used from an early period but examples have mostly survived only from around 1900. Bye-names could derive from a physical characteristic such as Gowp i' the Lift ('look at the sky') from an upward cast in the eye or Lang Hairry (Henry), a tall man. Others could derive from some incident or habit: Sodger Sy (Alexander Cargill, who served in the Boer War), Fechtin' Willie and Coffee Bets were all noted characters in Auchmithie in the early-20th century. Children sometimes bore their father's bye-name followed by their own Christian name, such as Cocker's Willie (William Swankie, whose father William was Cocker; his father, also Willie, was known as Breeks). Individuals could also be traced through more than one generation with accuracy in strings of names such as Willie's Meg's Jeemie's Sy to a noted great-grandparent. There were so many families with the same surname that certain families came to be identified by collective bye-names like that of the Polar Swankies of Arbroath or the four generations of Codlins of Ferryden. Some bye-names defy interpretation, their original meaning often lost in the peculiarities of local dialect.

Some examples of bye-names

Skateraw
Loupie, Jing, Dodge, Swack, Goshen, Sonter, Stroupie

Downies
Rodelty, Pannach, Dooney Dod, Doonie John, Sunny Ken, Snockie, Jumbles George, Shakie's Doddie, King's Alec, Fish Agnes, The Lairdie (owned own house) and five Leipers – Po, Tam, Chuckle, Bomber and Nack.

Findon
Drottie (the last line fisherman).

Portlethen (c.1900)
Goshen, Songie's Ondra, Bell's Joe, Muckle Ann, Cockie, Luckie, Babbie, Babbie's Willie, Lairdie, Lairdie's Robbie, Tetumie, Captain, Wildie, Luckie Deddy, Fite and Blackie, Pooby Bella, Sannasse's Sandy, Pizzie. Also Buckie Andrew (Wood), Little Geordie (Craig), Mighty James (Craig), Deaf Man (John Craig). The leading fisherman was known as The Provost (c.f. Usan, while at Ferryden there was a King of the Fishers).

Cowie

Tam, King, Scottie, Cockles, Cant, Waddy, Bannocks (all Christies); Ridley, Tan, Jonas, Curly (Massons); Merry, Totley, Tirley, Do (Adams); Stoo, Bass, Saut, Feem, Collie, Brosie (Taylors).

Stonehaven

Adam Nippy, Corkie, Cruse, Dunkie Donald, Fidgie Dorrit, Goshen, Gabert, Humpie Colman, Kaysie, Lichtie Hoo, Laddie Daw, Pimp Wid, Perlib, Potty's John, Baboon, Scutter's Rob, Snorie, Slob, Tather, Torry, Tod, Vie-you-go.

Ferryden (1855)

Taktime, Red Robbie, Shet Perlie, Tam Tuke, Willie Buckie, Jamie Wee, Water Willie, Lazy Jamie, Nicky, The Barnet (hence Barnet's Willie/Bob/Davie), Smoky, Elicky Tosslie, Tokie, Bob Teet, Lachadenny and the Codlins. In setting out the fishers took their cue from James Bull West, King of the Fishers, whose word was gospel.

Usan (1920s)

Archie's Bob, Margaret Ann's Peter, Willie's Granny Betsy, Jean's Wilt, Dey's Jock, Jemima's Geordie, Watch Toor Peter, Cartie Willie, Auld Diddlie, Grannie ower the green, Annie ower the green, Fiddler Davie.

Auchmithie

Coffee Bets, Babbie, Bo, Cock's Jock, Moggy, Davy Bow Cargill.

Broughty Ferry

Cathy Tam, Willsay, Carver Robbie, Quack, Annie the Tweenie, Happy Annie, Tammie Mannie, Tappy.

Appendix II: Fisher surnames

Ordinary folk in lowland Scotland only began to acquire surnames from the 14th century but such lowly folk as fishers are rarely documented before 1600 and few much before the 1660s from when many parish registers begin. The earliest record of fisher names in the district is from Montrose in 1470, when three skippers from some outlying fishertoun were each sold a boatload of mussels. Their names were very ordinary and modern sounding: John Anderson, David Wright and Andrew Wilsone. Only Anderson is later found as a fisher surname in the district.

Surnames have four origins: from occupations, such as Taylor, Smith or Soutar; from an ancestor's name, such as Alexander, Wat(t) or Adam, sometimes with –son added as in the case of Thomson or Anderson; from some personal epithet such as Brown, Reid, Swankie or Blaber; or from the place of origin, such as Cargill, Coull or Bridgeford. Early examples of the latter were prefixed de or 'of' and were used by high-ranking persons in the 12th and 13th centuries but around 1400 to 1450 prefixes were dropped when such names began to be used by ordinary folk. Thus de Berkeley became Barclay and de Kethenis became Caithness. Victorian antiquarians found many surnames peculiar to individual fishertouns and came to the erroneous conclusion that many Scots fisherfolk were descended from settlers of Norwegian, Dutch or even Spanish origin, the latter from the 1588 Armada! The fishers themselves began to believe this but in fact there is not a single surname, even the rarest or most unusual, which is of exotic origin. Although there are surnames of Gaelic, Anglo-Saxon, Middle English or Scots, Old French, Breton, Anglo-Norman, Flemish and Scandinavian origin, none were peculiar to fisherfolk and most are recorded earlier among landward folk in Scotland. In the 17th and 18th centuries, and sometimes later, the surnames current in fishertouns can sometimes be found among the landward population in the same area, which demonstrates that they emerged from the local population and did not arrive by sea from foreign parts. Since fishers only rarely migrated before the 18th century their surnames often became very rare outside a particular community. This, together with the peculiarities of their micro-dialects, gave rise to the theory of exotic origin. The dialects, too, were simply a variation of local speech, reinforced by inter-marriage almost exclusively among fisherfolk in the same village or parish, while many words were technical terms peculiar to their occupation. In some communities continuity in surnames continued through several centuries but few sets of names remained static. Some surnames became more common simply because some families had more sons than daughters. The names below are almost all of males, since only they could transmit their surnames to the next generation. Scottish women, however, never took their husband's surname until the first household census of 1841, when all were given the same surname as their husbands owing to the rules having been drawn up in London. Some communities shared a handful of surnames while others of a similar size had no predominant names. Fishertouns in the same parish usually shared some surnames, while those in the next parish might have a completely different set of names. So it is usually possible to tell exactly where incomers to existing or new-founded communities originated.

Only surnames which occur more than once in one place, or once in at least two different places, however far apart in time and distance, are listed below. In a couple of cases non-fishers with sea-faring connections have been included but with their occupations noted in brackets. Migration became more common in the 19th century as some new villages were founded and the movement which came about with herring fishing from the 1830s sometimes induced fishers to settle elsewhere for various reasons. Where such common names as Smith or Watt appear spread widely in time or distance there is no reason to assume that they originate from a common ancestor, as is likely in the case of such localised names as Swankie, Cargill, Blues or McBay. Most of the sources used were no later than 1900 but of the names recorded then, most have remained common in the same community. The main sources were the parish registers, only a few of which start before the late-17th century, some not until the early-18th, so the earliest record of a surname is not necessarily the earliest occurrence in a particular community. Since few registers give place of residence within a parish or occupation before the mid-18th century it is the registers of births which are the most useful as the wife was recorded under her own name and there were two male witnesses. If the husband and any of the others, but especially all four, have surnames commonly found as fisher names later in the same community, or at the same time in neighbouring ones, then it is safe to assume that the husband was a fisherman. The household census returns, every ten years from 1841 and open at time of writing to 1901, are a sound source, giving the occupation and relationship of every person. Not every census book was gone through, nor were all later records such as valuation rolls. So if 1881 or 1891 is given as the last date this does not mean that the surname did not continue to be common, only a date up to around 1900 was generally sought. The most commonly accepted spellings are quoted first.

ADAM
>a very common personal name in the 12th and 13th centuries, later a surname. Johnshaven 1720; Montrose 1720–50; Cowie 1727–28, 1739, 1771, 1841–91; Stonehaven 1841–81; Crawton 1861; Catterline 1890.

ALEXANDER
>from the personal name. The name of the ancient Greek hero became popular in Scotland since it was also the name of three medieval Scottish kings. Found as a surname from around 1400, and once pronounced Elshinder. Although found in the district before 1841, a few also migrated from Buchan in the mid-19th century. Johnshaven 1720, 1841–91; Ferryden 1753–56; Catterline 1772; Stonehaven 1800, 1841; Arbroath 1871; Ethie Haven 1881.

ALLAN/ALAN
>from the Celtic personal name. Although the Gaelic equivalent was *Ailene*, in lowland Scotland the name probably originated from the Breton *Alain*, which became a surname by 1400. Arbroath 1650–1700 (female); Cove 1676, 1734–44, 1841–91; Montrose 1700–20, 1779–90; Johnshaven 1710–50; Stonehaven 1722–25; Gourdon 1730; Milton 1746–1778; Torry 1813, 1841; Portlethen 1841.

ALLARDYCE/ALLARDICE
>from the barony in Arbuthnott parish. Ferryden 1714–23; Milton 1732.

ANDERSON
>from Andrew's son. A common Scots surname from the 15th century. Recorded as the surname of a fishing skipper visiting Montrose in 1470. Broughty Ferry 1646–54, late-17th century – 1784, 1841–95; Findon 1691; Ferryden 1753–56, 1841, 1895; Montrose 1779–1840s; Usan 1787, 1861; Milton 1841.

ANDREW
>from the personal name. It occurs as a surname from 1330 and is recorded in Aberdeen from 1399. Crawton 1841–61; Gourdon 1891.

AITON/AYTON see Eaton

BARCLAY
>probably from Berkeley, Gloucestershire. Found in Scotland from the 12th century. Alexander de Berkeley married the heiress of Mathers. Crawton 1698–1767.

BAXTER
>from the occupation of bakester, a baker (originally applied to women). Found in Fife 1200–40 and in Angus from 1296, where the first Baxters may have been royal bakers. Still a common name in Angus. Torry 1743, 1807, 1813; Ferryden 1841.

BEATTIE/BEATTY/BEDDY/BEDDIE/BEDIE/BIDDY/BATY
>from a diminutive of Bartholomew. At first common in the Borders in the 14th century, it occurred in Aberdeen by the 15th century and in Montrose and the Mearns from 1500. Usually spelt Beattie from the 1740s. Arbroath 1656–1700 (female), 1780, 1821, 1826 (mariner), 1841–91; Auchmithie 1669–1890s; Johnshaven 1710; Torry 1743; Stonehaven 1745; Tangleha' 1921.

BISSET

diminutive of Old French *bis*, a rock dove. As a surname it occurs in southern Scotland from the 12th century and in the north-east from 1364. West Haven 1841–1891.

BLABER/BLABAR/BLAIBER/BLEBAR/BLEBBAR

from Scots *blaber/blabber*, an inarticulate speaker. As a surname it occurs in Aberdeen from 1408 and Arbuthnott in 1626. The earliest spelling was Blaiber. Portlethen 1691, 1716, 1739, 1766; Crawton 1703–08, 1725; Stonehaven 1722–30; Skateraw 1758, 1765.

BLAIR

from the commonly occurring Gaelic place-name *blar*, a clearing, plain or battle. It occurs as a surname de Blare in 1204 and as Blair by around 1400. Stonehaven 1822, 1861–81; Cowie 1841.

BLUES/BLEWS/BLEWIS

the earliest form was Blewhouse, from a place-name ('blue' possibly referring to a slate roof). This form was recorded in Bervie parish around 1600 but the descendants later spelled the name Blewis or Blews and from around 1840 Blues. Johnshaven 1684–1780, 1841–91; Gourdon 1698, 1770–80, 1841–81; Milton 1706–1803; Tangleha' 1820s.

BONNER

from Old French *bonair*, gentle, courteous. As a surname it occurs in Aberdeen in the 13th century. Cove 1730; Stonehaven 1881.

BRAND

from the Old Norse personal name *Brandr*. As a surname it is found at Irvine in 1323 and Edinburgh from 1512. Milton 1717–20; Torry 1743, 1791, 1813; Altens 1807–13; Cove 1841.

BREMNER/BREMER/BREBNER/BRYMER

from Brabener, a native of Brabant in the Netherlands, but which came to mean 'weaver' in Scots. William Brabner was a white-fisher in Fittie, Aberdeen, in 1601. Ferryden 1714–23; Muchalls 1764; Stonehaven 1776; Arbroath 1837, 1841, 1871.

BRIDGEFORD/BRIDG(E)FOORD/BRIGFUIRD

from the lost barony of Bridgeford in Dunnottar parish on the Catterline Burn near East Mains of Barras. The earliest spelling was Brigfuird. Stonehaven 1637, 1672–1728, 1881 (harbourmaster); Crawton 1708–75; Catterline 1732–76.

BRODIE/BRODDIE/BREDDIE/BRYDIE/BRIDIE

from the barony of Brodie in Moray but probably confused with another name, Bridie, once common in Lochwinnoch, Renfrewshire. Originally de Brodie in the 14th century, by 1492 simply Brodie. Muchalls 1716; Skateraw 1727, 1757–60, 1871, 1890; Cove 1738, 1743; Torry 1760s, 1813; Cowie 1841–81; Stonehaven 1861; Crawton 1861–91; Catterline 1881–90.

BROWN

from Anglo-Saxon *brun*, brown. Found as a surname in Annandale around 1200, at Elgin in 1261 and Dundee and Aberdeenshire around 1280. Spelt Brown but in Scots pronounced Broon. Stonehaven 1725, 1841–61; Stranathro 1841.

BRUCE

from Brix in Normandy. Originally de Brus in Scotland, by 1400 it became a common Scots surname as Bruce. Found in Ferryden in the 18th century but the later Bruces in Arbroath came from Buchan. Ferryden 1723, 1753–56, 1841; Arbroath 1891.

BRYMER see Bremner

BUCHAN

from the province, a common surname in Buchan fishing communities from where they migrated south from the mid-19th century. Crawton 1861; Catterline 1861–81.

BURNET(T)

from the Anglo-Saxon personal name *Beornheard* or Bernard. Found as a surname Burnard at Melrose around 1200, later spelt Burnett. Cowie 1725; Torry 1881.

CAD(D)ENHEAD

from Calden-head on the Calden Water, Selkirkshire. Found as a surname Caldenhed in south-east Scotland from the 15th century. Archibald Cadenheid was a fishing skipper in Fittie, Aberdeen, in 1601. Cowie 1720–32; Muchalls 1720–64.

CADDEL

a form of Calder, from the place-name Cawdor. Muchalls 1720; Cowie 1721–23.

CAIE/KAI/KAY

from Cai or Kei, one of the legendary knights of the Round Table, fashionable as a personal name in the 12th and 13th centuries. It occurs as a surname in Aberdeenshire from the 15th century. It was originally spelt Kay or Kai in the Mearns but from 1790 Caie. Cove 1677, 1742, 1789–91, 1841–91; Torry 1841–81.

CAITHNESS

from the parish of Kettins in south-east Perthshire. It occurs as de Kethenis in 1345, after 1400 Catnes or Ketenis. It occurs in Aberdeen in 1454, Panbride parish in 1626 and Montrose in the 1660s in a non-seafaring context. Arbroath 1660, 1821 (mariner), 1826; East or West Haven 18th century, 1800; Broughty Ferry 1759–1801; West Haven 1841–95.

CANT

a Flemish name occurring in Fife in 1376. The provost of Montrose in 1430 bore the name and it later occurs on the east coast sometimes borne by seafarers and merchants. Crawton 1672–97.

CARCHRIE/KERKARY

from Carcary, Maryton parish, Angus. A very rare name not in any book of Scottish or British surnames. Milton 1723–31, 1758.

CARGILL

from the lands of Cargill, near the confluence of the River Isla and the Tay. Borne as a surname by landsmen connected with Coupar Angus Abbey and Arbroath and its abbey in the 15th century, sometimes as Kergyll. It may have occurred in Auchmithie long before records begin in the 1660s, and was the commonest fisher surname there. Many migrated from Auchmithie to Arbroath, where it was also previously found, from 1829. Arbroath 1660, 1694, 1772, 1783 (shipmaster), 1841–91; Auchmithie 1669–1930; Ethie Haven 1770s, 1851–81; Montrose 1779–90; Usan 1787, 1841, 1861; Johnshaven 1841; Ferryden 1841,1895.

CARMICHAEL

from Carmichael in Lanarkshire. Broughty Ferry 1654; Montrose 1720–50.

CARNEGIE

from the barony of Carnegie, Carmyllie parish, Angus. Originally de Carnegy and borne by a landowning family, it became quite a common Angus surname by the 15th century. Gourdon 1841–61; Shieldhill 1871; Torry 1881.

CARRIE

an abbreviated form of Macharrie, from Irish *Mac Fhearadhaigh*, son of Feradach. A Galloway name, found in Ayrshire by the 15th century. Arbroath 1871.

CHRISTIE/CHRYSTIE

from a diminutive of Christopher. A very common surname in eastern Scotland from the 15th century. Stonehaven 1672–97, 1881; Arbroath 1680s (female); Skateraw 1724–58, 1785, 1841 onwards; Catterline 1803; Stranathro 1841–71; Cowie 1841–90; Shieldhill 1871–81.

CLARK

from *clerc*, clergyman, the only literate class of people in the early middle ages. It occurs as a surname from around 1400. East or West Haven 1600–24, throughout 18th century; Usan 1657; Milton 1705–20; Broughty Ferry 1715; Arbroath 1781; West Haven 1800–1930s; Crawton 1828–81, Stonehaven 1881; Montrose 1880s–90; Ferryden 1895.

CLOUDSLIE/CLOUDSLY

from Cloudesly, a Sussex surname, probably from a place-name. It occurs as the name of burgesses and merchants in Montrose from 1638 into the 18th century. Milton 1723, 1730–36.

COBBAN (see also Gibbon)

from the Old Norse personal name *Kolbein*. As a surname it occurs in Aberdeen as Coban in 1486. It may later have been confused with Gibbon found at nearby Cowie in 1724. Muchalls 1720.

COLLIE/COLY (see also Cowie)

from Gaelic *coille*, a wood. The surname probably derives from the barony of Collie or Cowie. It occurs as a surname as de Coly in 1296, and as Coly in Aberdeen in the 15th century. Findon 1691; Crawton 1709; Stonehaven 1841; Gourdon 1841–61, 1891.

CORMACK/CARMACK/GARMACK/KERMACK/KERMAG

from Kermuck, Aberdeenshire rather than the Gaelic personal name *Cormac*. It appears as a surname in Aberdeenshire as de Carmuick, Carmuk and Kermaghe around 1382–1552. Montrose (Garmack) 1636, (Kermuck/Kermack/Cormack) 1685–1720; Shieldhill 1678, 1861; Johnshaven 1687; Gawpol 1731–34, 1784; Catterline 1755; Muchalls (Kermack/Cormack) 1757–64; Cowie 1759.

COULL/COUL

probably from Coull, Tannadice parish or Coul, Lintrathen parish, Angus. This commonly occurring place-name is from Gaelic *cùil*, a neuk, secure place or retreat or *cùl*, back as in 'at the back of'. As a surname it probably arose independently elsewhere. It was borne by a Dundee merchant skipper around 1625–35 and must have been of Angus origin although it occurs in Aberdeenshire as de Cull around 1230, and in Glasgow in 1458 as Cowl. It also occurs as a fisher name in the Buckie area, Banffshire, from where fishers migrated to Ferryden. It became the commonest surname there. Ferryden 1686–1895; Arbroath 1727 (female); Usan 1841, 1861; Ethie Haven 1841–81; Shieldhill 1851; Tangleha' 1881; Montrose 1890–1915; Gourdon 1891; Johnshaven 1891.

COUPER/COWPER

from Cupar, Fife or the occupation of cooper. It occurs in Aberdeen in 1281, 1468 and 1477, Berwickshire in 1296 and was common in Fife. Cove 1676; Portlethen 1691.

COWIE (see also Collie)

from Gaelic *coille*, a wood. The surname probably derives from the barony of Cowie. It was also a common fisher surname at Buckie and was found at Macduff and Charleston-St Combs in Buchan but probably arose independently. Johnshaven 1720–30; Montrose 1819, 1841.

COWPER see Couper

CRAIG

from Gaelic *creag*, a rock, a commonly occurring place-name. Locally probably from the parish of Craig in which Ferryden and Usan lie. As a surname it occurs as de Crag in Aberdeen around 1278–1358, and from 1400 as Crag or Craig. Johnshaven 1684; Portlethen 1718–71, 1816–1907; Cowie 1727–39; Stonehaven 1746, 1841–81; Skateraw 1758, 1890; Downies 1803; Cove 1803, 1841, 1891; Burnbanks 1804–81; Stranathro 1819, 1841; Torry 1881; Gourdon 1891; Broughty Ferry 1895.

CRAIGIE/CREGIE

from a place-name (see also Criggie). Portlethen 1691; Milton 1697–1707; Johnshaven 1841; Montrose 1880s.

CRAMOND

from Cramond near Edinburgh. Originally de Cramond 1289–1388, by 1476 simply Cramond. Milton 1716–21.

CRAWFORD

from the barony of Crawford, Lanarkshire. Originally de Crawford, from 1400 found without a prefix. It also occurs among the Fraserburgh fishers. East Haven 1800–91.

CRIGGIE/CRIGIE/GRIGGIE

from Criggie near St Cyrus (see also Craigie). Johnshaven 1684–1775; Gourdon 1698, 1730–70, 1841–91.

CRUICKSHANK

possibly a geographical name (shank is a projecting hill-slope as well as a leg) rather than a personal epithet. It occurs as a surname in Haddington in 1296. Johnshaven 1700; Crawton 1706; Shieldhill 1861.

CUSHNIE

from Cushnie in Leochel parish, Aberdeenshire. It occurs as a surname in Aberdeen from 1500. Montrose 1815–48.

DAVIDSON

from David's son. Robert Davidson was provost of Aberdeen 1408–11, killed at Harlaw. Later widespread from Ayrshire to Dundee, arising independently in more than one place. Crawton 1775–1920s; Johnshaven 1841; Shieldhill 1861; Catterline 1881–91; Gourdon 1891.

DICKIE

from a diminutive of Dick, itself derived from Richard, and must have arisen independently in other areas. It occurs as a surname in Glasgow in 1504 and a David Dickie was a burgess of Montrose in 1627. Gourdon 1698–1730; Milton 1710–24; Johnshaven 1720–50.

DICKSON/DIXON

son of Dick (derived from Richard). William Dicson was a bailie in Aberdeen in 1398. Milton of Mathers 1861; Johnshaven 1881.

DOERS

a version of Dewars, derived from Gaelic *deradh*, keeper of sacred relics, or from the place-name Dewar, Midlothian. Montrose 1700–20.

DONALD

from the common Gaelic personal name *Domhnall*. It occurs as a surname in Kinross in 1328, Aberdeen in 1398, Kelso in 1567 and Jedburgh in 1641. Cove 1677; Gawpol 1733; Ferryden 1753–56.

DONALDSON

from Donald's son, or translated from Gaelic *Mac Domhnall*. Recorded as a surname from the 14th century. Tangleha' 1881–1902.

DORWARD/DURWARD/DORRIT/DORRAT

from the honorable position of the king's door-ward. Alan (the) Durward was a very important Angus landowner in the 13th century. Lesser lords, and abbeys and cathedrals, could also have had door-wards from which the name could have arisen. It occurs fairly frequently as a surname in Angus and Aberdeenshire from 1500. Milton 1739–40; Montrose before 1750; Crawton 1828; Broughty Ferry 1895.

DOUGLAS

from the lands of Douglas in Lanarkshire, from which Sir James Douglas, henchman of King Robert I, took his name. It became a fairly common Scots surname from 1400. Johnshaven 1841; Gourdon 1841–91.

DUNCAN

from the common Gaelic personal name *Donnchadh*. It is found as a surname from 1367, and in Aberdeen from 1402. Johnshaven 1687, 1891; Arbroath 1792; Ferryden 1841, 1895; Stonehaven 1861; Ethie Haven 1895–1901.

DURWARD see Dorward

EATON/AITON/AYTON

from Ayton near Eyemouth in Berwickshire. It occurs as a surname by 1400. Locally it was spelt Eaton from around 1800. Auchmithie 1776–1930s; Arbroath 1891.

ESPLIN

from the Old Testament name Absalom. It occurs as a widespread if uncommon surname in lowland Scotland from around 1500. Ferryden 1716; East Haven 1891.

EWAN

from the Gaelic personal name *Eoghann*. Apparently a surname from around 1200. Ferryden 1753–56; Montrose 1819.

FAIRWEATHER

of sunny disposition. Recorded in Perth in the reign of James II (1437–60). A branch of the family originated in the Menmuir district of Angus. Arbroath 1713 (female); Cowie 1890.

FALCONER

from the occupation. A burgess of Montrose in 1350 bore the surname. Cowie 1627–36; Stonehaven 1708–30 (boatbuilder).

FALT

probably Scots *falt* (pronounced faut), fault, blame or injury. Gourdon 1710, 1750, 1770; Shieldhill 1749 (female).

FERRIER

from Scots *ferrier*, a farrier, one who shoes horses. Broughty Ferry 1749, 1757, 1776, 1841–95; Johnshaven 1891.

FIFE see Fyffe

FINDLAY/FINDLOW/FINLAY/FINLAW

from the Gaelic personal name *Fionnlaigh*. As a surname it occurred in Brechin as Fyndelai in 1526. Also a common fisher surname at Cullen, Banffshire. Catterline 1627; Ferryden 1696, 1723, 1753–56, 1819, 1841, 1895; Broughty Ferry 1761.

FITCHET

perhaps from a place-name, Montfitchett. Found in Suffolk and Devon in the 13th century and in north-east Scotland from the 14th century. A Walter Fitchet held land in Aberdeen in 1317. Usan 1787.

FORBES

from the lands of Forbes in Aberdeenshire. Originally de Forbes, by 1500 Forbes, a fairly common surname in the north-east. Torry 1742–44, 1760s, 1813, 1841–81.

FOWLER/FOULLER/FOULER

from the occupation of fowler (bird catcher). It occurs as a surname at Berwick in 1370, in Edinburgh in 1358, and as the name of an Aberdeen burgess in 1451. Cowie 1618, 1622–36; Cove 1676; Johnshaven 1685; Torry 1744, 1813, 1841.

FRASER

originally French *de Frisell*. Recorded as Fraser in 1160 and 1210, it later became a fairly common Scots surname. Montrose 1700–20.

FREEMAN

from Anglo-Saxon *freo mann*, a freeman (as opposed to a slave or serf). As a surname it occurs as Freman in Peebles-shire in 1296. Cove 1677; Gourdon 1730, 1841–91; Skateraw 1732, 1758, 1767–68; Catterline 1802, 1841–61; Crawton 1841–61; Tangleha' 1940s.

FYFFE/FIFE

from the county of Fife. Originally de Fyff, after 1400 it occurs without the prefix in various spellings such as Fieff or Fyff from Angus to Aberdeenshire. Broughty Ferry 1841, 1895.

GADIE/GADY

possibly from Gadie, Aberdeenshire. Ethie Haven 1770s; Usan 1787.

GALL/GAUL

from Gaelic *gall*, foreign, applied to the lowland Scots. It occurs as a surname in Perth in 1334, Glasgow in 1397 and Aberdeen in 1399. It also occurs as Gaul in Aberdeenshire. Broughty Ferry 1776, 1807, 1841, 1895; Auchmithie 1841; Ferryden 1895.

GARMACK see Cormack

GEMLO/GEMLOE/KEMLO/KEMLAY

of uncertain origin, possibly from a place-name. It occurs as a surname from Ayrshire to Angus between 1280 and 1477 as Kemblock, Kemloc or Kemlok. Johnshaven 1720–30; Montrose before 1750; Ferryden 1895.

GIBB

from a diminutive of Gilbert. David Gyb is recorded in Cupar in 1521. Johnshaven 1891.

GIBBON (see also Cobban)

from a diminutive of Gilbert, with the French diminutive ending *–on*. It occurs as a personal name in Ayrshire and Galloway in the 15th century, later it was a fairly uncommon surname. In the Mearns it may have been confused with Cobban found at nearby Muchalls in 1720. Cowie 1724.

GORDON

from Gordon in Berwickshire. It occurs first as a surname as de Gordon around 1150–60. The Gordons acquired Strathbogie (Huntly) and became the most powerful landed family in the north-east; from 1400 Gordon became a common north-east surname. Skateraw 1735; Downies 1812.

GOVE/GOAVE

from Gaelic *gobha*, a smith. The surname Gow is a variant. In the Mearns spelt Goave before the 1770s. Johnshaven 1668, 1716–70; Milton 1696, 1702–46, 1782; Stonehaven 1706; Gourdon 1710, 1841–61, 1891; Catterline 1881–91.

GOWAN

from Gaelic *gobhainn*, a smith (genitive of *gobha*). Stonehaven 1672–97, 1786; Gourdon 1698, 1710, 1770, 1810, 1891; Shieldhill 1742.

GOWANS

a variant of the above. Montrose 1636; Auchmithie 1669; Gourdon 1698–1810, 1841–91.

GRAY (see also Grey)

from Gray, a town in Normandy. A Hugo de Gray is recorded in Scotland in 1248. The name occurs as Gray from the 14th century and there was an important landowning family of the name in Angus. It could also have arisen as a personal epithet. Milton 1740; Ferryden 1753; Gourdon 1891.

GREGORY

from the personal name. William *filius Gregori* was provost of Crail in 1330. The surname occurs in Aberdeenshire from the 16th century. Auchmithie 1674; Stonehaven 1709.

GREIG

from the Pictish king Giric or his patron saint St Cyricus. The latter occurs in St Cyrus (formerly Ecclesgreig). Ferryden 1698; Stranathro 1841.

GREY (see also Gray)

possibly from an epithet referring to the colour of hair or clothing. A much less common spelling than Gray. Muchalls 1764.

GRIEVE

from the occupation, Anglo-Saxon *gerefa*, bailiff or steward. It occurs as a surname in Berwickshire in 1296 and at Fyvie, Aberdeenshire, in 1382. Crawton 1704–9; Milton 1745–63, 1769; Johnshaven 1841.

GUYON

from the personal name Guy with the French diminutive *–on*. It occurs as a surname in England from the 13th century as Guiun, Gwiun, Gyan and Wyon. Cove 1677, 1743, 1760, 1841–91; Altens 1807–08; Gourdon 1891.

HAMPTON

from the common English place-name Hampton. It occurs in Scotland as de Hamptone in Peebles-shire in 1233, as Hanton, the name of a Montrose burgess, in 1600, and at Brechin as Hampton in 1657. Gourdon 1698–1700; Milton 1731–37; Johnshaven 1810; Catterline 1841.

HERD

from the occupation, a herdsman or shepherd. East Haven 1841–1930s.

HILL

location or place-name, recorded as de la Hyll in 1271, de la Hill in 1321, later in the 14th century as de Hill and del Hylle. It occurs as Hill in Aberdeen and Midlothian from the 15th century and a Ninian Hill was a burgess of Montrose in 1592. Broughty Ferry 1711–13; Ferryden 1723.

HOGG/HOG

possibly from an epithet or from Anglo-Saxon *hoga*, careful or prudent. As a surname in Scotland it occurs as Hog, Hoge and Hogg from the 13th century. Also found as a fisher name at Cromarty. Gawpol 1732–43; Crawton 1828.

HOSACK

probably from Hossack, the name of the east mouth of the River Thurso. The surname occurs mainly in Inverness, Ross and Moray and as a fisher surname at Cromarty. Montrose 1815–48.

HUTCHEON

from French *Huchon*, a diminutive of Hugh. A personal name into the 15th century, from the 16th century it occurs as a surname. Milton 1716; Usan 1753.

INGLIS

from Scots *Englis*, English. It occurs as le Engleys in the 13th century and from 1400 as Inglis in Aberdeen, Glasgow and St Andrews. Arbroath 1700 (female); Johnshaven 1710–20; Usan 1723; Ferryden 1753–56, 1841, 1895; Montrose 1815–48; Crawton 1841.

JAFFREY

from the personal name Geoffrey, the French version of Germanic *Guthfrith*. It occurs at Peebles in the form le fitz Geffrai in 1296, by the 15th century as Geoffrey, and in Aberdeenshire from the 16th century as Jaffray. Johnshaven 1730–40, 1790.

JAMIE/JAME

diminutive of James, found as a surname from 1500. Milton 1697–1764; Gourdon 1740–60; Johnshaven 1750–70; Stonehaven 1822.

JAMIESON

James's or Jamie's son, a surname from the 15th century. Auchmithie 1669; Ferryden 1694; Stonehaven 1881.

JARVIS

from *Gervas(e)*, a Middle English personal name. Catterline 1745; Crawton 1767, 1775.

JOHNSTONE/JOHNSTON

from the barony of Johnstone in Annandale. Originally de Johnston(e), by the later 14th century without the prefix. Crawton 1709; Ferryden 1753–56, 1895.

KAY/KAI see Caie

KEMLO/KEMLAY see Gemlo

KERKARY see Carchrie

KERMACK/KERMAG see Cormack

KIDD/KID/KYDD:

from the Anglo-Saxon personal name *Cydd(i)* or possibly from Kit, a diminutive of Christopher. It occurs as a surname in Dundee from the 14th century. Arbroath 1695 (female), 1784, 1788 (shipmaster), 1891; Broughty Ferry 1718–84, 1841; Auchmithie 1720; Milton 1740.

KNIGHT

from Anglo-Saxon *cnicht*, a boy or serving-lad. Robert Knycht was a burgess of Arbroath in 1331, John Knycht was a canon of Brechin Cathedral in 1435. The surname occurs in Monifieth parish from 1650. Broughty Ferry 1710–21, 1761, 1781, 1841–91, 1895; Arbroath 1826 (mariner).

KNOWLES/KNOWS/KNOLLS

from knoll, a small rounded hillock, from a location or place-name. Findon 1738, 1756–72, 1841–81; Downies 1841–71; Torry 1881; Stonehaven 1881.

LAMANS/LEMANS

possibly from a Middle English or Scots epithet *lem(m)an*, lover, sweetheart; a very rare surname. Crawton 1841–61; Stonehaven 1881.

LARGIE

from Largie, Insch, Aberdeenshire. Alexander Largie in Kirkton of Fetteresso is recorded in 1656. Johnshaven 1685–1770, 1830–41; Catterline 1734.

LAW/LAWE

from a place-name, Middle English or Scots *law*, a conical hill. It occurs as a surname from the 15th century. Cowie 1627–36; Stonehaven 1672–97; Johnshaven 1700–80; Milton 1717–74; Gawpol 1742–44; Montrose 1779–90; Stranathro 1841–71.

LAWRENCE

from the personal name. It occurs as a surname from the 16th century. Milton 1729; Usan 1787; Broughty Ferry 1895.

LAWSON

from Laurence's son. It occurs as a surname from the 14th century. Broughty Ferry 1650s–1711, 1784; Usan 1716, 1776, 1787; Ethie Haven 1763–74, 1841; Montrose 1776; Auchmithie 1780–1800.

LEES/LEYS

probably from a commonly occurring place-name: leys is fallow ground. It occurs as a surname from the 15th century at Ellon, Aberdeenshire, and Dundee in various spellings, including Leis. Cowie 1762–85, 1841–91; Skateraw 1786, 1809–19, 1841–71, 1890; Stonehaven 1822–81.

LEIPER/LIEPER/LEPPER/LEPER/LEAPER/LIPPER/LIPER

from Anglo-Saxon *leapere*, a basket-maker. It appears as a surname in Edinburgh in the 12th century. Cowie 1618–36, 1727, 1841–90; Findon 1691, 1717–54, 1841–81; Muchalls 1720–37, 1758–59; Stonehaven 1722, 1861–81; Skateraw 1732–35; Portlethen 1771–1907; Burnbanks 1802, 1841–81; Cove 1803, 1841; Downies 1803–90; Stranathro 1814–19, 1841–71; Stonehaven 1822–81; Torry 1881.

LEMANS see Lamans

LINDSAY:

from the district of Lindesay in Lincolnshire. It occurs in Scotland as de Lindesey in 1124 and 1174, later as Lindsay, a fairly common surname in Angus. Johnshaven 1684; Usan 1694–1716, 1776; Montrose before 1750, 1776; Arbroath 1891.

LORIMER

from the occupation lorimer, a maker of bits, stirrups and other metal parts of horse-harness. It occurs as a surname in Perth in the 13th century and by the 15th century was widespread in lowland Scotland. It occurs in Monifieth parish in 1710 and at Monifieth itself (so probably a salmon fisher) in 1715. Broughty Ferry 1775, 1841, 1895.

LOW

uncertain, possibly a personal epithet in origin. A common Scots surname pronounced to rhyme with cow. Crawton 1698–1722; Johnshaven 1776.

LOWNIE

probably from the place-name in Dunnichen parish, near Forfar. Johnshaven 1710; Gourdon 1770 (sailor), 1841–91; Stonehaven 1861.

LUMSDEN

from the manor of Lumsden, Berwickshire. It occurs as de Lumisden in the 12th century and de Lummysden in 1335, by the 15th century as Lumsden. Crawton 1672–1728.

LYALL/LYELL

from the Anglo-Saxon personal name *Liulf*, but possibly confused with another Scots surname, Lyle, derived from French *de l'Isle*. It is recorded in Scotland from 1170 and by the 15th century it was quite a common surname in Angus and Aberdeenshire. Arbroath 1650s (female); Broughty Ferry 1719; Panbride parish (probably East Haven, as later) 18th century; Usan 1787; East Haven 1841–90.

MCBAY/MCBEY

from the Gaelic personal name *MacBeatha*, son of life. As a Gaelic patronymic it was *Mac mhic Beatha*, simplified to MacBeth, MacBey or MacVey. Although spelt McBay in recent times in the Mearns it is pronounced Mcbei. Milton 1777–1803; Tangleha' 1820s; Johnshaven 1830–91; Catterline 1881–93.

MACGREGOR

from Gaelic *Mac Griogair*, son of Gregory, a fairly common surname originating in the central Highlands. Milton 1723, 1790.

MACKAY/MACKIE

the Gaelic patronymic *Mac Aoidh* arose independently in Strathnavar and in Argyll. It became confused with another Gaelic name, Mac Kie, from Galloway, and the spellings MacKay and Mackie were often used interchangeably of the same person, although Mackie has the emphasis on the first syllable. MacKay also occurs as a fisher surname in Buchan and Easter Ross, but one MacKay in Catterline was a native of Caithness, unconnected with the earlier Mackies or MacKays in the area. Montrose (Mackie) 1636, (Mackie/Mackay) 1700–20; Johnshaven (Mackie) 1717; Stonehaven (Mackie) 1841–61; Catterline (MacKay) 1881.

MAIN

said to be from the Norse personal name *Magnus*. Main was a common fisher surname in Nairn, Hopeman and Burghead but may have originated in Orkney. Portlethen 1716–1907; Cowie 1725; Ferryden 1757; Downies 1777, 1780, 1800–90; Burnbanks 1803, 1841–81; Skateraw 1809; Stranathro 1819–71; Stonehaven 1861–81; Torry 1881.

MARSHALL

literally a horse-servant, or groom. Philip Marescallus (fl. c.1200) became through marriage the ancestor of the Keiths, Earls Marischal. Arbroath 1822 (pilot), 1841.

MARTIN

from the personal name. As a surname it is recorded in Edinburgh in 1386, becoming more common from the 15th century and found throughout the highlands and lowlands. Findon 1691; Johnshaven 1702.

MASSON/MASON/MESSON

from the occupation, a stonemason. Stonehaven 1672–97, 1725, 1861–81; Torry 1676, 1813; Cowie 1716–85, 1841–90; Muchalls 1723; Skateraw 1735, 1841–90; Crawton 1841–91.

MAXWELL

from Maccus Weil, a salmon pool in the Tweed near Kelso. It occurs in the 13th century as de Maccuswell, later Maxwell. Johnshaven 1687, 1720.

MEARNS

from the county name, Gaelic *a' Mhaoirne*, the Stewardry. As a surname it occurs as de Mernys in Aberdeen in 1401 and 1469 and at Brechin in 1435, later without the prefix. Johnshaven 1684–1802, 1841; Ferryden 1714, 1753–56, 1819, 1841–95; Montrose 1720–50; Usan 1723, 1787; Shieldhill 1749.

MELVIN

a form of Melville (from Malavile in Normandy) with which it was often interchangeable. Andrew Malvyn was a burgess of Arbroath in 1387. Catterline 1890.

MILNE/MILN/MILL

from Anglo-Saxon *myln*, a mill. As a surname it occurs as Myll around 1492–1528. Before 1800 Milne and Mill were often used interchangeably of the same person since the pronunciation is the same. Montrose 1636, 1700–20, 1815–48, 1880s; Arbroath 1670s (female); Johnshaven 1687, 1720–30; Stonehaven 1709, 1841; Milton 1728; Gourdon 1780–91.

MITCHELL

from the personal name Michael. It occurs as a surname spelt Michell from the 15th century. Cowie 1727; Torry 1797, 1841; Stonehaven 1861–81; Montrose 1880s.

MOFFART/MUFFART

of uncertain origin and very rare, possibly a version of Moffat, derived from the town in Dumfries-shire. Johnshaven 1685, 1687, 1720, 1770; Crawton 1672–97; Gourdon 1710.

MOFFAT

from the town. Nicholas de Mufet witnessed a charter by the Bishop of Glasgow before 1232. Ferryden 1841, 1895–98.

MOIR

from Gaelic *mor*, big. It occurs as a surname in Aberdeenshire and among burgesses of Aberdeen in the 14th and 15th centuries. Shieldhill 1789; Arbroath 1831 (mariner); Montrose 1871–1900; Gourdon 1891; Tangleha' 1891, 1900.

MONCUR

originally de Moncur, so from a place-name, containing the Gaelic element *moine*, bog or moor. By the 15th century without a prefix. Crawton 1800, 1830, 1841; Johnshaven 1891; Gourdon 1891.

MONRO/MUNRO

originally de Monro from a Gaelic place-name including the element *moine*, a bog or moor. As the name of a landed family in Easter Ross in the 14th and 15th centuries it kept the prefix, later losing it as it became a fairly common surname. Montrose 1808, 1817, 1841.

MORRICE/MORICE/MORRIS/MORRES/MORES

from the French personal name *Maurice*, meaning Moorish or dark. It occurs as a surname in Scotland from the 16th century. Milton 1705; Montrose 1720–50; Tangleha' 1722; Ferryden 1723; Cove 1791, 1841–91; Torry 1841–81.

MOWAT/MOUAT

from an Old French surname *Mont Hault*, high mountain, sometimes Latinised as *Monte Alto*. It appears in Scotland as de Muhaut in the 13th century, and occurs in Angus and Aberdeenshire from 1400 as Mohat or Mohaut. Gourdon 1861–91; Tangleha' 1902–14.

MUFFART see Moffart

MUNRO see Monro

MURRAY

from the province of Moray. It occurs in the Latinised form *de Moravia* in the 13th century and from the 14th century as Moray or Murray. It was also a very common fisher surname in Buckie. Milton 1717; Johnshaven 1750–60, 1841; Auchmithie 1841; Gourdon 1841–61.

NAPIER/NAPER

from the office of napier, a court official in charge of napery or table linen. A John Naper is recorded around 1290, and the form le Naper in 1296, but by around 1450 Naper or Napier occur without a prefix. Locally pronounced 'Naper' regardless of spelling. Torry 1677, 1813; Muchalls 1717, 1768; Johnshaven 1720.

NEILSON

from Niall's (Neil's) son. It appears in the 14th century independently in Ayrshire and Caithness. Cove 1677, 1742–3, 1841–91; Portlethen 1691; Montrose before 1750; Cowie 1841; Torry 1881.

NICOL/NICOLL

from a diminutive of Nicholas. John and Alexander Nuckall, white-fishers in Fittie, Aberdeen, are recorded in 1592. It also occurs as a fisher surname at Macduff. Milton 1790; Johnshaven 1841; Ferryden 1841, 1895.

NOBLE

from a French epithet *le noble*. It occurs around 1200 in the Latin form *Nobilis* and in 1296 as le Noble, but as Nobil in 1398 and Nobile in 1464. The name was later common among the Fraserburgh fishers, some of whom migrated to the Mearns from the mid-19th century. Crawton 1861–81; Stonehaven 1881; Catterline 1881–91.

NORRIE/NORIE/NORRY

from the Orcadian Norn *Norre*, Norway. As a surname it occurs in eastern Scotland around 1360–1408 as Nory and became widespread later in the 15th century. Broughty Ferry 1718, 1749, 1773–81, 1841, 1895.

OGILVIE

from a barony of the name in Glamis parish, Angus. It occurs as de Oggilvi in 1290 and de Ogilby in 1425, the name of a landholding family. From the 16th century it became a fairly common surname in Angus. Gourdon 1841–61, 1891.

ORKNEY

from the island name. It occurs in 1405 as a surname and at Arbroath in 1457, later widespread if uncommon. Montrose 1720–50.

PARIS

originally de Paris recorded from 1202 to 1506 in various spellings but simply Paris in 1489. It has been suggested that rather than being derived from the French capital city, it originated from a district of Lincolnshire, but this is unproven. It is quite a rare surname still found in the Dundee and Carnoustie area of the Angus coast. West Haven 1790–1841.

PATERSON/PATTERSON

from Patrick's son. It occurs in Aberdeen in the 15th century and Dundee from 1544 and has long been a common name in the district. Usan c.1650, 1723; Cove 1677; Montrose before 1750; Ferryden 1895.

PATON/PATTON

from a diminutive of Patrick with the French diminutive suffix –on. A surname from before 1500, it became quite common in Angus. Ferryden 1666, 1753–56, 1819, 1841–91, 1895; Usan 1666, 1685, 1697, 1723, 1753, 1787, 1841–1900; East or West Haven 1693, 18th century; Montrose 1815–80s; Auchmithie 1841–61.

PERT/PEART

probably from the parish of Pert near Northwater Bridge. The name is still localised in the coastal towns and villages of the district. Ferryden 1686, 1753–1895; Usan 1686, 1697, 1714, 1723, 1753, 1787, 1841, 1900; Montrose 1720–50, 1776, 1798, 1815–1915; Shieldhill 1851; Ethie Haven 1861, 1881; Torry 1881; Gourdon 1891; Arbroath 1891; Tangleha' 1914.

PETERKIN/PITTRECKEN

from a diminutive of Peter. It occurs as a surname in 1419, found in Aberdeen in 1468 and 1537 and in Moray in 1565. Usan 1757, 1787, 1798; Arbroath 1770–72 (female); Montrose 1776–90.

PETERS

from son of Peter. A not uncommon name in Angus and Aberdeenshire. West Haven 1841–90s.

QUHYT see Whyte

RAMSAY

from the district of Ramsay in Huntingdonshire. The first bearer of the name in Scotland was given land in Midlothian by King David I (1124–53). The name occurs as de Ramesie in the 12th century and as de Ramesay in 1395, later simply Ramsay. It is quite a common surname in Perthshire, Dundee and Angus. Johnshaven 1716–20; West Haven 1890–1930s; East Haven 1891–1920s.

RATTRAY

from Rattray in Perthshire. Montrose 1880s, 1915.

REID

from an epithet meaning red-haired. It occurs as le Rede in 1296 and in the 14th century as Reed or Rede, later Reid. It may also have been confused with the surname Reith. It also occurred as a fisher surname at Buckpool and Avoch. Johnshaven 1686, 1710, 1780–83, 1830–41; Stonehaven 1698–1700; Ferryden 1723; Cowie 1732.

RITCHIE

from a diminutive of Richard. It occurs from the 14th century as a surname at first spelt Richie, later Ritchie. It also occurs as a fisher surname at Rosehearty, Cairnbulg and Inverallochy in Buchan, from where some fishers migrated into the district in the 1860s. Stonehaven 1672–1709, 1820s–30s; Johnshaven 1702, 1720–50, 1830–91; Milton 1778–85; Gourdon 1790, 1841–91; Tangleha' 1841; Torry 1881; Arbroath 1891; Ferryden 1895.

ROBERTSON

from Robert's son, a name sometimes borne by members of the Clan Donnachie (Duncan) of Atholl, very rarely MacRobert. It is very common in the Tayside area and most Robertsons may in fact be descended from a Clan Donnachie chief called Robert who lived in the reign of King James I (1406–37). But the name arose independently in lowland Scotland and in England. A burgess of Montrose bore the surname in 1425 so he could not have been descended from the above Robert. Cowie 1618–36; Cove 1677, 1742, 1841–91; Johnshaven 1684–86; Altens 1807–08; Portlethen 1841; Torry 1841–81.

ROSS

from the province of Ross, also from Middle English *rouse* or Old French *rous*, red-haired. It occurs in the 12th century in Ayrshire as Ros, presumably derived from the latter. It was also a fisher surname at Burghead and Easter Ross, derived from the former. Montrose 1636, 1817; Broughty Ferry 1713–15, 1773–75; Milton 1782; Tangleha' 1841; Torry 1881.

SCOTT

from Scot, meaning a Gael and coined in Anglian south-east Scotland where Gaels were a tiny minority. It occurs from 1124 as le Scotte and in 1296 in south-east Scotland, and is found in Dundee as Scot in 1348. Usan 1612–1670s; Johnshaven 1702; Ferryden 1714, 1753–56; Milton 1734, 1767; Broughty Ferry 1841; East Haven 1841–91.

SHEPHERD

from the occupation. It occurs as a surname in Elgin in 1362 and in Angus from 1513. Auchmithie 1672–1930; Montrose 1720–50; Milton 1804; Ethie Haven 1841; Arbroath 1871–91; Johnshaven 1891.

SIM

from a diminutive of Simon, it is recorded as a surname from 1500. Usan 1714–16; Broughty Ferry 1841.

SIMPSON

from Sim's son. It occurs as a surname from around 1400 in various spellings such as Symsoun. Broughty Ferry 1711, 1718; Ferryden 1841; Johnshaven 1841–91; West Haven 1895.

SKIRLING

from Skirling in Peebles-shire. It occurs prefixed de in 1335, as Skyrlyn in 1520, and in Perth in 1607. Montrose 1636; Broughty Ferry 1711; Arbroath 1826–30 (pilot).

SMART

from the Old English personal name *Smert*. Found in Fife in 1376. A John Smert was a citizen of Brechin in 1452. Ferryden 1694; Montrose 1720–50.

SMITH

from the occupation. The commonest surname in the English-speaking world. The name was particularly common in Auchmithie from the 1660s and was the commonest fisher surname in Arbroath from 1841–71, only later outnumbered by Cargills. It was also a fisher surname in East Fife and on the Buchan-Moray coast from where some may have migrated into the district from the mid-19th century. Cowie 1618–36; Auchmithie 1669–1930s; Findon 1691; Stonehaven 1704–08; Milton 1739, 1761; Torry 1741–44, 1813; Ferryden 1753–56; Arbroath 1774, 1832, 1841–91; Cove 1841; Shieldhill 1841–51; Ethie Haven 1881; Gourdon 1891; Broughty Ferry 1895.

SOUTER/SOUTAR/SUTAR

from the occupation of soutar, a shoemaker. A fairly common Scots surname, arising independently all over lowland Scotland. It also occurs as a fisher surname at Lossiemouth. Milton 1729–44; Johnshaven 1891; Ferryden 1895.

SPINK

from Scots *spink*, active or agile. The earliest record of this very rare surname is of a Robert Spinc at Elgin in 1261. In Angus it appears almost solely as the name of fishers and seafarers. An Alexander Spink was shoremaster at Arbroath in 1624. East Haven 1600–24, 1800; Arbroath 1600, 1656–1891; Auchmithie 1669–1930s; Ferryden 1841, 1895.

STEPHEN (see also Steven)

from the personal name. It occurs in the Mearns fishertouns in the 18th century but from 1861 newcomers migrated from Fraserburgh, Cairnbulg and Inverallochy, where it was also common. Skateraw 1758, 1841–71; Catterline 1785–1891; Stonehaven 1800–41; Crawton 1861; Ethie Haven 1861; Johnshaven 1891; Ferryden 1895.

STEVEN/STIVEN (see also Stephen)

a Scots spelling of the personal name. It occurs as a surname from the 1470s. Stonehaven 1722–30; Skateraw 1732.

STEWART/STUART

from the office of royal steward, although it could also have arisen independently as others also had stewards, hence the saying 'Aa the Stewarts are nae sib tae the king'. It has been one of the commonest Scots surnames from the 14th century. It was the commonest fisher surname at Lossiemouth, from where some may have migrated from the mid-19th century. Gourdon 1841–91; Ferryden 1841, 1895; Broughty Ferry 1895.

STIVEN see Steven

STRACHAN

from the Deeside parish, originally Strathauchen. It occurs as de Strathekane in 1268, by 1400 without the prefix. It also occurs as a very common fisher surname in Buchan. Johnshaven 1716–20.

STUART see Stewart

STURROCK

from Middle English or Scots *storach/storrack*, a flock-master or store-master. It occurs as a surname in Aberdeen around 1448–53, at Dunnichen in Angus in 1509 and in Dundee in 1687. Broughty Ferry 1776, 1841–91, 1895.

STUTE

possibly from Scots for stout (pronounced 'stoot'). A Gilbert Stute was a burgess of Aberdeen in 1212; it also occurs as Stut in 1265. A very rare surname. Johnshaven 1710–30; Stonehaven 1861.

SUMMERS

from Somer (Old French *somier*), a sumpter or pack-horse (also applied to men). The Symmers or Somyrs of Balzeordie were an old Angus dynasty. Ferryden 1819, 1841.

SWAN

from the Anglo-Danish personal name *Swein*. It is found as a personal name in Anglian south-east Scotland in the 12th century and from 1250 it occurs as a surname in Fife. Arbroath 1678, 1841–91; Auchmithie 1686, 1820–61.

SWANKIE

from Scots *swank*, lithe, supple or a show-off. It occurs as Swanky in Dundee in 1578 and as Swankie in Angus in 1613, neither in a seafaring context. It has been virtually exclusive to Auchmithie from 1730 and Arbroath from the 1830s. Of 63 Swankies in the local telephone book at time of writing (c.1990), only nine were not residents of Arbroath or Auchmithie. It is so distinctive and exclusive to the area that seagulls in Arbroath are jokingly referred to as 'Swankie's doos'. It is so rare otherwise that it is not in any book on Scottish or British surnames. Auchmithie 1730–1930s; Arbroath 1837–91; Ethie Haven 1881–95.

TAILOR/TAYLOR/TAILYEOR/TYLIOR

from the occupation, originally French *tailleur*, literally cutter. It occurs as le Tayllur in 1276, Taillur in 1296. It was later a common Scots surname, often spelt Tailyeour. Crawton 1672–1700; Muchalls 1720, 1764; Milton 1720, 1736, 1768; Skateraw 1785; Cowie 1841–90; Catterline 1841–91; Stonehaven 1881; Gourdon 1891.

TAIT

from an Old Norse personal name *Teitr*, meaning glad or cheerful. In the 14th century it is found as a surname in Edinburgh and Montrose. It was also a fairly common fisher surname at Fraserburgh, Cairnbulg and Inverallochy in Buchan, from where they may have migrated. Arbroath 1830 (pilot), 1841–71; Torry 1881.

TAYLOR see Tailor

TEVIOTDALE

from Teviotdale in Roxburghshire. It occurs prefixed de in 1233 and 1328, later it occurs without the prefix. East or West Haven 1693, 18th century; Johnshaven 1720; Arbroath 1891.

THOM

from the diminutive of Thomas, found as a surname by the 15th century. Ferryden 1714; Gawpol 1750.

THOMSON

from Thom's son. It occurs in 1318 and since the 15th century has been a very common Scots surname. Cove 1677; Torry 1881.

THORN/TORN

from Turin, Aberlemno and Rescobie parishes, Angus. Recorded as de Torrin in Fife in 1231, and in Aberdeen as Turin in 1323 and Torne in 1493, but fairly rare. It occurs at Cotton of Usan around 1700. Two fishers called Torn or Thorn were the first settlers at Ethie Haven, also known as Torn's Ha'en. Ethie Haven 1701–42; Milton 1721; Arbroath 1781 (female).

TINDAL/TENDELL

from Tynedale, Northumberland. It occurs as de Tindal around 1208–13, later without the prefix in Angus and Dundee. Findon 1691; Crawton 1704–08; Montrose 1815–48.

TORRIE/TORRY

from the place-name. David Torry was a burgess in Elgin in 1590. The place-name also occurs in Fife and Dumfries-shire. Montrose 1880s–1915.

TRAIL

possibly from a place-name. It occurs from the 14th century in Aberdeen, Dundee and Fife, from where the Orkney Trails originated. Johnshaven 1720, 1750–60, 1841.

TWEDALE/TWEDDAL

from Tweed-dale in Peebles-shire. Recorded as de Tweddale in 1376 but Twedale from around 1400. Ferryden 1714, 1723; Montrose 1720–50.

TYLIOR see Tailor

WAITER

from the occupation of waiter, a Customs officer, sometimes called a tide-waiter, who could board any vessel. A very rare name not in any book of Scottish or British surnames. Johnshaven 1881 (female); Ethie Haven 1881–91 (salmon fisher); Gourdon 1891.

WALKER

from the occupation of waulker, a fuller of cloth. It occurs as a surname from the 14th century. Findon 1691; Ferryden 1723; Crawton 1750, 1780; Stonehaven 1822; Gourdon 1841–91; Shieldhill 1871–81; Torry 1881; Johnshaven 1891; Tangleha' 1902.

WAST see West

WATSON

from Watt's son. Found as a surname around 1400 in Edinburgh and Aberdeen and at Arbroath in 1450. It became a very common Scots surname by the 16th century and probably arose independently in various places. It was also a common fisher surname at Whitehills, Banffshire and Cromarty. Auchmithie 1669; Stonehaven 1672–1708; Crawton 1703–08; Ferryden 1714–16; Milton 1717, 1730–37.

WATT

from a diminutive of Walter, found as a surname from the 16th century, arising independently in many places. It was also a common fisher surname at Macduff, Gamrie and Pennan in Banffshire. Catterline 1627, 1750, 1861, 1919; Shieldhill 1678, 1732–1920s; East or West Haven 1693–18th century; Johnshaven 1700–70; Arbroath 1700s–1777, 1804, 1841–91; Crawton 1705–26, 1841; Stonehaven 1706, 1725–35, 1881; Muchalls 1720–40; Cowie 1725–35, 1771; Gawpol 1733–90; Gourdon 1740, 1861–91; Auchmithie 1766–1881; Usan 1787; Ferryden 1819, 1841–91, 1895.

WEBSTER

from the occupation webster, a weaver. It appears as a surname by the 15th century and must have arisen independently all over lowland Scotland. Broughty Ferry 1711–15, 1760, 1771–76, 1841–91, 1895; Cove 1760, 1841–91; Torry 1841–81; Crawton 1881.

WELSH/WELCH

from Middle English or Scots *walshe*, foreign. It occurs as a surname in Scotland from the 13th century. Crawton 1723–27; Gourdon 1920s.

WEST/WAST

from a person's origin in a westward location. It arose independently in several places, including Perthshire, West Lothian and in England. But the Ferryden Wasts or Wests traditionally migrated from Crovie in Banffshire. It was also a very common surname in neighbouring Macduff and Pennan. Ferryden 1731–45, 1760s, 1819, 1841–95; Shieldhill 1851.

WHYTE

from a personal epithet. It is found Latinised as *Albe* at Forfar and Dundee around 1200. Sometimes later spelt Quhyt. Broughty Ferry 1759; Tangleha' 1803; Milton 1841.

WILL

from the diminutive of William, found as a surname from the 15th century. Johnshaven 1760, 1841; Portlethen 1816; Cowie 1841.

WOOD

originally an epithet arising from residence in or near a wood, it occurs as a surname from 1295. It was also a common fisher surname at Banff, Portsoy and Portknockie. Findon 1737–54, 1841–81; Burnbanks 1804–41; Portlethen 1816–1907; Downies 1835–90; Torry 1841–81; Cove 1841–91; Stonehaven 1861–81; Gourdon 1891; Johnshaven 1891.

WYLIE/WYLLIE

from a diminutive of William, found as a surname from the 14th century. Crawton 1827–91; Gourdon 1891.

YOUNG

from a personal epithet; it occurs as a surname from the 14th century. Johnshaven 1710; Broughty Ferry 1714–18, 1747; Montrose 1720–50; Ferryden 1753–56, 1841, 1895; Arbroath 1871–91.

Appendix III: Sources and references

The basic sources, used for every community (and in the case of many of the small fishertouns the only available information) were: the Statistical Accounts of the two counties (First: 1790–95, New or Second: 1835–42 and in some cases the Third: 1950–65); the parish registers of births, in some cases extant from the later 17th century; the household census returns every ten years from 1841 to 1891; in some cases the valuation rolls; the Fishery Board records of Dundee, Arbroath, Montrose and Stonehaven districts and the published creek accounts of 1855, 1881 and 1928; Customs letter books and quarterly accounts; cartularies such as the Register of the Great Seal and the Arbroath Abbey register (which enabled some communities to be traced back to the middle ages) and burgh records. Oral evidence, where available, was also used. For the Mearns in particular *MacFarlane's Geographical Collections* include a list of Mearns fishertouns of 1642 and some 18th-century accounts of parishes. Headrick's 1813 account of the agriculture of Angus has useful descriptions of fishing methods, boats and curing. Robertson's account of Mearns agriculture, also of 1813, very usefully gives the number of boats and crew for each community. The above sources can be assumed for all communities, other specific sources are noted under the appropriate headings.

Note: where a bibliography or references are indicated after a book title, details of the sources are not given as they can all be found within that work.

General, including background and comparative studies:

Groome, Francis 1884 *Ordnance Gazetteer of Scotland*, 6 vols. Edinburgh.

Illsley, WA (ed) 1977 *The Third Statistical Account of Scotland 1950–65: The County of Angus*. Arbroath.

Knox, John 1786 *Observations on the Northern Fisheries*. London.

Lewis, Samuel 1847 *Topographical Dictionary of Scotland*. London.

Mitchell, Sir Arthur (ed) 1906 *MacFarlane's Geographical Collections*. Edinburgh: Scottish History Society.

Annual Reports of the Fishery Board and the Fishery Board for Scotland: creek returns for 1855, 1881, 1928.

Sinclair, Sir John (ed) 1791–99 (repr 1976) *The Statistical Account of Scotland*, vols XIII (*Angus*) and XIV (*Kincardineshire and South and East Aberdeenshire*). Wakefield: EP Publishing Ltd.

Smith, Dennis (ed) 1988 *The Third Statistical Account of Scotland 1950–65*, vol XXIX *The County of Kincardineshire*. Edinburgh.

The New Statistical Account of Scotland, vol X, 1845 (*Forfar and Kincardineshire*). Edinburgh and London.

Wilson, John 1882 *Gazetteer of Scotland*. Edinburgh.

Cartularies

Liber de S Thome de Aberbrothoc (Arbroath Abbey Register) 1848, 1856, 2 vols. Edinburgh: Bannatyne Club.

Parish registers 1553–1854.

Registrum Magni Sigilli Regum Scottorum (Register of the Great Seal of Scotland), 11 vols (new ed 1984). Edinburgh: Scottish Record Office.

Monographs etc

Coull, J R 1989 Fisherfolk and fishing settlements of the Grampian region. J S Smith and D Stevenson (eds) *Fermfolk and Fisherfolk*. Aberdeen: University Press.

Coull, J R 1996 *The Sea Fisheries of Scotland: a Historical Geography*. Edinburgh: John Donald.

Goodlad, C A 1971 *Shetland Fishing Saga*. Lerwick: Shetland Times.

Gray, M 1978 *The Fishing Industries of Scotland 1790–1914*. Oxford: University Press.

Howarth, P 1957 *The Life-boat Story*. London: Routledge and Kegan Paul.

Jervise, A 1885 *Memorials of Angus and the Mearns*, 2 vols. Edinburgh.

Martin, A 1981 *The Ring-Net Fishermen*. Edinburgh: John Donald.

Morris, J 1992 *An Illustrated Guide to our Lifeboat Stations*, part 7 (*Scotland*): *with a brief history of every station past and present*. Coventry: Lifeboat Enthusiasts' Society.

Pennant, T 1790 *A Tour through Scotland in 1772*, 3 vols. London.

Ports of Registry in Great Britain and Ireland, 1997. Anstruther: Scottish Fisheries Museum.

Samuel, A M 1918 *The Herring, its Effect on the History of Britain*. London.

Smith, P 1985 *The Lammas Drave and the Winter Herrin': a history of the herring fishing from East Fife*. Edinburgh: John Donald.

Summers, D W 1988 *Fishing off the Knuckle in the Fishing Villages of Buchan*. Aberdeen: Centre for Scottish Studies, University of Aberdeen (17pp, fully referenced).

Maps

Adair, John 1703 *The Coast of Scotland from the Red Head to Aberdeen*.

Gordon, Robert and Pont, Timothy 1641x50 *Maps for the Scottish section of Bleau's Atlas*.
New ed 1856. Edinburgh: W H Lizars (since reproduced 2006 Edinburgh: Birlinn/NLS).

Roy, William 2007 *The Great Map: the Military Survey of Scotland 1747–1755*. Edinburgh:
Birlinn.

Ordnance Survey 6 inches to 1 mile and 25 inches to 1 mile series: see under The Mearns and
Angus for details.

Fishing Technology

Fishing methods

Adams, D G 1983a Line fishing: techniques and terminology of an ancient craft on the Angus
and Mearns coast. *Arbroath Herald Annual 1983*.

Adams, D G 1985 *Report on the History of Salmon Fishing in the Montrose Area from c.1360 to
1835*. Typescript, 19pp., fully referenced (copies with Montrose Public Library, Montrose
Museum, Royal Museum of Scotland, Edinburgh and Scottish Fisheries Museum,
Anstruther).

Adams, D G 1986a Notes on long-line fishing from Arbroath, Ferryden and Gourdon. *Review of
Scottish Culture*, no 2, 37–42 (list of oral and published sources).

Martin, Angus 1995 *Fishing and Whaling*. Edinburgh: National Museums of Scotland,
Scotland's Past in Action series (bibliography).

Walker, Bruce 1985 Sma' line fishing as practised from Arbroath and Gourdon in the 1950s and
1970s. *Focus on Fishing* Edna R Hay and Bruce Walker, 1985. Dundee: Abertay Historical
Society Publication no 23.

Boats (general)

MacDonald, Bill n.d. [1990s] *Boats and Builders: the history of boatbuilding around
Fraserburgh*. Fraserburgh: Y MacDonald.

Stewart, R 1986 *Sail & Steam*. Elgin: Moray District Libraries (boatbuilding in the Buckie area
from Port Gordon to Cullen 1840s–1920s).

Tanner, M 1996 *Scottish Fishing Boats*. Princes Risborough: Shire Publications Ltd.

Sailing boats

Adams, D G 1984 Fishing boats on the Angus and Mearns coast before 1848. *Flowin' Tide*,
no 6, July 1984. Organ of the Scottish Vintage and Veteran Fishing Boat Owners' Society.

Hallewell, R 1991 *Scotland's Sailing Fishermen: the History of the Scottish Herring Boom*.
Strathtummel: R Hallewell.

Knox, John 1786 *Observations on the Northern Fisheries*.

March, E 1972 *Sailing Drifters: the Story of the Herring Luggers of England, Scotland and the
Isle of Man*. Chapters 1/2/3/11/12. Newton Abbott: David & Charles (measured drawings
and technical terms).

Steam and motor boats

Smith, P 1998 *The History of Steam and the East Fife Fishing Fleet*. Leven: J Corstorphine.

Wilson, G 1995 *Scottish Fishing Boats*. Beverley: Hutton Press (bibliography).

Coasting vessels

Moyse-Bartlett, H 1946 *From Sail to Steam: the final development and passing of the sailing
ship*. London: The Historical Association (pamphlet).

Simper, R 1974 *Scottish Sail: a forgotten era*. Newton Abbott: David & Charles.

The Mearns

Monographs

Kinnear, G H 1921 *Kincardineshire* (Cambridge County Geographies). Cambridge: University
Press.

Mitchell op cit vol II.

Robertson, G 1813 *A General View of the Agriculture of Kincardineshire or the Mearns*. London (lists fishertouns, numbers of boats and fishers).

Watt, J C 1914 *The Mearns of Old*. Edinburgh and Glasgow: Wm Hodge & Co.

Maps

Garden, W 1797 (surveyed 1774) *Map of Kincardineshire*. London: A Arrowsmith.

Ordnance Survey 6 inches to 1 mile series *Kincardineshire* 1865 (surveyed 1860); 25 inches to 1 mile series 1864, 1904, 1927. Southampton.

Robertson, James 1822 *Topographical and Military Map of the Counties of Aberdeen, Banff and Kincardine*. London.

Thomson, John 1822 *Atlas: Kincardineshire*. Edinburgh.

Torry

Ogilvie, T W 1901 *The Book of St Fittock*. Aberdeen.

Altens

Adams, D G 1993a The Fishing Village of Altens. *Leopard Magazine*, no 182, August 1993, 24.

Burnbanks

Adams, D G 1993b The Lost Village of Burnbanks. *Leopard Magazine*, no 183, September 1993, 20.

Cove

Murray, Janet 1975 Going back to Cove. *Leopard Magazine*, vol 1, nos 8–9, April-May 1975.

Findon

Christie, A 1897 *The Finnan Haddie*. Aberdeen.

Henderson, J A 1892 *History of the Parish of Banchory-Devenick*. Aberdeen.

Portlethen

Henderson, J A op cit.

Downies

Information from Jean Nicoll, Downies.

Elsick and Skateraw

Adams, D G 1993c The Fishertoun of Elsick. *Leopard Magazine*, no 184, October 1993, 24.

Barron, Douglas G (ed) 1892 *Court Book of the Barony of Urie in Kincardineshire 1604–1747*. Edinburgh: Scottish History Society.

Christie, W 1968 Sketraw, a North-East Fishing Village. *Scots Magazine*, November 1968.

Garioch, Alexander 1722 Description of the parish of Fetteresso. In Mitchell, op cit, vol I, 247.

Information from John Masson, Skateraw Road, Newtonhill.

Stranathro

Information from John Masson, Newtonhill.

Muchalls

Aberdeen Journal, 13 December 1758.

Adams, D G 1993d The Fishertoun of Muchalls. *Leopard Magazine*, no 185, November 1993, 24.

Barron op cit.

Donald, James (Logie Farm, Stonehaven) 1919 The Seatown of Muchalls. *The Mearns Leader*. Stonehaven: D G McLaren (photocopy in Stonehaven Library).

Hill, J P 1956 *The Episcopal Church at Muchalls*. London: Mowbray and Co.

Mitchell op cit.

Information from John Masson, Newtonhill.

Cowie

Barron op cit.

Christie, E 1974 *The Empty Shore: the story of Cowie, Kincardineshire*. Cowie: E Christie (bibliography).

Mitchell op cit.

Stonehaven

Christie, E 1977 *The Haven under the Hill: the story of Stonehaven*. Cowie: E Christie (bibliography).

Keyth, J 'sometime minister of Dunotir' c.1642 Description of some remarkable things within the Sheriffdom of the Mearns. In Mitchell, op cit, vol III, 236.

Souter, R 1988 *A Wild and Rocky Coast*. Stonehaven: Stonehaven Ladies Lifeboat Guild (Stonehaven, Gourdon and Johnshaven lifeboats).

Crawton

Adams, D G 1994a The Ancient Village of Crawton. *Leopard Magazine*, no 187, January 1994, 24.

Catterline

Information from John Watt, Catterline.

Gawpol

Adams, D G 1994b The Lost Settlement of Gawpol. *Leopard Magazine*, no 188, February 1994, 40.

Shieldhill

Arbuthnott Muniments, Aberdeen University Archives (lease of 'Newhaven of Kinneff' 1678).

Information from John Watt, Catterline and Alex and Rena Welsh, Gourdon.

Inverbervie

Gibson, C 1964, 1969. From his Nature Diary column in *The Courier*, 5 December 1964 and 12 July 1969 (about salmon and the mouth of the Bervie Water).

The Royal Burgh of Inverbervie: official guide 1984. Inverbervie: Inverbervie Community Council.

Gourdon

Gove, Robert 1983 *Gourdon in the 19th Century* (pamphlet).

Souter, R 1994 *Call Out: service records of the Gourdon lifeboats 1878–1969*. Gourdon: Gourdon Lifeboat Committee.

Walker op cit.

Johnshaven, Milton and Tangleha'

Adams, D G 1991 *Johnshaven and Milton; a social and economic history*. Brechin: Chanonry Press (bibliography).

Souter 1988 op cit.

St Cyrus Bay and North Esk salmon fishings

Adams 1985 op cit.

Angus

Monographs

Edwards, R 1678 (translated J Trail 1793) *Description of the County of Angus*. Dundee. Reprinted in Warden, vol 2, 234–52 (see below) and by Forfar and District Historical Society, 1967.

Headrick, J 1813 *A View of the Agriculture of Angus or Forfarshire*. Edinburgh.

Ochterlony, J c.1682x85 Account of the Shire of Forfar. In Mitchell op cit. Also published by Forfar and District Historical Society, 1969.

Warden, Alexander 1880–85 *Angus or Forfarshire*, 5 vols. Dundee.

Maps

Adair, J 1693 *The Town and Water of Montross with the neighbouring Country & Coast from the Red-head to the North-water.*

Adair, J 1703 (surveyed 1688–1693) *A True and Exact Hydrographical Description of the Sea Coast and Isles of Scotland.* Edinburgh.

Ainslie, J 1794 (pub 1801) *Map of the County of Forfar or Shire of Angus from an Actual Survey.* Edinburgh.

Blackadder, William 1825 *Map of Angusshire* (2 sheets). Edinburgh.

Ordnance Survey 6 inches to 1 mile series *Forfarshire* 1865 onwards (surveyed from 1858); 25 inches to 1 mile series 1901–02, 1924. Southampton.

Montrose

Adams 1985 op cit.

Jackson, G and Lythe, S G E (eds) 1993 *The Port of Montrose: a history of its harbour, trade and shipping.* Wainscott, N Y: Georgica Press/Tayport: Hutton Press. Instigated by and with contributions from David G Adams. (See especially chapters 13/14/15/16 on whaling, salmon fishing and sea fishing before and since 1800; fully referenced.)

Montrose Yearbook 1884–1920s (lists fishing boats, giving owners and type).

Ferryden

Douglas, A 1857 *A History of Ferryden.* Montrose.

Edwards, D H 1930 *Among the Fisherfolks of Usan and Ferryden.* Brechin: D H Edwards.

West, J n.d. [1980s] *A Personal History of Ferryden.* Ferryden: J West.

West, J and Morrison, D 1985 *Old Ferryden: a history of an Angus fishing village in words and pictures.* Forfar: Angus District Libraries and Museums.

Usan and Boddin

Adams D G 1983b *Usan or Fishtown of Ullishaven: with notes on St Skaes and Boddin.* Brechin: Chanonry Press (bibliography).

Information from J Patterson, one-time resident of Usan.

Lunan Bay salmon fishings

Information from Dr M Halliday, W Shearer and the salmon fishers of Usan.

Ethie Haven

Adams, D G 1986b Ethie Haven or Torn's Ha'en: the story of a forgotten Angus fishing hamlet. *Arbroath Herald Annual*, 1986.

Information from Dr G Burgess, Forfar (proprietor of a flat in Ethie Haven).

Auchmithie

Adams, D G 1995 *Auchmithie: home of the smokie.* Forfar: Angus District Libraries and Museums (bibliography).

King, Margaret H 1992 Blue Coats, Skate-Mooed Pooches and Strippet Brots: Auchmithie and Arbroath Fisher Dress. *Arbroath Herald Review of 1992.*

King, Margaret H 1997 Free Men or Serfs? Auchmithie Fishers Denied Justice in 18th Century Legal Farce. *Arbroath Herald Review of 1997.*

Arbroath and Cove Haven

Adams 1983a op cit.

King, Margaret H 1990 Herring Heyday. *Arbroath Herald Review of 1990.*

East Haven and West Haven

Adams, D G and Falconer, Bob 1990 *The Ha'ens o' Panbride and roond aboot: a history of East Haven, West Haven & district.* Brechin: Chanonry Press (bibliography).

Buddon Ness salmon fishings

MacLeod, Colin R 2005 Barry Buddon: a major Scottish sand dune system. *The Scottish Naturalist,* vol 117 (2005), 5–127.

Information from newspaper cuttings supplied by Gillian Zealand about Barry Links lighthouses and lifeboat, written by her and her father Colin Gibson.

Broughty Ferry

Davey, C 1991 *The Last Toot: the end of salmon fishing in Broughty Ferry*. Dundee: Association for Fife and Tayside Historical Research.

Davey, N and Perkins, J 1976 *Broughty Ferry: from fishing village to suburb*. Dundee: Dundee Museums and Art Galleries.

MacMillan, R undated (1970s) *Broughty Ferry in the Days of Sail*. Broughty Ferry: R MacMillan.

Malcolm, J 1910 *The Parish of Monifieth in Ancient and Modern Times*. Edinburgh and London.

Mudie, Sir Francis et al 1970 (repr 1979) *Broughty Castle*. Dundee: Abertay Historical Society Publication no 15.

Dundee

Dundee Year Books

Henderson, D S 1972 *Fishing for the Whale: a guide-catalogue to the collection of whaling relics in Dundee Museum*. Dundee: Dundee Museums and Art Galleries (includes a historical account of the industry and a bibliography).

MacDonald, R and Small, A 1993 Reconstructing 12th and 13th century Dundee. *Northern Studies*, vol 30, 1–18.

Martin, A 1995 op cit.

Maxwell, Alexander 1884 *The History of Old Dundee*. Dundee: Wm Kidd.

Proceedings of the British Association for the Advancement of Science 1912. Dundee.

Torrie, Elizabeth P D 1990 *Medieval Dundee: a town and its people*. Dundee: Abertay Historical Society Publication no 30.

Whatley, C et al 1993 *The Life and Times of Dundee*. Edinburgh: John Donald (chapters 1/2/3).

Sprat fishing

Smith, Alexander 1952 *The Third Statistical Account of Scotland: the County of Fife* (Newburgh). Edinburgh and London: Oliver & Boyd.

Indexed newspaper cuttings in Dundee Central Library local collection.

Information from Charlie Johnston, Newburgh.

Appendix II: Fisher Surnames

Black, George 1946 *The Surnames of Scotland: their origin, meaning and history*. New York: New York Public Library.

Dwelly, Edward 1988 *The Illustrated Gaelic-English Dictionary*. Glasgow: Gairm Publications.

Reany, P H 1977 *A Dictionary of British Surnames*, 2nd ed. London: Routledge & Kegan Paul.

Robinson, M 1985 *The Concise Scots Dictionary*. Aberdeen: University Press.

Watson, H D 1982 *The Swankies of Arbroath and Auchmithie: an unusual fisher surname*. Typescript in Arbroath Library.

Pers. comm. from Ian A Fraser and Simon Taylor.